LOST in the Grooves

D0141437

Contributors

Brooke Alberts, Mike Appelstein, Jake Austen, Peter Bagge,
Ken Barnes, The Bengala, Tosh Berman, Jon Bernhardt,
Gene Booth, Derrick Bostrom, Joe Boucher, Carl Cafarelli,
Kevin Carhart, Sean Carrillo, Hayden Childs, Genevieve Conaty,
David Cotner, Robert Dayton, Jean-Emmanuel Deluxe,
Stuart Derdeyn, Deke Dickerson, Brian Doherty,
Jonathan Donaldson, Philip Drucker, SL Duff, Andrew Earles,
Becky Ebenkamp, Russ Forster, Phil Freeman, Ron Garmon,
Doug Gillard, Chas Glynn, Gary Pig Gold, William Ham,
Doug Harvey, Max Hechter, Richard Henderson,
Elizabeth Herndon, Tim Hinely, Jay Hinman, Andrew Hultkrans,
Elizabeth Ivanovich, Kris Kendall, Kelly Kuvo, P. Edwin Letcher,
Ted Liebler, Michael Lucas, Michael Lynch, Erin McKean,
Richard Meltzer, Rick Moody, Jim O'Rourke, Alec Palao,
George Pelecanos, James Porter, Mark Prindle, Domenic Priore,
Howie Pyro, Ken Rudman, Metal Mike Saunders,
David J. Schwartz, Gene Sculatti, Greg Shaw, Jack Shay,
Matthew Smith, Matthew Specktor, Vern Stoltz, Deniz Tek,
Michele Tepper, Dave Thompson, Gregg Turkington, Jillian Venters,
Elisabeth Vincentelli, Ed Ward, Steve Wynn and Jacqueline Zahas.

LOST in the Grooves

Scram's Capricious Guide to the Music You Missed

Edited by **KIM COOPER** and **DAVID SMAY**
Illustrations by **TOM NEELY**

Routledge   New York & London

Published in 2005 by
Routledge
270 Madison Avenue
New York, NY 10016

Published in Great Britain by
Routledge
2 Park Square
Milton Park, Abingdon,
Oxon OX14 4RN

Copyright © 2005 by Kim Cooper and David Smay
Routledge is an imprint of the Taylor & Francis Group.

The Everly Brothers *Two Yanks in London*, Patto *Roll 'Em Smoke 'Em Put Another Line Out* reprinted by permission of Ken Barnes.
Elvis Presley *Elvis Sings the Wonderful World of Christmas* reprinted by permission of Richard Meltzer.
Curtis Mayfield *Back to the World* reprinted by permission of International Creative Management, Inc. Copyright © 2004 by George Pelecanos.
Alvin and the Chipmunks *The Alvin Show*, Dolly Parton *Hello I'm Dolly* reprinted by permission of *Roctober Comics and Music* magazine.
The First Team *Chevrolet Sings of Safe Driving and You*, Mort Garson & Jacques Wilson *The Wozard of Iz: An Electronic Odyssey*, Judee Sill *Judee Sill/Heart Food* reprinted by permission of Scram.
Meic Stevens *Outlander* reprinted by permission of *Scram*. Copyright ©2004 by Ron Garmon.
Badfinger *No Dice*, Blue Ash *No More, No Less*, Bob Mosely *Bob Mosely*, The Mugwumps *The Mugwumps*, The Raspberries *Fresh* reprinted by permission of Metal Mike Saunders.
David Cassidy *Cassidy Live!*, Colours *Colours/Atmosphere*, Graffiti *Graffiti*, Barry McGuire *This Precious Time*, P.F. Sloan *Songs Of Our Times/Twelve More Times* reprinted by permission of Gene Sculatti.
The Raspberries *Fresh* reprinted by permission of Greg Shaw.
Dillard & Clark *Through the Morning, Through the Night*, Dan Hicks & His Hot Licks *Where's the Money*, Martin Mull *Martin Mull*, Mike Nesmith *Nevada Fighter*, Brinsley Schwarz *Despite It All* reprinted by permission of Ed Ward.
Sex Clark 5 *Strum & Drum!* reprinted by permission of *Worldly Remains* magazine. Copyright © 2003 by Kim Cooper.

Printed in the United States of America on acid-free paper.

All rights reserved. No part of this book may be reprinted or reproduced or utilized in any form or by any electronic, mechanical, or other means, now known or hereafter invented, including photocopying and recording, or in any information storage or retrieval system without permission in writing from the publisher.

10 9 8 7 6 5 4 3 2 1

Library of Congress Cataloging-in-Publication Data
     Lost in the grooves : Scram's capricious guide to the music you missed / edited by Kim Cooper and David Smay.
        p. cm.
     Includes index.
     ISBN 0-415-96998-0 (pb : alk. paper)
     1. Rock music—United States—History and criticism.   I. Cooper, Kim. II. Smay, David. III. Scram.

ML3534.L685 2005

781.66'0973—dc22
2004017253

Dedicated to *Mojo Navigator, Bomp, Teenage Wasteland Gazette, Back Door Man, Phonograph Record Magazine, Creem, Crawdaddy* and every writer who ever danced about architecture out of a compulsion to share the music.

Acknowledgments

David Smay would like to thank Jacqueline Zahas for her red pencil and the ice skating bruises she suffered for this book. He'd like to thank his son, Emmett, for generously donating Dad-time that could've been spent on baseball and board games. He'd also like to thank The Buffistas who helped shape this book, and Anne Weber in particular for her sense of urgency in sharing music.

Kim Cooper thanks the first wave zinesters (Barnes, Saunders, Sculatti, Shaw, Andy Shernoff and Don Waller) for their recollections; Richard Carlin and Dave McBride at Routledge; Phil Drucker and Meg Maryatt for envisioning a larger *Lost in the Grooves* on the Web and beyond; Colin Blunstone, Stephen Friedland, Linda Perhacs, Emitt Rhodes, Mark Taylor and the Sex Clark 5 for putting facts to her fancies; all the devoted contributors; her grandparents; and *especially* David Smay.

Reconsider, baby.

Scram is a magazine that for a dozen years has been tweaking the critical consensus with sly reappraisals of artists deemed insignificant, unimportant, or just far outside the hipster ghetto. We're the ones who shouted there was more to bubblegum than the obvious epithet. We raved about Radio Birdman when few north of Sydney cared, unearthed a great folk-rock disc tucked between Dion's heroin and homegrown eras and celebrated the earthy brilliance of Jackie DeShannon's forgotten recording career. Now we've called upon scores of *Scram* writers and folks who share our iconoclastic passions to bring you *Lost in the Grooves*, a collection of miniature love letters to albums (and a few singles and EPs) that at least one person considers iconic.

We see ourselves as part of a long tradition of buttonholers—evangelizers spreading the good word about our faves with an unshakeable faith that your physical and spiritual well-being depends on it. (See "Mimeos and Cut-Out Bins" for more on the early history of zines, and the vintage reprints spread throughout the book.) Thing is, we're worried about you. You're listless, your skin is sallow, you're sprouting unsightly blemishes and developing a funk in your trunk—and we think this probably has something to do with the absence of the Potatomen in your record collection. You're teetering on the edge of an abyss, and the only thing that might *possibly* save you is John Cale's *Paris 1919*. We're sure of it. Perhaps you somehow missed Michael Mantler's Edward Gorey tribute. Or maybe you don't have any Swamp Dogg. It's almost unimaginable, but some people don't own any Swamp Dogg at all.

Dozens of factors have conspired to prevent you from finding your favorite record. You're an inadvertent victim of narrowly focused marketing strategies. History, geography, even the limits of your own taste have thwarted you. What you need is an enthusiastic record geek friend to lead you through the bins. You need somebody to pull you away from your beloved indie rock 45s, drag you grudgingly into the country section and thrust a David Allan Coe record into your mitts. What you have in your mitts right now is your own portable geek.

We want crate-diggers to read about Tony Joe White, Schoolly-D fans to hear about Pentangle, Mekons fans to check out Kylie Minogue. No, really, we insist. Because somewhere in the cut-out bin of a record store in Tulsa is your favorite record and you've never even heard of it. Or it's hiding in plain sight, overshadowed by that same musician's acknowledged master-pieces. Maybe it's the one great record in an otherwise mediocre career. Or it's in this very book, in an essay you're going to skip. So many random events conspire to prevent the two of you from finding each other.

At the same time, we want *Lost in the Grooves* to be a record guide, subject to dog-ears and Post-It noting. David spent years tracking down Hackamore Brick and Savage Rose after Greil Marcus wrote about them in *Stranded*; *Breakfast without Meat* magazine's intelligent adoration of Jimmy Webb made Kim rethink her aversion to that artist; and we were both bub-blegumized by exposure to Lester Bangs.

This book exists to nudge the canon so that lost records tumble out. We want to highlight subgenres that produced great music but have fallen out of critical favor, assuming they were ever in it. One thing we *didn't* want was a record collector smackdown, vying for pack status with the obscurity of their treasures. Nor did we want to focus on works solely for their freakish novelty. So bad it's good? Nah, just so good it's gotta be heard. Not every record here is a masterpiece, but each is distinctive, original and fascinating.

But the standards for which records are unsung, forgotten or undervalued are incredibly slippery. There are plenty of records famous for being obscure, a countercanon of influential cult classics. So we don't really need to write about *Gilded Palace of Sin* or *Radio City* or *One Nation under a Groove*. They have graduated beyond the scope of this book. Now they're a part of the canon.

We analyzed the small geographies between cult and canon, charting the ever-shifting border and reviewing case histories to get a feel for the terrain. Inevitably, our criteria for inclusion were both subjective—we asked the contributors to pitch their favorites, filtering the list for cohesion and breadth—and a snapshot of how we see the canon right now. It was impossible to ignore how often reputations rise or fall on completely extra-musical terms. Consider, for example, the unexpected impact of one car commercial.

Nick Drake's star rose precipitously in 2000 when Volkswagen appropriated "Pink Moon." *Pink Moon* sold a reported 74,000 copies that year (up from 6,000), as Drake's doomed romanticism found a crop of receptive ears that dwarfed his longtime cult following. His winsome looks and tragic fate rendered Drake the perfect Shelleyan poster boy for the Belle & Sebastian generation, though many new fans made uncomfortable noises about coming to his music through the "dirty" scrim of commerce. But with the artist long dead and unable to approve such marketing plans, Drake retained his creative dignity, and his music still seems primally, perfectly pure.

Others nurture a cult in the shadows of mainstream success. Scott Walker began as one of the Walker Brothers, British girlhood's very own golden California fantasy. In 1967, Scott commenced a series of outré louche pop albums steeped in Brelian archetype and an ever-rising pool of sap. Late sixties Walkersong could be exquisitely heartfelt, or schlock city; hits came even as he veered into easy listening territory. But by the time of his masterpiece *Scott 4* (1969), the fans had tuned out. It remained for Julian Cope to restore his reputation with a 1981 compilation subtitled *Godlike Genius*. Scott returned with *Climate of Hunter*, an extension of the powerful electronic material he'd slotted into the Walker Brothers' reunion disc *Nite Flights*, to little notice by critics then plotzing over Bowie's similar experiments with Eno. Recently honored with a five-disc box set, Scott's canonical status is assured.

With an eerie ability to ride the zeitgeist, the Beach Boys have kept their summer on life support for nearly forty years. Regular revivals remarketed the Boys as good-time music for successive generations. Meanwhile, a passionate cult clung tightly to *their* private version of the subchart Beach Boys: the Beach Boys of Manson covers, *Sunflower* and that terrifying board tape of Murray Wilson haranguing his sons. Underground scholars like Domenic Priore compiled essential field guides as bootleggers continued assembling endless jigsaw puzzles of *Smiles* that might have been. Eventually Capitol recognized the market for such effluvia and issued a *Pet Sounds Sessions* box. Brian returned to the stage backed by a band of pop freaks who encouraged the master to replicate *Pet Sounds* and *Smile* live. Ironically, as their more arcane music finally finds an audience, the classic early kar kulture tracks are being neglected. But we think there's room on any discriminating shelf for both "Chug-a-lug" *and* "Cabinessence."

Some artists get lost despite continued strong work. The aviaphobic Byrd, Gene Clark left the band as their touring commitments intensified, slipping off to forge a distinctive brand of mournful, harmony-drenched country-rock through collaborations with the Gosdin Brothers and Doug Dillard. While respected, these recordings sold sparingly. The eighties Paisley Revival scene was the creative boost Clark needed. Bands like the Bangles and Three O'Clock worshipped at his jangled boots, and pulled Clark back into the spotlight. In the last years of his life, he recorded duets with Carla Olsen, their *So Rebellious a Lover* selling better than any previous Clark release. As the Byrds' output has been subjected to box sets and expanded reissues, the strength of Clark's early contribution is undeniable. But his very accessible and pretty solo material has failed to find any real posthumous life. While Gram and the Burritos loft up into the firmament, Gene Clark remains incomprehensibly earthbound.

Now Sly and the Family Stone are properly in every credible rock history and sitting safely in the Rock Hall of Fame. But because Sly Stone remains inconveniently alive and unproductive, because James Brown's iconic status overshadows his peers, because George Clinton's a cuddlier interview for VH-1, the history of funk and rap becomes subtly distorted over time. Undoubtedly, Sly doesn't exist without the whipcrack rhythmic innovations of JB (starting with "Out of Sight" in the mid-sixties). Still, funk as we know it starts on the thumb-callous of Larry Graham on "Thank You (Falettinme Be Mice Elf Agin)"—and all things funky roll outward from that low, seismic tremor. Context is lost, images dominate. The Family Stone's epochal Woodstock performance date-stamps them as Hippie Rock in a way that muddles the clear line from *There's a Riot Goin' On* through every Dr. Dre production. Sly crawled up a hole in his nostril thirty years ago, and that's a loss comparable to Hendrix's death.

The late nineties saw a flurry of interest in the DIY Elephant 6 collective. While the Apples in Stereo and Olivia Tremor Control got more attention at the time, it's the marching band psychedelia of Neutral Milk Hotel that's proved the movement's legacy. *In the Aeroplane over the Sea* received warm notices on release, but no one could have predicted the record's inexorable rise to the top of the postpunk indie canon. Although bandleader Jeff Mangum broke up the band after their 1998 tour, his weirdly beautiful love letter to Anne Frank went out and did its own promotion, passing from hand to hand in a truly underground, ever-expanding cult. When *Magnet* magazine listed the best releases of the last ten years, *Aeroplane* soared comfortably above the rest.

Deep catalogs that resist easy summary create their own problems. The book on Jonathan Richman says: proto-punk innovator with the Modern Lovers and faux-naïf kiddie songster thereafter. But that book's wrong. The kid songs were only a brief transitional period to stake out a new sound and songwriting territory that had a huge influence on the nineties indie lo-fi scene. We review *Modern Lovers 88* in this book, but could have just as easily highlighted *Rock 'N' Roll with the Modern Lovers* or *Rockin' and Romance* or *I, Jonathan*, each stellar, distinct, and scattered across his career. Curtis Mayfield's 1970s work similarly suffers from his very consistency. It doesn't provide an easy hook for critics, and so the story stops after *Superfly*.

Box sets present key opportunities for revaluation; the Byrds, Zombies, and Beach Boys all got significant boosts with their career summaries. But it doesn't always work. Even as we go to press, the Talking Heads' box seems to be actively souring their reputation simply because the packaging is so pretentious. How else to account for Robert Christgau all but anointing them as the best rock band in the world in 1982, then dismissing the whole of their work with a dyspeptic C? The Jefferson Airplane's box set couldn't pry them loose from their era to be heard as *music,* and that's an entirely different issue. Music at the core of specific scenes struggles to be heard for its merits instead of as a lifestyle soundtrack. Goth is one obvious example, where Bauhaus drew from the same peculiar mix of dub, Krautrock, prog, punk and processed guitars as Joy Division and PiL, but can't shake its subcultural associations long enough to be heard by anyone inexpert in liquid eyeliner.

So many factors play into a band's rediscovery: the advocacy of a superstar fan (Kurt Cobain's penchant for Pastels t-shirts and Vaselines covers), an emergent scene with obvious forebears (the White Stripes and the long-standing garage rock underground), fads in sonic recycling (analog synthesizers coming back into vogue causing an outbreak of Moog farts and blurps everywhere). Rap's insatiable beat craving created a permanent market in yesterday's sounds that slopped over into every sample-happy subgenre.

It's such a crapshoot, you need a tool to help even the odds. The subject's far too large to be covered comprehensively, so we designed this book as more than a record guide. It's a provocation, an outline, a dialogue, a shortcut, a rabbit hole. If you follow just a few of its paths, you'll find whole unexplored continents of music. We've set you on shore; here's a map into the interior.

Mimeos and Cut-Out Bins: THE EARLY HISTORY OF

Mimeos and Cut-Out Bins

THE EARLY HISTORY OF ROCK ZINES

Kim Cooper

Until the mid-sixties, press coverage of popular music was limited to the giddy burble of fan mags or the stolid cant of the trades. Rare exceptions—such as the progressive Jim Delehant-edited *Hit Parader* and Ralph Gleason's criticism in the *San Francisco Chronicle*—were treasured by pop fans looking for more meat than Ringo's ring size or Herman's favorite cake. Then rock fanzines arrived on the scene, courtesy of science fiction freaks familiar with the genre's self-publishing traditions. Zines contributed to an evolving critical language that would ultimately take two paths: into the gut or to the academy. The most compelling zines fused the two.

Starting in 1966, Paul Williams edited *Crawdaddy*, a somewhat high-toned and visually understated East Coast journal given to rhapsodizing over L.A.'s Love, Beach Boys and Doors. Budding critic Andy Shernoff found it "important but way too serious." In the Haight, multicolored weekly *Mojo-Navigator* (co-edited by David Harris and seventeen-year-old Greg Shaw, of whom more later) offered a fan's eye view of the San Francisco scene, with gossip, interviews and a critique of an antirock editorial in the underground *Oracle*.

Zines were widely traded, sold in hip shops, at gigs and on the street. Future *Creem* publisher Barry Kramer distributed titles through the Midwest. Greg Shaw and Chester Anderson launched the Underground Press Syndicate, a list of forty-plus mags that serviced each other with free copies.

Mojo-Navigator folded in late 1967, having overextended itself by switching from mimeograph to offset printing to meet national orders. In 1970, Shaw launched *Who Put the Bomp* (later just *Bomp*), which through the seventies would provide a home for rabid Merseybeat fandom, garage rock research and unabashed affection for then-unpopular artists like the Beach Boys. *Bomp*'s enthusiastic tone, combined with the cheapness of many of the out-of-print platters touted, made it appealing for readers to experiment with unknown acts.

Creem began as an underground tabloid covering the sociopolitical scene, but by 1971 found its voice as a snotty, often hilarious chronicler of rock and roll excess. Cover stories on popular acts frequently found the writer belittling them, while interior pages raved about more modest-selling staff favorites. Tuning into these discs made a reader feel part of the ultra-cool insider clique led by Lester Bangs. The reader might even get a letter printed in the magazine, with the editorial rimshot serving as proof of acceptance.

Boston's *Fusion* packed windy gee-whiz cultural commentary and photo essays in the front of the book, but was an open door to freelance reviewers who section editor Gary Kenton allowed to freely pan big-label releases. Compelling longer features included Richard Meltzer's affectionate ruminations on Johnny Mathis, and Mike Saunders ranking every recorded Zombies tune.

Around 1970, United Artists assigned publicist Greg Shaw to edit *Phonograph Record Magazine*, a house organ given away by radio stations and subject to minimal label oversight. *PRM* soon became paycheck and playground for a terrific crop of writers who could vote their conscience on discs new, notable, or noxious, while giving inches to pets like the Dolls, Todd Rundgren and the Move. Within a few years *PRM* would cut the corporate cord entirely, before ceasing publication in 1975.

And then there was *Rolling Stone*, which initially looked and functioned like an underground, but fast proved itself more concerned with maintaining a self-consciously hip tone than with passionately addressing the culture. Editors would routinely ask writers to change reviews if the thoughts expressed were critical of artists deemed above criticism. While many important pieces appeared in its pages, the organ inspired little affection, and some writers started their own zines in reaction against *RS*.

By the early seventies, rock critics formed networks of like-minded scribes who'd collide over junket appetizers or at the legendary 1973 Rock Writers Convention in Memphis, aka Day Zero for Big Star's reputation. A critic-friendly band like the Raspberries would garner interchangeable reviews across the print spectrum (see Greg Shaw's review of *Fresh* in this volume): a little moaning over such obvious derivative riffage, giving way to a shout of pure glee to have such perfect Beatlesque confections back on the airwaves again.

Leafing through a stack of vintage zines, well-known names are everywhere, from the mastheads to the letters columns. But look too for the ace craftsmen who wrote for love and never went pro, like Gene Sculatti's faves Crescenzo Capece of *Cretinous Contentions* and "Hot" Scott Fischer, "a nutty St. Louis guy who, in '73 or so, dug only noise and space-rock." Greg Shaw has warm memories of (girl group and exploitation mag scholar/future *New York Rocker* publisher) Alan Betrock's exhaustively researched *Jamz* and *Rock Marketplace*. Before forming the Dictators, Andy Shernoff published *Teenage Wasteland Gazette* out of his folks' house. *TWG* took delight in razzing foppish Jon Tiven, whose *New Haven Rock Press* featured columns by Nick Tosches and Richard Meltzer, and positive reviews of records ignored or maligned in *Rolling Stone*. Circa 1971–1972, Mark Shipper published two hilarious, ahead-of-their-time issues of *Flash*, dedicated to digging up great sounds in America's bargain bins while attempting to restore the reputations of the DC5 and Paul Revere & the Raiders. The staff—including Saunders, Sculatti, Shaw, Ken Barnes, and Ed Ward—was solicited from a letter printed in *Creem* asking if anyone else was seeking out unknown cheapie discs. (You'll find some of their favorites reprinted in this book.) In the mid-seventies, *Back Door Man's* Don Waller and company covered the pre-punk, post-glitter L.A. scene with grit, style and just the right amount of arrogance.

A common scenario had zinesters realizing they could turn more people on, and even make a few bucks, by jettisoning print for vinyl. Miriam Linna teamed with Billy Miller and launched *Kicks*, which taught punks and would-be rockabillies about the deep back-story of hepness in America. They started releasing recordings under the Norton imprint and stopped zining. *Bomp* magazine folded as the label of the same name got busier with its Stooges and Stiv Bators releases. *Slash* had a few influential years of L.A. punk scene chronicling before issuing the debuts of X, the Germs and the Blasters. Meanwhile, V. Vale and Andrea Juno transformed their San Francisco punk zine *Search & Destroy* into the culturally influential RE/Search book series, offering ahead-of-the-zeitgeist titles on industrial culture, pranks, B-movies and zining itself.

In the eighties, zines became specialized: *Ugly Things* reported on lost sixties legends (and punk, as the contributors' interests evolved), hardcore bible *Maximum RocknRoll* was the outlet for regional scene reports and insular Berkeley politics, while *Forced Exposure* celebrated the dark, noisy edges of the expanding alternative scene. By the early nineties, zines began their flirtation with the mainstream—review mags like *Factsheet 5* conferred status on "Editor's Choice" titles and listed hundreds of disparate publications in each issue, anthologies were published and some zinesters got book deals.

But the explosion of the zine scene coincided with the rise of the Internet, a medium that offered most of the pleasures of self-publishing without the pesky need to sell ads, negotiate distribution or pay the printer. Online, special interest list-servs and message boards allowed like-minded collectors to communicate, critics began keeping music-themed blogs and well-funded websites like allmusic.com became the URLs of record almost by default.

And yet, paper zines survive, many of them cleaving to the tradition of passionate advocacy that distinguished the *Mojo-Navigator* and its immediate descendants. This book's contributors include the folks behind such worthy recent ventures as *Cannot Become Obsolete, Caught in Flux, Cimmaron Weekend, Dagger, 8-Track Mind, Garage & Beat!, Roctober,* and *Worldly Remains,* among others. If you dig their reviews, check out the contributors' notes for ways to get their magazines.

A

THE ACTION

Brain* aka *Rolled Gold **(Recorded 1967–68, released Parasol, 2002)**
Five young men from Kentish Town whose singles won repute at the height
of Carnaby-era Britpop, the Action had daring, ability, imagination and no
less a personage than George Martin as producer. They did tight, distinctively Anglo R&B rungs above other worthy background noise by the Birds
or Downliners Sect. Reg King was one of the era's great soul-crooners, classy
as Pickett, expressive as Covay. Amazingly, the Action failed to chart in the
cutthroat U.K. market and elsewhere drew no water at all. Their later band-
written songs took a left-hand veer into brittle, understated psychedelia.
Demos for the unreleased album reveal grainy textures, tough fragments of
melody and a glass-skulled Panavision unity of mod perception so staggering
one half-suspects that they were carelessly left behind by prankster kids from
another dimension.

The Action swiped songcraft from Curtis Mayfield and Holland/
Dozier/Holland and assurance from entertaining fickle London mods, but
sound here as if they'd been marinating in mescaline on the Strip. Since they
only made double-A sides, there was no history of failure or limits. The
opener is "Come Around," a dry Movement anthem they dress up in G.
Harrison motley to cut acid capers. Swooping harmonies and artful time
changes prove they've got the whole 1967 clever-bastard thing wired. As the
songs flash past, the critic hears innocent wonder, loneliness in the middle of
a gigantic youth culture and the rolling clang of cash registers. London label

execs heard no such thing, and the Action died in an attar sweeter than the Zombies.

Reg King checked out for a solo career. The addition of Ian Whiteman on keys eventually turned the Action into underrated acid-jazzbos Mighty Baby, whose 1969 self-titled debut stands with *Atom Heart Mother* and *Mr. Fantasy*. Five bonus tracks on the CD were the Action's last demos, with "Only Dreaming" and "A Saying for Today" as lovely as anything from *Brain*. (Ron Garmon)

ADAM AND THE ANTS

Kings of the Wild Frontier   (Epic, 1980)

There's a difference between destroying things out of anger and destroying things because you're so happy that your limbs and head just can't control themselves. The Greeks understand this, the Jews understand this, and Adam and the Ants understood this. In terms of sound recordings documenting pure anarchic joy, *Kings of the Wild Frontier* may be the later twentieth century's most effective call to bruise oneself by flailing too close to the furniture, or at least to slash and burn one's face using eyeshadow as lipstick and vice versa.

The second Adam and the Ants album may seem an odd choice as a neglected album, since it garnered three U.K. top tens. However, history has marginalized *KOTWF* as a novelty album of the "new wave" or "New Romantic" variety, albeit one employing two drummers playing African Burundi beats.

As for punk cred, the Ants apparently have none subsequent to *Dirk Wears White Sox*. The truth of the matter, however, is that *KOTWF* embodies the original spirit of seventies punk—not the anger of sixties punk/garage, but the childlike hurrah of being pretty without being precious, having a knowledge and real command of one's instrument (as did Adam with his voice and the perpetually underappreciated Marco Pirroni with his guitar), and the fearlessness to combine aesthetic influences that made no sense intellectually (simultaneously identifying with the English pirate pillager and the Native American pillaged is no small task, folks).

It really doesn't matter that the Ants are neither embraced by the retro–new wave nor the retro-punk culture. Adam knew when he made the music that it didn't fit into these genres, and was further aware of the irony that the genres he didn't fit into both espoused destruction of genres. The important thing is that he went forth and made the music, his own tribalspaghettiwesternR&Bbaroquebubblegumgrindhousetapdancesurfmetalgothpop view of the world. (Elizabeth Herndon)

HERB ALPERT & THE TIJUANA BRASS
Whipped Cream & Other Delights
(A&M, 1965)

If you don't believe *WC&OD* belongs in this book because it's so unapologetically mainstream, here's a pop quiz: name two songs on the LP. Stumped? I rest my case.

Exaggerating just slightly, a friend called *WC&OD* the record "everyone's dad owned." A&M co-founder/trumpeter Alpert's fourth TJB release and sales/artistic peak, it initially sold 500,000+ copies, all but seventeen of which can be accounted for in an audit of our nation's thrift stores.

The genius begins with the cover's delectable Dolores Erickson, who models the non-dairy dessert topping (actually, dollops of sturdier shaving cream) on her décolletage. More importantly, she's pretty on the inside. *WC&OD*'s musical menu is a medley of buoyant, brilliantly arranged gastronomy-themed instrumentals—a genre, it's worth noting, that makes titles hard to recall. Two tunes ("Whipped Cream," "Lollipops and Roses") introduced *The Dating Game*'s bachelorettes and their Hai Karate–slapped suitors. "Bittersweet Samba" has been hilariously mashed with Public Enemy's lyrics.

If influence signals greatness, the TJB was the Dylan of hombre horns. It spawned hundreds of studio-concocted copygatos devised to divert dinero from A&M. Among them: the Guadalajara Brass, the Acapulco Brass, the Mariachi Brass (with Chet Baker!). Other "groups" conjured up less exotic locales: Erin Go Brass, Swedish Brass, the San Fernando (yep, the Valley) Brass. *WC&OD*'s sexy sleeve has been parodied by comic Pat Cooper, who sports a pasta-concocted frock on *Spaghetti Sauce & Other Delights*, and Soul Asylum, whose *Clam Dip & Other Delights* features its frontman smeared with schmear. In the sixties, only the Beatles, Elvis and Sinatra outsold the TJB, but *WC&OD* can still be Filed Under: Underrated. The TJB's sheer omnipresence rendered it nearly invisible, inconspicuous to Boomers and future generations despite its generation-gapless appeal.

Fascinated initially by an artifact that ignited a *muy-más* swingin' era, Xers scouring Goodwill bins in the go-go eighties eventually grew immune to Erickson's charms, which—as the great LP-to-CD switchover began— were as bountiful as Mitch Miller and Mantovani. The surefire five-servings o' *Whipped Cream* per store left even those with exotica-craving palates staving off the platter until later. Patrons who did pick up the 50–cent treasures often had camp motives: more than one fabulous individual has hoarded Doloreses for decor—*Whipped Cream* wallpaper!

Which begs the question: Did anyone ever actually play this mostscrumptious musical morsel, or simply stare at it? Go ask dad . . . (Becky Ebenkamp)

ALVIN AND THE CHIPMUNKS
The Alvin Show   **(Liberty, 1961)**

This subversive children's record is the soundtrack to the Rodent Rockers' primetime cartoon. On it we meet Mrs. Frumpington, an anti-Rock crusader from the Society for Quiet and Universal Appreciation of Refined Enterprises, who demonstrates the most heinous of all music by playing snippets of several rockin' Chips' tunes. Alvin curses her out, but human mentor David Seville (a.k.a. Ross Bagdasarian, the Armenian-American genius behind the 'munks) stops him. So Alvin goes into plan B: he goes to her house and gives her a flower while his brothers hide outside with instruments. He has her consider her love of the wind through the branches (guitar plucking), the sound of the bullfrog (bass) and the birds (a fake woodpecker playing percussion). As she starts to get more and more swept up into the rhythmic groove he asks, "Do you like families? Don't you just love a baby, a baby…?" She responds, "A baby? A baby, a baby baBY BABY!" Now that he has her worked up he asks, "And how about a daddy, a daddy…?" She has now lost control to the demon rhythms and starts screaming. A full horn section kicks in as she works herself into an erotic climax, "*BABY BABY BABY, DADDY DADDY DADDY BABY BABY BABY! Ohhhhhh!*" She howls her orgasmic rock 'n' roll vocals until men in white coats take her away. Thus, the most sexually charged kiddie record ever proves everything she feared was true. Side 2 opens with the boys singing a wholesome song about what they like to do (baseball, swimming, watching *Gunsmoke*), but then Alvin reprises the tune with new, naughty lyrics. "I like to break dishes and fight with the squirrels, I like to pull pigtails when they're on girls, we like to eat candy and talk in school." "I knew it," laments David. As the album ends with a reprise of the TV theme, children everywhere, exhausted by the erotic anarchy of Alvin and his brothers, basked in the afterglow of the wildest Alvin album ever. (Jake Austen)

APPALOOSA
Appaloosa
(Columbia, 1969)

Decades of absorption in rock criticism never gave me a hint that this existed. In a critical-historical world where being a hairy, smelly, misshapen evolutionary link earns more props than being a beautiful, fragile insect inhabiting a dead-end evolutionary niche, this Al Kooper–produced record has had its fossils swept unnoticed into the used vinyl bins. Little noted nor long remembered, *Appaloosa*—masterminded by singer/songwriter John Parker Compton—is as uninfluential as a record could be.

Still, it should have been. Anyone with a yen for smart, decadent, delicate and lovely has a lot to learn—or just to love—from this languorously smooth and sweet combo. Yet, like the sea of crème de menthe Compton sings of, it has an intoxicating bite. It came from nowhere and went nowhere, waving no flags for any trends or theories, yet even today sounds like it could represent a new advance in out-of-nowhere chamber baroque pop. It should be of enduring interest to fans of Nick Drake, Pearls Before Swine or Elliott Smith.

In a bit of studio chatter prefacing the LP's first, and best, song, "Tulu Rogers" (who, the chorus tells us, "listens to Sebastian Bach/she loves John

Locke"—the song is strong enough to bear such name-dropping pretensions with an easy, mysterious smile), Compton can be heard saying "this isn't an easy song to do" and I'm sure he's right. Still, the band makes it sound like it is. On this record, even cornflakes are eaten from silver bowls (with Kandinsky prints on the wall), and the music sounds like the pure-light glints of candlelight off those bowls. (Brian Doherty)

THE AUTEURS
New Wave   (Hut, 1993)

Luke Haines can't resist poking a finger into the suppurating wound of the English class system. He swans about singing superbly bilious songs about burglars in training, murderous chauffeurs, resentful valets and domesticated showgirls, with wicked glee and an unerring knack for shiv-like guitar hooks. The Auteurs purvey a distinctly British rock and roll dressed in shabby music hall piano tinkles, and that guitar crunch derived primarily from Mick Ronson's Les Paul (with flashes of Townshend). Haines rarely sings full-throated. Like most Brits, he prefers to keep something conversational in his tone to allow room for vicious asides and mewling plaints. More than Blur or Pulp or Suede, the Auteurs stand as the definitive example of the grand Kinks/Bowie splice that became Britpop.

There's a playfulness in British rock, a flash and snarl to it—the energy pent up and explosive. Though he's wry, Haines doesn't seem particularly playful, and his songs sport the most unreliable narrators this side of Nabokov. Don't trust the man singing "Junk shop clothes will get you nowhere.../Chaim Soutine never spent/A thrift shop dime/In his life/Lenny Bruce never walked/In a dead man's shoes/Even for one night."

Haines never wrote a boring lyric, but the reason I'm not pushing his chapbook on you is because he's also a brilliant architect of guitar hooks and fetching, flashy melodies that get you singing along before you realize he's made you complicit in some rotsome crime. He's the leader of a band of Dickensian cutpurse urchins; he's a backstage brat. He's Roald Dahl's louche and caddish nephew armed with a Rickenbacker, and if you're moneyed I advise you not to turn your back on him. (David Smay)

BADFINGER

No Dice   (Apple, 1970)

If you pride yourself on being a member of the generation that battles hypocrisy, shuns prejudices and easy labels, and fights to the death to tell the pigs (boo) what it's all about (yay)—and won't listen to Badfinger's *No Dice* because they're a "teenybopper group," then it's your own tough luck.

Not to mention that the *No Dice* album sounds like what the Beatles might have done had they gotten it together after their white album—and we all know how hip a record that is—and not to mention that Badfinger is one of the best songwriting groups around, one of the best singing groups anywhere, and now has an absolutely great lead guitarist in Pete Ham, they're really one fucking whale of a group anyway.

It's really late-Beatles music Badfinger does, if you'll check out the white album/*Abbey Road* style of production and the distinctly similar instrumental sound.

Then there's even exact imitation Ringo ker-plod drumming. However, in songwriting and singing Badfinger shuts the post-*Pepper* Beatles down cold, and that, I feel, is something most comparisons of the two groups sneakily evade talking about.

Finally, if you can sit around grooving on Paul McCartney's solo album, when there's a group right around the corner—Badfinger—that can do everything McCartney can do (Pete Ham sings, writes, and even has the gall to *look* like McCartney), that's your tough luck too, I guess. When Badfinger gets around to making the record they're capable of making, it may be as good as everything the Beatles ever did after *Rubber Soul*, all rolled into one. In the meantime, *No Dice* is merely great.

(Metal Mike Saunders, *Creem*, March 1971)

B

THE BARRY SISTERS
Our Way/Tahka Tahka   (Roulette, 1973)

In 1937, Clara and Minnie Bagelman listened to their radio horrified as the Midwest, white bread Andrew Sisters achieved breakout success with a swing version of one of the Bagelman Sisters' very own Yiddish standards, "Bei Mir Bist Du Schoen." They changed their names at once to Merna and Claire Barry and set out to take advantage of the new trend, landing a high-profile job on a radio show newly created to exploit the emerging genre, *Yiddish Melodies in Swing*. The rechristened Barry Sisters went on to become a regular fixture on the American showbiz landscape of the forties and fifties.

In 1973, the Barry Sisters thumbed their noses at the Andrews Sisters and other gentile appropriationists when they released *Our Way/Tahka Tahka*, an absurdly hilarious lineup of American popular classics sung in Yiddish. In these songs, Yiddish imbues humor in a way that English never could. Through translation, the Barry Sisters tap into a fresh aspect of musical enjoyment—the magic that supercedes melody, the sound of the words. Even the listener who speaks nary a word of Yiddish will not be able to resist the delicious marriage of highly improbable, yet perfect, words and music. "Mame" in Yiddish? We can't help but giggle helplessly, as we tap our feet and hum along to the Barry Sisters' riotous renditions of "Tea For Two" ("Tay Far Tzay"), "My Way" ("Mein Vaig") and, the ultimate, "Raindrops Keep Falling on My Head" ("Trop'ns Fin Regn Oif Mein Kopf")! If Eastern European klezmer music contributed to the birth of American popular music, and Jewish theater influenced American musical theater, then the Barry Sisters turned the tables—reclaiming the Jewish roots inherent in both. (Sean Carrillo)

JOE BATAAN
Subway Joe   (Fania, 1968)

The Filipino/African-American Bataan is virtually unknown to white record geeks, despite his superstar status in NYC's late-sixties/early-seventies Latin music scene. He even created his own genre of "Soul Latin" or "Salsa Soul" (shortened to "SalSoul"—also the name of his record label). Before taking the unsurprising path into disco, then the unwise path into rap, Bataan recorded six good-to-great-to-amazing LPs for the Fania label between 1967 and 1972. This was the second.

Playing the advantageous best song/first song card, the title track will have you whored out for the rest of the album. It's one of those tunes that has an immediate impact after twenty seconds—heads are turning, guests are asking you what it is, meaningless babble stops. "Subway Joe" was a regional hit (more so on Latin radio, natch), but Bataan had already scored one or two of those with lesser songs from his 1967 debut *Gypsy Woman*. Bataan and his Latin Swingers didn't fit in visually or logistically with the late sixties. The back of the album is cheaply laid out around a photo of a trad-suited mid-sized band, and is very reminiscent of a cruise ship vanity LP. *Subway Joe* was an as-yet-unheard hybrid of sixties pop, Motown, and Cuban musics. Each track is cleverly credited to whatever subgenre of Latin music from which it originated: Boogaloo, Guaguanco, Bolero-Cha-Cha, Jala Jala, or Descarga. Until these early LPs were recently reissued, Bataan was unjustly remembered as the poor man's Gil Scott-Heron (a collaborator), and for the proto and mainstream disco and Sugarhill Gang–style mishaps of his post-Fania days. Another wrong has been righted. (Andrew Earles)

PETER BAUMANN
Romance 76   **(Virgin, 1976)**

I've never understood why everyone thought the Sex Pistols were such a big deal. So what if they couldn't play their instruments? Tangerine Dream couldn't play their instruments, and for the longest time I'm not even sure you could classify what they did play as musical instruments. In 1971 Peter Baumann became a member of Tangerine Dream and helped expand the parameters of electronic music through his contributions to several landmark recordings including *Zeit, Atem* and *Phaedra*.

Baumann began his solo career with the release of *Romance 76*. Not surprisingly, *Romance 76* is an electronic instrumental album highly reminiscent of the best Baumann-related Tangerine Dream recordings. What is surprising is that *Romance 76* attains a personal quality Tangerine Dream was never able to achieve. There is an element of the subconscious within the collection of moody, introspective compositions that indicates a *human* origin. There is a direct desire to communicate, to hear and be heard, that was never present in Tangerine Dream music. Peter Baumann *wants* something. It is dark, it is mysterious, and it yearns to be found. There is an odd confessional (and quite possibly unrepentant) quality to *Romance 76* that, considering there are no lyrics, is a remarkable achievement itself. Like the best Tangerine Dream albums, the only true indicator of completion is the needle lifting off the surface of the vinyl. *Romance 76* is no different. After 25+ years of ownership, I still don't know the titles of the individual tracks. I just know I like Side 2 better than Side 1.

Stranded on a desert island with Johnny Rotten? Not my cuppa tea. But Peter Baumann? That might be a different story. (Philip Drucker)

THE BEACH BOYS
Shut Down, Volume 2   (Capitol, 1964)

Consider the value of the 5- and 10-cent store. In the days before floodlit "drug" emporia sold everything from soap to chardonnay and patio furniture, a Woolworth's or Sprouse Reitz proffered a manageable mix of the practical and the playful. The very incongruity of its parts (thread and thimbles, crayons and plastic soldiers) enhanced the whole: always something new down the next aisle. This album is like that. Its unholy alliance of ambitious and expedient music is the source of much of its charm.

Here, on their fourth LP in eighteen months, are the Beach Boys' most expendable toss-off (the instro "Denny's Drums") and their most indelible keeper ("Don't Worry Baby"). Here, too, are the acknowledged classics "The Warmth of the Sun" and "Fun Fun Fun," its glassine guitar bright as Cali light.

But there's also a no-sweat cover of "Louie Louie" that closely follows Richard Berry's original; another butter-rich ballad, "Keep an Eye on Summer," that matches "Warmth" (gorgeous falsetto fade); and the redundo sax/guitar title track. "Why Do Fools Fall in Love" is Brian's first full Spector tribute (despite all those claps and castanets, it's amazingly light on its feet). There's the pep-rally paean "Pom Pom Play Girl" and, best among the genre songs, the "pre-school" car tune "In the Parking Lot," with Mike Love's galloping make-out tale bookended by an intro and outro of ridiculously beautiful jet-age falsetto.

It took Elvis till the '68 comeback before he could kid his image, and the Beatles till '67 before they could lighten up enough to flick "She Loves You" into the finale of "All You Need Is Love." Three years earlier, on *SDV2*'s audio-vérité playlet, "'Cassius' Love vs. 'Sonny' Wilson," Mike and Brian diss each other in a faux fight that good-naturedly—and revealingly—shows how the band members saw and felt about each other.

Finally, wonderfully, there's the sleeper, Dennis's soulful minute-and-a-half "This Car of Mine." Nominally "filler," this Dion-derived shuffle finds him singing, imperfectly, honestly, his seventeen-year-old heart out: "I remember the day when I chose her over all those old broken junkers/But I could tell underneath the coat of rust she was gold ... no clunker." Too much. (Gene Sculatti) (See also: Dennis Wilson)

Adult Child   (unreleased, recorded 1976–77)

You gotta love any album that opens with the lines, "Life is for the living!/Don't sit around on your ass smoking grass/That stuff went out a long time ago ..." *Adult Child* is one of the finest Beach Boys albums of the 1970s, but it never saw the light of day. A damn shame, but at least bootleg collectors can enjoy it.

During this period, Brian Wilson was pushed back into the creative spotlight and he was in a most curious headspace. The title conveys so much. The childlike and playful do an uneasy dance with the responsibilities and troubles of adulthood. The whole wonky package is similar in tone to the Beach Boys' *Love You* album. There are so-called Beach Boys fans who say anybody who applauds *Love You* and this album is being ironic. I say fuck those tight-arsed naysayers! Both of these albums showcase a truly original mix of humor and sadness. The original numbers always dance just a step away from cliché, dealing with simple lyrical themes that make you wonder why they had never been explored before. Two songs are about healthy eating and exercise. Another is about ecology. "Lines" is simply about waiting in line for a movie. All of the songs are infectiously catchy, including the ballads, which are possibly the saddest ballads known to humankind. And there are a few classic covers, including an unhinged "Shortenin' Bread."

Brian Wilson intended *Adult Child* to be his Big Band album. Some songs have those lavish arrangements, some even swing! Most feature deep, warm keyboards accompanied by Brian's cigarette-burned voice and the voices of the rest of the gang, including then-wife Marilyn. One may quickly pass *Adult Child* off as being disturbed, but its brilliant charms can't be denied. Warts and all? Warts can be gems. (Robert Dayton) (See also: Dennis Wilson)

L.A. (Light Album)   (CBS, 1979)

When the Beach Boys played Radio City Music Hall in 1979, their ten-minute disco version of "Here Comes the Night" was vehemently booed and a near-riot occurred. Rod Stewart was a sissy who could swallow cum and sing "Do You Think I'm Sexy" as far as these hard-boiled New Yorkers were concerned, and the Bee Gees were has-beens who'd sold out in desperation to sing bad falsetto to a tepid "beat" … but the Beach Boys, the last link to *The T.A.M.I. Show* and Murray the K goodness, *playing disco?* Eat Shit!

That ten minutes blew it for *L.A.* Left in the can was Brian Wilson's true masterpiece of the seventies, "California Feeling," where the Beach Boys sang about Laguna's Three Arch Bay and the smell of orange groves … real *Southern California Pastoral.* Then you had this nice little Al Jardine nature suite, "Santa Ana Winds/Lookin' Down the Coastline/Monterey," a cool extension of the stuff he'd done for *Holland.* Jardine shelved a less saccharine version of "Lady Lynda" and with Mike Love cowrote a pretty good "let's go back to the old days" rocker, "It's a Beautiful Day."

Had these tracks, plus the 3:28 DJ-only 45 of "Here Comes the Night," been part of *L.A.*, they would have joined Dennis Wilson's excellent "Baby Blue" and "Love Surrounds Me" to make for a fine LP. Dennis sang Carl Wilson's heartfelt "Angel Come Home." Carl took on a David Crosbyesque dreamer mode for "Full Sail" and "Goin' South," in which baby brother "thinks" of joining the birds on their annual trek to Baja. Brian pitched in a cover of "Shortenin' Bread" that may not be as balls-out as the one by the Readymen in 1964, but works as whacked fifties R&B. Brian's last chart song for the Beach Boys was 'Good Timin'," a cool "Surfer Girl"-style record. Like "California Feeling," it featured a track recorded in the pre-"Brian is Back" days of 1974. (Domenic Priore) (See also: Dennis Wilson)

BE-BOP DELUXE
Futurama (Harvest, 1975)

I first encountered *Futurama* at a library book sale in the late seventies. It turned out to be my initiation into the mysteries of the electric guitar, revealing dimensions that Ted Nugent only hinted at. It is also the record that usually springs to mind when I hear the phrase "wall of sound."

Futurama is so crammed with screaming guitars and thundering pianos and layered harmonies and orchestras that there is no room to think or even breathe throughout its nine gloriously overproduced tracks. If you can imagine all of your Bowie, Queen, and ELO records playing simultaneously, then you might have some idea of what this LP is all about.

Be-Bop Deluxe was a U.K. outfit fronted by the previously obscure psych-folk guitarist Bill Nelson. Their debut *Axe Victim* is a credible exercise in Ziggy-style glam rock. However, it is their second LP that stands unchallenged as the towering Mount Everest of seventies guitar overdub excess, with an absolutely massive-sounding Roy Thomas Baker production dominating a Hendrix/Spector trip encompassing glam, power pop, heavy progressive rock, and psychedelia. It overflows with moments of real beauty and inspiration. "Sound Track" sounds like a squadron of lead guitarists engaged in a battle of decibels. "Maid in Heaven" binds this sort of chaos with numerous hooks to create an incredibly catchy pop single.

After *Futurama*, Be-Bop Deluxe toned it down and spent a few years sounding like mid-period Cockney Rebel until Bill Nelson eventually reinvented himself as a new wave and ambient pioneer. (Matthew Smith)

THE BEE GEES
Mr. Natural (RSO/Atlantic, 1974)

Mr. Natural is the last LP the Bee Gees released before "going disco," and its poor sales suggest that their (literal) change of pace was as much a desperation move as it was pure inspiration. The reason I suggest this is that this LP is itself quite inspired—the most satisfying LP they ever made, in my opinion. "Charade," "Throw a Penny," "I Can't Let You Go," as well as the title track—which has nothing to do with R. Crumb's comic book character—are all masterpieces and are beautifully produced (by Atlantic vet Arif Mardin).

The lyrics and vocal performances on these tracks in particular are deeply moving and profound, almost on a par with *Pet Sounds*.

Ironically, the weakest track, "Heavy Breathing," is a remarkably failed attempt on the Brothers Gibb's part at making danceable R&B—all the more surprising because their future output would be more of the same, albeit of a much high caliber. My hunch as to why *Mr. Natural* may have sold so poorly is the record's sleeve, which features a moon-faced drunkard sitting alone at a bar. While amusing and quite appropriate to the record's lyrical content, I can't imagine such high-concept artistry appealing to the Bee Gees' mainstream fan base! (Peter Bagge) (See also: Robin Gibb)

COLIN BLUNSTONE

One Year   (Epic, 1971)

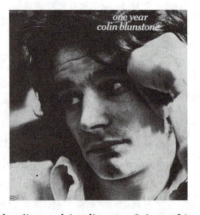

Celebrated as the Zombies are today, during the actual British Invasion the spectacled rockers couldn't buy a break. Yes, "Tell Her No" and "She's Not There" were U.S. hits in the winter of 1964–65, but for a group whose output rivals the Kinks for ace originals, their failure to break bigger is galling and mysterious. After "Care of Cell 44" flopped, the band splintered in disgust. *Odessey & Oracle* was released posthumously—with "Time of the Season" emerging as an unexpected smash soon after—but the band had already scattered. Vocalist Blunstone took a straight gig as an insurance clerk as balm for postbreakup depression.

One Year was Blunstone's formal return to music, not counting the singles he did as "Neil MacArthur" for Cat Stevens' producer Mike Hurst, and it's very nearly a lost Zombies album. Better still, it's a marvelous Colin Blunstone album. The disc was produced by Zombies Chris White and Rod Argent, includes three Argent/White compositions, and Argent-the-Group plays on several tracks. It did in fact take a year to complete, during which time the players came upon the idea of pairing Blunstone's husky, whispery

The following is an excerpt from the review that appeared in the

June 1973 issue of *Phonograph Record Magazine*.

BLUE ASH

No More, No Less (Mercury, 1973)

"I Remember A Time" could do for Blue Ash what "Mr. Tambourine Man" did for the Byrds: the start of a brilliant career, a Number One hit, instant mythology. The guitar intro lasts all of five seconds before Jimmy Kendzor and Frank Secich's voices come in, oozing of everything the Byrds and Lovin' Spoonful ever promised, the soaring harmonies in the chorus driving over jangling lead guitar work. It's the sound of tomorrow right here today, it's the perfect folk-rock single. It's beautiful, that's what.

This is one of the most spirited, powerful debuts ever from an American group. *No More, No Less* opens with "Have You Seen Her," a fast rocker kicked off by four whomps on David Evans' snare. This is the one that makes me think of The Who; the lead guitar is pure West Coast, though.

"Just Another Game" is the one quiet song, an effective tonedown before "I Remember A Time." "Plain To See" is simi- lar to "I Remember A Time" in the way its simple, compelling melody rocks out with vocal harmonies framed over a trebly Byrds guitar sound.

"Here We Go Again" follows, midway between the hardest and softest numbers on the first side. What's great here are the group vocals on top of the tuff folk-rock cum hard rock instru- mental sound; it's like killing two birds with one stone, the whole premise behind the old and new Mod groups (Small Faces, early Who, the Sweet), not to mention the hard pop mas- terpiece known to the world as "Do Ya."

By the time this album ends, there's no doubt about it, Blue Ash have got themselves one hell of a debut LP that may send fellow stateside groups like Stories, the Raspberries, and Big Star running back to the woodshed to come up with music even better than their present stuff. (Metal Mike Saunders) vocals with a string quartet. On tracks like the haunting "Smokey Day," "Her Song," and "Caroline Goodbye," Blunstone sounds like a ghostly choirboy in some Edwardian parlor, his pure tones reaching through time's mists to find a sun-dappled spot to materialize.

The closing track, Denny Laine's "Say You Don't Mind," was the last thing recorded for the album. Blunstone's final utterance is a stunningly raw falsetto swoop that sounds like nothing he'd ever done before. It heralds the independence of an astonishing singer and songwriter, who the next year would record the equally fine *Ennismore*.

Blunstone and Argent are again touring and recording as the Zombies, and play many of these songs in concert. (Kim Cooper)

WILLIE BOBO

Do What You Want to Do   **(Sussex, 1971)**

As a child I spent hours poring over my sister's albums. My sister Julia only listened to music by people with strange names like Cal Tjader, Yusef Lateef, Hugh Masekela and my favorite, Willie Bobo.

In 1971 Willie Bobo released a masterwork accompanied by a group made up of friends old and new (billed as the "Bo-Gents") and deftly orches-trated by Steve Huffsteter (father of Steven Hufsteter of Quick and Cruzados fame). Although not as famous as Bobo's Verve releases, nonethe-less *DWYWTD* captures a special moment in the career of a jazz genius. It was released the same year as Isaac Hayes's *Shaft*, which set the standard for this type of sax-heavy sound; perhaps this explains why *DWYWTD* did not garner the same attention. It is, however, a subtler, more finely-crafted gem of an album.

The album is an uncanny blend of jazz, funk, and soul. Imagine a jazz cruise with eight very fine musicians, including percussion masters Victor Pantoja and Willie Bobo. Five of the eight songs on this LP are by members of the band. Also included is a funky, laid-back version of the Beatles' "Come Together" that fits nicely in the context of the album.

The real standout, though, is the Antonio Carlos Jobim classic "Dindi." It is so well executed here that all other versions pale by comparison. The bass and drums lay down a mellifluous carpet of sinuous rhythm, while the electric piano accents in perfect time; Barry Zweig's guitar licks subtly accentuate Bobo's utterly disarming phrasing, and the flugelhorn solo captures the feeling of the entire arrangement in a few short bars. This is "Dindi" as it has never been done, apologies to Astrud and kudos to Mr. Huffsteter. Bobo's classic deserves to be moved from the archives and put back on the turntable. (Sean Carrillo)

CURT BOETTCHER

There's an Innocent Face   **(Elektra, 1973)**

A select few pop wunderkind were given the keys to the toyshop in the late sixties. Beach Boys' lyricist Van Dyke Parks was granted free reign behind the mixing console for his *Song Cycle* LP; Association producer Curt Boettcher, less known for his membership in baroque pop ensembles Sagittarius and the Millennium, was comparably endowed with studio time. Neither would make appreciable commercial inroads with their own idiosyncratic, meticulously constructed recordings. Boettcher, in particular, seemed to slip below radar as the halcyon sixties era of California pop gave way to uninspired early seventies chart fare.

Yet it was precisely in this period, when androgynous English pop vied with Southern bar bands for the attention of record buyers, that Boettcher's final stab at a solo career made its quixotic appearance. This record was issued with negligible promotion and disappeared immediately, which is a shame because it contained some of Boettcher's best work. The songs reflect what the Everly Brothers might have achieved had they had a vested interest in studio craftsmanship (and a slightly drug-tinted perspective on same) to match their brilliant harmonies. The latter abounded on Boettcher's album, his voice paired perfectly throughout with that of collaborator Web Burrel. (Though, as was revealed in the reissue liner notes nearly thirty years later, Burrel expected the album to be issued as Curt & Web. The playing, writing, and singing was, for the most part, divided evenly between the two. Boettcher's solo credit on the sleeve effectively ended a marvelous partnership.)

Time has not dimmed the luster of songs such as "I Love You More Each Day," with its stop-on-a-dime arrangement (and a bass part performed on tuba!) or the phase-shifted marvel of "Malachi Star." Now as then and undeniably true to its title, *There's an Innocent Face* radiates sunlight with every play. (Richard Henderson) (See also: Sagittarius)

BOOGIE DOWN PRODUCTIONS
Sex and Violence   (Jive, 1992)

Not one track from *Sex and Violence* appears on KRS-One's 2000 best of, *A Retrospective*. That's because it's as shocking an explosion of pure hip-hop id as anyone's ever released. Seemingly tired of the professorial role he'd assumed on *Edutainment*, KRS-One burst forth on *Sex and Violence* with some of the kickingest beats he ever mustered, a fistful of dancehall/ragga flavor, and lyrics about ... well, let's take "13 And Good" as Exhibit A. It's a life-affirming jail-bait story about a girl who lies about her age to bed KRS, and when her dad finds out, he wants a piece of KRS for himself—prison style! Ha!

Of course, it's not all polymorphous sexual perversity and ballistic battle rhymes. KRS gets political on *Sex and Violence*, too. On "Drug Dealer," he advises the corner boys to "organize yourselves and open up a school." His argument is that just as previous minority groups (he cites Jews and Italians) started out as criminals and became respectable, it's time for crack dealers to do the same.

Ignore his wack stabs at social engineering, though, because *Sex and Violence* is KRS-One's best-sounding album. The beats are massive, easily better than anything on more acclaimed releases like *By Any Means Necessary* and *Return of the Boom Bap*. "Duck Down," "Like a Throttle," and "Build and Destroy" are anthems any MC would be proud to have written. And how many other rappers would choose cover artwork by Pop surrealist painter Robert Williams? No wonder this album sank beneath the waves: it's way too insanely individualistic for "the streets." *Sex and Violence* is a genuine work of hip-hop art. (Phil Freeman)

JAMES BOOKER
Resurrection of the Bayou Maharajah   (Rounder, 1993)

The most improbable character in New Orleans' storied line of piano players was a one-eyed, toothless, gay junkie with paranoid delusions. Did I mention the eye-patch? Or that he might've been the greatest of them all? No small

6 Greatest Midget Rock & Roll Records

1. Bushwick Bill, *Little Big Man* (Virgin, 1992): On "Ever So Clear" the small but powerful Bill ("Size Ain't Shit" was his mantra) raps in a natural munchkin voice about making his girlfriend shoot him in the eye. Photos of his bloody eye socket became an LP cover for his band the Geto Boys.
2. Johnny Puleo and His Harmonica Gang, *Vol. 1* (Audio Fidelity, 1958): Harmonica virtuoso Puleo, 4' 6," was a vaudeville star in Borah Minevitch's Harmonica Rascals before fronting his own band. Because of the distinctive fidelity attributes of an all-harmonica band, Johnny's records were used to test stereo equipment, so everyone who bought an early stereo system was likely to own a Puleo record.
3. Lowell Mason, *The Gospel Midget* (Diadem, 197?): Not to be confused with the seminal nineteenth-century hymn composer of the same name, who was more than 46-inches tall.
4. Nelson Ned, *Si Las Flores Pudieran Hablar* (WS Latino, 1975): The Brazilian Ned is still one of the most popular romantic singers in Mexico, Spanish-speaking United States, South America and his home country.
5. Michel Petrucciani, *Pianism* (Blue Note, 1986): A piano prodigy and virtuoso despite stubby little fingers.
6. Children of the World, *Children of the World* (Epic, 1978): Herve Villechaize (of TV's *Fantasy Island*) sings a song with these thoughtful children called "Why" that set dwarf performers back to before court jester days. (Jake Austen)

claim for a city home to Jelly Roll Morton, Professor Longhair, Fats Domino, Huey Smith, Allen Toussaint, Ellis Marsalis and Mac Rebennack.

It was said of the great stride piano players that they had "a left hand like God." Booker's got that kind of thundering majesty, and a right hand like John the Baptist—still touched by God, but a little loopy after wandering around in the desert for years eating bugs. His hands skitter with Tatum-like dexterity, drawing the entire history of the Crescent City through his keyboard, a flow of rhythm and melody as inexorable as the Mississippi and no less capricious.

Rounder culled *Bayou Maharajah* from sixty hours of live tape recorded between 1972 and 1982 at New Orleans' historic Maple Leaf. (The companion release, *Spiders on the Keys* is entirely instrumental.) Don't be put off by the potentially cheesy medley structure of the track listings—Booker's style was endlessly discursive, the songs but a pretext for him to unfurl his gift. I doubt he ever played a song the same way twice. It's difficult to describe the appeal of Booker's singing—he's no Aaron Neville—but it allows him an added dimension to express his innate, distinctive musicality. Whether he's inserting a warning about the CIA into one of his signature tunes, "Papa Was a Rascal," or flitting through the "Minute Waltz" with the facility that earned him the nickname "The Chocolate Liberace," or making a jaw-dropping boogie woogie run on a Fats Domino standard like "All By Myself," Booker plays inimitably. He was a cracked vessel for all that talent, but nothing's closer to the Creole soul of New Orleans. (David Smay)

THE BOYS FROM NOWHERE

The Young Lion 45s

The Highway to Hell is paved with bad imitations. Discarded tubes of lipstick and the sloughed-off leathers of Stooges-wannabes stand by to warn the hopefuls who stagger along the time-honored—and widely dishonored—passage. In the late eighties, the LIE and Mass Pike were crowded with bands who fancied themselves the new Stones or Dolls (allegiance shifted around 1985 from *Pebbles* comps to MC5 reissues), but these outfits disappeared in the hair-apocalypse that was Guns N' Roses. Which is a crooked way of approaching Boys From Nowhere, the greatest garage band you've never heard.

While Lyres and the Chesterfield Kings were trying to drag us back to sacred-mono, Mick Divvens was shaking his mane to Uriah Heep records. While Jeff Conolly was struggling to accept that the world hadn't ended in 1967, Mick was on about the merits of Ratt's first 45. Yet brushing aside specious punk notions of purism, the fact remains that Divvens recorded some of the finest singles ever waxed by a guy named Mick. Vaulting over the usual obstacles—slack-jawed drummers with lucrative sidelines in armed robbery, feckless sidemen too busy griping to show up for practice—Divvens did it the hard way, playing organ, guitar, duck-call, and hair-on-fire screaming for a series of self-released singles that need to be heard to be believed.

Combining the pant-pissing heaviness of the best Detroit thug-rock with prime sixties 'tude, these were a far cry from the fey recidivism of bands I won't name, unless I already have; "Beg," "Jungle Boy," and (especially) "I Don't Bother" approach Stooges-like levels of intensity without sacrificing melodic interest, and—with that duck-call—nodding toward the retarded art-punk of fellow Ohioans Pere Ubu. These were subsequently reissued on a series of Spanish, German and Australian 12-inches that sounded as if they were mastered in a laughing-gas factory. Tinny, cruddy (the original pressings were both, in a good way) and sped-up, they led some to wonder what the fuss was about. An album on Skyclad followed. But the best are still those early singles, and it's a crime against humanity that Divvens still has boxes of 'em in his garage. He ought to be sending children to college on their backs. Maybe then someone could come forward to show the Hives, White Stripes, etc., how it's done. (Matthew Specktor)

BRICK

Brick   (Bang, 1977)

The second Brick LP is revered among the heads, but you may not be a disco-funk head, and this may not be a disco-funk album. Like their Midwest brethren Slave, the very special Brick are champs in the innocuous tar pit of Soul/Funk/R&B "Old School" radio syndication.

Roll around inside this record however you wish, but start with the third track—then try to get that one out of your mind for the rest of the day. The best example of What You're Dealing With, "Happy" is a semi-improvised, sunshiny pop song sucking up to difficult chords and the multi wind and brass wizardry of leader Jimmy Brown (who favored the flute). He was a sort of Rahsaan Roland Kirk of live action dance funk, making an onstage spectacle of his switcheroo antics. The stretched-out jam "We Don't Wanna Sit

Down" has postpunk-worthy scratch guitar, and you know the Pop Group and Gang of Four (there, I guess we're talkin' your talk now) got into these bands (see also the aforementioned Slave, early Cameo and second wave Bar-Kays).

Brick peaked with the two chart-burners on the album, "Dusic" and "Ain't Gonna Hurt Nobody." In the case of the latter, Brick should've had the world by the balls; there isn't a catchier, nor more credible, radio hit on the Urban dial. And anyone who doesn't acknowledge its genius in immediate, to-the-gut hooks could only be one of those "I'm not really into music" co-worker types (or a relative of the same stripe).

This album saved Atlanta's ass from the embarrassment of mid-to-late seventies James Brown (a solid case of drugs equaling bad music). (Andrew Earles)

IAN BROWN

Golden Greats   **(Polydor, 1999)**

In typically iconoclastic fashion, Ian Brown does his Stone Roses–based experimentations with dance backbeats one better on his second solo effort. The album forges a marriage of pop-rock accessibility and electronic fluidity that has seldom been achieved before or since.

Golden Greats is an inscrutably interesting animal from its first moments: versatile Aziz Ibrahim's muscular guitar heroics burst from his jangling quasi-Asiatic introduction, while Brown the singer abandons his previously trade-marked fey tonality, projecting a newly strong, moody and confident artist. As usual, his lyrics are often utter bollocks ("Dolphins were monkeys/That didn't like the land"), but in the mode of muse-worship (e.g., "Set My Baby Free"), Brown delivers occasional poetry as welcome counterweight.

Words notwithstanding, the genius here is the songcraft. Masterful pop chord progressions guide the rhythmic side of a heavily electro mix, producing a relentlessly engrossing, Mobyesque effect. Although Brown is contextually closer to Seal than Moby—and more complex and rough-hewn than either artist—the appeal is to the same self-serious club-goers and couch-stoners. Brown's real talents aren't vocal or instrumental—they're collaborative. On most tracks here, Dave McCracken, Tim Wills and Inder Goldfinger alternate guitar, percussion, keyboard, and production with a recently self-taught Brown. Why the work was so alchemically catchy this time around, however, is a true enigma.

Despite its innovative meld of rock bombast and trance-inducing electronics, *Golden Greats* was doomed almost immediately after release by Brown's unfailing knack for self-sabotage. The Roses' debut full-length inarguably changed the tone of British rock, but Brown and company waited four years to release a follow-up, during which time Oasis famously stole the Roses' swagger and the Beatles' songbook. If *Golden Greats*, which debuted in the U.K. at #9, might have given Brown a second chance to reclaim British music stateside for the forces of good, we'll never know. Citing family obligations, he pulled out of all promotion of the album mere days before major PR for his U.S. tour was to begin. (Jack Shay)

BUCKNER & GARCIA
Pac-Man Fever (CBS, 1982)

Look, I'm not saying we should *all* go out and write a bunch of songs about videogames, but it worked for Jerry Buckner and Gary Garcia, and look where they are now! (They merged into one guy, formed the Grateful Dead, and died of a marijuana attack.) That's right! They're the president!

Being an adult with unlimited access to gambling and naked people, I don't normally listen to children's music. But something keeps calling me back to the eternal critics' nonfavorite *Pac-Man Fever*—even more now than when I was a child. But then, how could I have appreciated the full rewards of this masterwork when I was too young to understand the heartbreak of having to chase a centipede? Or the devastating horror of … something to do with a mousetrap?

I may sound serious, but I'm actually being deadly facetious. It's the music that brings me back. Driven by synth, piano, and guitar, these pop hooks are far too ingenious for children's music, careening maniacally between sugary peaks ("Pac-Man Fever," "Do The Donkey Kong," "Hyperspace"), soul-wrenching balladry ("Goin' Berzerk," "Ode to a Centipede," "The Defender"), swaggering electronics ("Froggy's Lament," "Mousetrap"), and frolicking billiard-enhanced trepanni—oh. No, I guess that's all the songs.

But what truly separates Buckner & Garcia's sole release from Bruce Springsteen's *Nebraska* and other hits of the day is that every song incorporates actual videogame sounds in such a way that the bleeps and bloops become an integral part of the song's mood! Who else could have pulled this off?

No wait—I spelled that wrong. I meant, "Who else would have had so little self-respect as to release this uproarious embarrassment?" Maybe Fuckner & Garshitta (AHAHHA!) should be kicked in the assbutt for wasting so many stupendable melodies on lyrics like "I'm the defender—a mind-bender!"—but that doesn't make the melodies any less stupendable. (Mark Prindle)

RICHARD BUCKNER
Devotion + Doubt/The Hill   (MCA, 1997/Overcoat, 2000)

An adventurous songwriter who treats country and folk conventions as a diving board into the psyche, Richard Buckner explores high-pressure depths with *Devotion + Doubt*, which balances bleak and beautiful on a knife-edge equally recalling Big Star's *3rd* and Dock Boggs. *The Hill*, on the other hand, is a breathtakingly virtuoso adaptation of Edgar Lee Masters's *Spoon River Anthology*. Both albums exemplify Buckner's reckless willingness to follow his muse regardless of the challenges and personal cost.

Devotion + Doubt is Buckner's journal of his emotional plague years. Many people have gone through alcohol-soaked reflection after a relationship, when one is still in love and bitter about it. Buckner saw fit to capture his letters from hell, seemingly written at 4 A.M. on motel notepads next to near-empty whiskey bottles. "Pull" sets the stage: 2:40 minutes that epitomize the album's complex, understated instrumentation; besides several guitars, bass, and drums, there are fiddles both plucked and bowed, organ, vibes and pedal steel, all quietly building ambience. This is deconstructed country, sometimes quiet, always emotional, an introspective honky-tonk. Buckner sings about alcohol, ghosts, bitter loss and restless wandering with an eye for exhibitionism and an hallucinatory pen. Of particular note are "A Goodbye Rye," which interrupts the quiet flow of the album with up-tempo drumbeats; "Fater," an *a cappella* kiss-off to a faithless love; "On Travelling," a particularly naked raw nerve; and "Song of 27," which makes resolution sound like defeat. Although *D+D* can be overwhelming on first try, if the listener grasps the warmth of humanity underneath the despair, they can keep afloat and learn to roll with the waves, reaping the rewards of the experience.

On *The Hill*, Buckner abandons his own bitter poetry in favor of selections from *Spoon River Anthology*. The album is a single track. There are eighteen poems listed, but only about half appear as lyrics ("Mrs. Merritt" is a musical interlude before "Tom Merritt," and so forth). Masters' death-obsessed free verse works surprisingly well in Buckner's rebuilt-country style. The speakers of the *Spoon River* poems are all crying out from the grave, telling their stories of adultery, marital bitterness, suicide, and murder, and they sound like Buckner himself. The tracking of the album is problematic for those who, like me, are obsessive compilationists, but it makes sense artistically, which is all the justification it needs. (Hayden Childs)

DORSEY BURNETTE
Here & Now   (Capitol, 1972)

By 1972, the middle-aged Memphian's Rockabilly Trio days were behind him. So were the hits he gave Ricky Nelson, his own pop stardom ("Tall Oak Tree," the affecting "Hey Little One"), and his pill-fueled fall (his inability to say no suggests a Deep South Dennis Wilson). Burnette was saved—literally by religion and family, professionally by the early-seventies crossover tide that pushed country acts like Charlie Rich, Donna Fargo, and Tanya Tucker up the pop charts in record numbers.

Back from the brink, Burnette sounds like a soul saved. *Here & Now*, his Capitol debut, is an L.A.-recorded, big-production countrypolitan album, the perfect habitat for that soulful booming baritone. Think P. J. Proby, minus the overt mannerisms, with a Tennessee accent. It's a joy to hear him take on "Daddy Don't You Walk So Fast," vocally supercharge the honky-tonk ballad "I Love You Because" and roll through the mid-tempo hit original "In the Spring (The Roses Always Turn Red)," itself a remarkable confessional to a late soulmate. But it's in the upbeat tunes that Dorsey excels—"Lonely To Be Alone," a Dobro-powered, John Hartford-ish original, and, best of all, "I Just Couldn't Let Her Walk Away." Over a driving bass, banjo, chorale and pedal-steel (the arrangement is almost bluegrass Spector), he just soars. By the last verse and chorus, riding the harmonies and rhythm, he and the whole massive track sound like they're about to lift off the terra altogether. It's a pure pop moment, really, in the midst of a country album: robust, real, life-filled, worth it.

The Dorsey Burnette album followed in 1973, and it's strong too ("Keep Out Of My Dreams," "It Happens Every Time"). Burnette passed away in 1976. (Gene Sculatti)

C

JACKIE CAIN & ROY KRAL

Double Take   (Columbia, 1961)

One of the most enduring (and endearing) partnerships in show business began in the late 1940s when Roy Kral met "girl singer" Jackie Cain. Her crystal clear voice proved the perfect complement to Kral's deft arrangements and smooth baritone, and in 1948 they embarked on a musical and personal collaboration that spanned over fifty years. Like Glen Miller's classic sound of clarinet over saxophone, Kral sang his vocals a full octave below Jackie's. This parallel harmony created the irresistible, optimistic feeling that is at the center of their distinctive signature sound.

On *Double Take*, accompanied only by bassist Ted Snyder and Stan Harris on drums, Kral weaves a surprisingly full-sounding tapestry of standards, cabaret and jazz. Whimsically, Snyder switches instruments on the final number, Sondheim/Stein's "Together Wherever We Go," and provides us with what is surely the only three-part harmony with tuba.

This delicious sense of play infuses the entire album with fun and sets it apart from all other Jackie and Roy endeavors. Song by song, Jackie and Roy joke, banter, argue, kiss and make up. By turns droll, wry, charming and sarcastic, the couple poke fun at modern relationships and one another. Cain and Kral's own composition "Glasses and Ashes and Bottles and Cans" is the quintessentially perfect party postmortem. When Roy sings brashly "I like Scotch on the rocks" Jackie's understated "I know ..." speaks volumes.

Fresh and appealing, light and lively, *Double Take* is a triumph of harmony and wit, substance and style. Never before or since have two people created such unmitigated joy on vinyl. From the opening "Cheerful Little Earful" to the masterwork of vocalese called "Daahoud" by Clifford Brown, Jackie and Roy embark on a musical journey on which one is thrilled to be a stowaway. (Sean Carrillo)

JOHN CALE
Paris 1919   (Reprise, 1973)

I was a teenage Velvets freak who overplayed their records until they sounded like dishwater sloshing around the room. Happily, John Cale's solo albums continue to provide aural pleasure, and none more so than this intricate pastoral, recorded with Little Feat's Lowell George and Richie Hayward, and orchestral backing from the UCLA Symphony. (Only in researching this piece did I discover this record was made in Los Angeles, which is hard to reconcile with the cosmopolitan lyrical content and the white-on-white cover image of the bent sometime-rocker in a bentwood rocker, looking like he's auditioning for the Bogarde part in *Death in Venice*.) *Paris 1919* is an understated beauty of a disc, mysterious and gentle, with Cale's echoey Welsh-accented vocals coasting over the proceedings like a waft of incense.

"Child's Christmas in Wales" borrows Thomas's title and substitutes the singer's own arcane memories. The gorgeously melodic "The Endless Plain of Fortune" tells a cryptic tale of greed and emotional distance, its multiple characters making brief appearances before passing offstage. "Andalucia" is maybe a girl, maybe a place, but only John Cale could rhyme it with "when can I see ya?" and have it sound so clever. The side ends with "Macbeth," a surprise rocker anticipating the rougher-edged work that would come as Cale moved to Island in 1974: not quite "Chickenshit," but still completely out of place here. On the flip, the title track's an historical ghost story with a bridge of orchestral birdsong, and the cockeyed reggae of "Graham Greene" makes great fun of British hoity-toity society, sung in a Davies leer. The record drifts prettily off into disconnection with the sleepy train window travelogue of

"Half Past France" and "Antarctica Starts Here," a whispered postscript to the Velvets' "New Age."

John Cale then became a rock star, but left his tenderest parts behind for us to taste. (Kim Cooper) (See also: Lou Reed)

GLEN CAMPBELL

Reunion: The Songs of Jimmy Webb   **(Capitol, 1974)**

After Jimmy Webb's explosion onto the late sixties scene as a hitmaker, he released records as a singer-songwriter. But nobody delivered Webb's songs like Glen Campbell, so the old friends decided to work together again. Webb arranged and wrote all but two songs on *Reunion* (Lowell George's "Roll Me Easy" and "About the Ocean" by Jimmy's sis, Susan Webb). Glen was at the absolute peak of his vocal powers on this record. The way he turned a line like "I don't think you're human, but I miss you anyway" into an angerless surge of melody is evidence of his chemistry with Webb. Though every track on this record rewards close listening (like the rousing, minor-key waltz "It's a Sin [When You Love Somebody]"), two are jaw-droppingly beautiful, "You Might As Well Smile" and "Adoration." "Smile" features some of Webb's best lyrics, and amazing vocal acrobatics by Campbell. Listen to the way Glen croons the second verse ("I remember times when you held me/You'd freeze my spine/We were looking in the mirror/At the time I got confused and/I thought your eyes were mine") over gently changing chords and those trademark high-register strings. "Adoration" is a gorgeous, ominous barb delivered to a soon-to-be shit-canned lover. The majestic arrangement starts slowly, building into a dramatic chorus, followed by a strangely sped-up second verse, then slowing down again to normal for the second chorus. Campbell shows off his range as he hits a high A on the song's bitter last line: "I'm gonna show you how it feels to feel goodbye." Wow. This is one of those albums so well done that you never get sick of it no matter how many times you play it. Though this was not the end of Webb and Campbell's collaboration, it was the last in the organic, soaring pop style they had pioneered. (Doug Gillard) (See also: Bobbie Gentry, Jimmy Webb)

CAPTAIN BEEFHEART
Safe as Milk (Buddah, 1967)

As one who, after listening to *Trout Mask Replica* years ago, had written off Captain Beefheart as having even more of whatever it was that annoyed me about Frank Zappa, I was floored to discover that he and his band had once put out a record that, well ... rocked. Beefheart purists may dismiss it as being too conventional, with fairly traditional structures and time signatures, and lyrics that are only somewhat incomprehensible, but *Safe as Milk* manages to capture Beefheart in a half-frog, half tadpole state as he and his band were emerging from (relatively) conventional sixties blues-rock into their better known, art/freak/dada/uncategorizable incarnation exemplified by *Trout Mask Replica*.

This album features an early lineup of the Magic Band: Jerry Handley, Alex St. Claire, John French and a guest appearance by a young Ry Cooder on guitar and bass. While "Abba Zabba" is considered by the faithful the most "Beefheartlike" song, to my ears "Zig Zag Wanderer" and "Dropout Boogie" are the standouts, combining driving beat, fuzzed-out guitar and lunatic vocals to produce something that evokes the Monks, Kinks and Crazy World of Arthur Brown. Another notable track is "I'm Glad," a conventional-sounding pop song with an oddness that only later creeps up on you. Then there's "Electricity," with distorted vocals that recall Chrome, and on which, during recording, Beefheart's voice alone reportedly shattered the microphone.

Although later Captain Beefheart releases have overshadowed *Safe as Milk*, listeners who are turned off by their willful abstruseness will find it a surprisingly listenable piece of acid rock. (Chas Glynn)

CARDINAL
Cardinal (Flydaddy, 1994)

I think I first read about it on the back of a Sub Pop press release. Flydaddy was a Sub Pop–distributed label and publicist Nils Bernstein was talking about this record that was coming out. He described it as sounding a bit like early Bee Gees and the Left Banke and then went on to say, "... no kidding, this Cardinal record is one of the greatest pop records I have ever heard."

Cardinal was the work of Richard Davies, an Australian lawyer living in the United States, and Eric Matthews, a classically trained composer from outside of Portland, Oregon. Their pal (and Sebadoh drummer) Bob Fay thought that if they combined Davies's songwriting skills with Matthews's arranging, this duo might create magic. Which they did.

Davies wrote the songs on an acoustic guitar and Matthews added his deft touches with strings, trumpet, and a harpsichord, and it truly sounds like music piped in from another era, not the miserable grunge era we were just exiting. Listen to the magical opener "If You Believe in Christmas Trees" (with its perfect trumpet toots), the breathtaking harmonies of "Last Poems," the string-soaked "Big Mink" or the delicate cover by obscure sixties band Mortimer, "Singing to the Sunshine." They even take a stab at something a bit grittier in Matthews's "Dream Figure," then save the absolute best for last in the exquisite "Silver Machines" with its triumphant chorus, "… everything in my life is coming true." Truly a thing of lasting beauty. (Tim Hinely)

AARON CARTER
Oh, Aaron   **(Jive, 2001)**

The downside to pop record collecting is that most records consist of one, two, or three good cuts (the hits), while the rest is generic, interchangeable filler. This is more true now than ever, when the last seven or so songs on, say, a Christina Aguilera CD sound like the *same exact* songs filling out a Mandy Moore CD. But every now and then you get the unexpected surprise of putting on a disc and being entertained by it all the way through. No such surprise was ever more unexpected than with pre-fab, pre-teen "rapper" Aaron Carter's third CD.

Everything about Aaron Carter would make anyone over the age of twelve hate his guts right off the bat. His talents are limited, and it's safe to assume the only reason he's making records is because his older brother is Backstreet Boy Nick. Plus the words "white" and "rapper" together are usually a recipe for awfulness.

And make no mistake: Aaron's a lousy rapper. Yet I *love* his rapping. For one thing, he doesn't indulge in any wiggerisms. He never pretends to be anything other than whiter than Wonderbread—and unapologetically so, as he shouts with glee about his new dirt bike or Sony Playstation. The result is surprisingly amusing and appealing (thanks mainly to writers such as Andy Goldmark, and my current favorite hacks/geniuses Brian Kieruf and Josh Schwartz). Plus, all of Aaron's records have hooks galore, as anyone who's listened to Radio Disney for more than thirty minutes would be forced to concede.

My one complaint is that, like Nick, Aaron Carter actually has a very good, nasal "rock" singing voice (as evidenced on the great Archies-sounding song "Baby, It's You"). I wish they would phase out this whole "rapper" thing—I wish the *whole world* would phase out this "rapper thing"—and just let the kid sing rock songs from now on. (Peter Bagge)

JOHNNY CASH

Bitter Tears: Ballads of the American Indian   (Columbia, 1964)

You don't become legendary without taking risks. *Bitter Tears* was part of the Man in Black's "Americana" series, which pioneered the concept album before anyone had heard the term. *Bitter Tears* was not commercial; it was angry and political, with songs that address Native American themes and draw upon the rhythms and vocal styles of the 500 Nations. Cash was inspired by the songs of the Nargaset Indian folksinger Peter LaFarge, an important figure in the Greenwich Village folk scene. Five of the eight songs here are LaFarge covers, including the album's classic track, "The Ballad of Ira Hayes."

Cash became incensed when country radio shied away from playing "Hayes." In a move that presaged his middle-finger "Thank You" to the country music industry after he won the Grammy for "Unchained," he took out a full-page *Billboard* ad accusing the record industry of wishing to "wallow in meaninglessness." Not surprisingly, the ad did nothing to help the album's airplay.

Cash had immersed himself in research about injustices committed against Native Americans, and his passionate outrage complements the material. His cavernous voice is the ideal instrument for LaFarge's lyrics of alienation, isolation and betrayal, fueled by helpless—though not humorless—rage. When Johnny sings, on "Drums," of "drums beyond the mountains," his voice becomes that of the stony peaks themselves; and when he tells of U.S. government mistreatment of the Seneca tribe on "As Long As the Grass Shall Grow," his voice turns the spoken-word verse into a grave call to witness. Cash's own "Apache Tears" and the Johnny Horton contribution "The Vanishing Race" are both haunting in their spare otherworldliness. No one song or LP could bear the weight of Cash's legacy, but *Bitter Tears* captures both his artistic courage and his humanism. (David J. Schwartz)

THE CHILLS
Brave Words   (Homestead, 1987)

The Chills were an ever-shifting outfit from New Zealand with only singer/songwriter/guitarist Martin Phillipps staying the course. This was their first organic full-length to reach America's mopey undergrads and sun-starved record collectors. The singles collection *Kaleidoscope World* preceded it, and it was followed with two strong-to-excellent CDs on Slash/Warner in the early nineties.

This one, though, best gets across their work, the band's spooky strength, a power that doesn't smack or bludgeon but sneaks up with a muted intensity. They showed up on our shores in an early wave of American indie record collector seasonal obsessions, this time with all the otherworldly, smart, guitar-based pop-rock arising out of New Zealand in the late eighties. Of that batch, only the Verlaines and the Bats came close to the Chills' genius.

The band was reportedly unhappy with Red Krayola mainstay Mayo Thompson's misty, gauzy production. But what do bands know? That sound is a vital component of the pale ghostliness that makes this a uniquely moving pop artifact. This is one of those rare records that creates a new sonic and emotional world to live in, a world that no one, even the Chills, ever returned to explore more fully. But there's enough here for a lifetime of exploration. The sound amps up from a (lost) loving whisper to a careening train of dense, tense rock rumble from track to track. The locales shift from a creepy dark carnival to Dan Destiny preparing to launch off to a mysterious silver dawn. Throughout, Phillips comes across as that rarest of rock voices, the wise friend: hurt and sometimes confused but optimistic, sweet, caring, and strong. The band strums and pumps and bears down and relaxes and transmits all those qualities as well. (Brian Doherty)

DAVID CASSIDY

Cassidy Live!   (Bell, 1974)

Here's a guy with some claim to status. His dad's distinguished himself, right alongside Claude Akins, as one of the slimiest heavies ever to grace the TV cop shows, and his mom runs a tight musical ship nightly, riding over a rowdy herd that includes Danny Bonaducci and Dave Madden.

Where Cass Jr. shines is up onstage, out in front of maybe six or eight thousand screaming Briton boppers. He's got a lot of what pre–rock 'n' roll audiences used to clamor for—polish, showbiz spunk, and that trouper stamina occasioned by plenty of public pratfalls on the boards. Davy's thoroughly pro; slick and choreographed, well versed even in intra-song patter and convivial coyness. Since these qualities are generally associated with another, older brand of performer, and since his vocal skills, while impressive, are hardly commensurate with that kind of bravado and slickness, he comes off beautifully—as a precocious star-kid having way too good a time to worry about credibility or critics or anything. He's a natural ham, takes to smalltime Bigtime like Anka or Darin did.

Who's to say this isn't the best live "rock" album of the year? I'll take this Dave over that downhill skidding other one any day. Coiffed and spangled, this one sounds like a cross between a 38–year-old karate chopping Presley and the grinning, apple-cheeked Wayne Newton. He picks killer material, strokes it with a gentle show biz hand ("Some Kind of Summer" and the slowed-down "Breaking Up Is Hard to Do" sound like companion pieces to sloppy El Pres glut like the live "Suspicious Minds," all over-recorded rhythm and trashy tambourine-on-highhat), and walks away a winner every time.

His versions of oldies by the kiddo Beatles ("Please Please Me") and Rascals ("How Can I Be Sure") are double-sided xerox, his rock medley (a gruntoid "C.C. Rider," "Jailhouse Rock," etc.) irreverent, and his job on Stills' hoary "For What It's Worth" the best that song's ever had; the band goes crazy once Cass burps up his helium vocal, running amok like

continued

1969 G. Dead turned loose on 12,000 Haight St. regulars on a 1967 Sunday. "Mae" is classic Dennis Yost and "Delta Dawn" out-bludgeons Cocker and Russell's well-known assaults on subtlety.

Slicker than the once-blissful Bonos, almost as powerful as Rory Gallagher, twice as hammy as the Hudsons, Jack and Shirley's firstborn has distinguished himself this time. Are you ready, brothers & sisters?

(Gene Sculatti, *Creem*, December 1974) (See also: The Partridge Family)

LOU CHRISTIE

Lightnin' Strikes (MGM, 1966)

I'm a big fan of Lou Christie's hits, but I'm even fonder of his early misses. This album was a decent seller because the title track was so hugely popular. "Lightnin' Strikes" was the masterpiece from Lou and his writing partner, Twyla Herbert, that earlier works "The Gypsy Cried" and "Two Faces Have I" admirably presaged. The hit generated an excess of sales, but the album became a frequent piece of thrift store fodder in its day. I believe it was too silly even for your average young music fan of 1964. As fun as the hit is, it's just one example of the genius of Lou's unique vocal style, the campy arrangements, and the oddball background vocals. Side 1 of *Lightnin' Strikes* is comprised of six remakes of hits of the day, such as "You've Got Your Troubles" and "Going out of My Head." While they exhibit plenty of offbeat charm, it's the zany teen love originals on the flipside that will forever entrance the few folks who have fallen under Lou's spell. Lou's range allowed him to be a sort of self-contained 4 Seasons, doing the suave low parts as well as the soaring falsetto choruses. The female background singers (including Twyla's daughter) were every bit as over the top as Lou and added just the right amount of ridiculous moxie. "Trapeze," "Diary," "Jungle," "Crying in the Street" and "Baby We Got to Run Away" were cut from the same cloth as "Lightnin' Strikes," but were tailored for a more flamboyant fan. They were too quirky to stand much of a chance with a wide audience. His first album is good too, and he made plenty of decent ones afterward, but this is the acme. (P. Edwin Letcher)

GENE CLARK

Gene Clark & The Gosdin Brothers (Columbia, 1967)

The tastemakers regularly declare the cocaine-fueled *No Other* Gene Clark's masterpiece, but for my money it's the tunesmith's first long-player that deserves the *número uno* slot. Never mind that it presaged the country-rock of his former bandmates the Byrds, this is a superb collection of emotionally complex pop-rock that was ignored at the time and continues to be overlooked.

Gene Clark & The Gosdin Brothers was recorded after an aborted album attempted with the singer's live backing combo. Nominally produced by Gary Usher, it was Clark's manager Jim Dickson who brought in Vern and Rex Gosdin as featured accompaniment. The Gosdins were not really utilized to their full capacity, but some beautifully dissonant bluegrassoid harmonies add an exotic undertow to the doomed romanticism of Clark's leads. Musically, the album resonates with the twang of pickers as cool as Clarence White and Glen Campbell—not to mention the idiosyncratic rhythm section of Clarke and Hillman.

Five Great Songs from Dunedin, New Zealand

1. The Chills, "Pink Frost": A schizophrenic introduction segues into one of the most haunting songs ever written.
2. The Clean, "Tally Ho": You need listen to this only once and the Farfisa riff (played by the Chills' Martin Phillipps) will be etched into your brain for weeks.
3. Look Blue Go Purple, "Cactus Cat": Frantic Jangly Guitar + Killer Female Harmonies = Smiling Music Fan.
4. The Verlaines, "Death and the Maiden": The best 4/4 to 3/4 time change since "We Can Work It Out."
5. Sneaky Feelings, "Pity's Sake": Includes the lyric "You don't need a change of heart. What you need is a change of your brain is what you need." 'Nuff said. (Jon Bernhardt)

And oh, what songs. Dylanesque wordplay is rampant on the superbly orchestrated "Echoes" and the what-the-hell's-he-on-about "So You Say You Lost Your Baby," but for the most part the album continues the introspective air found on Clark's superlative Byrds material, creating a deliciously somber mood on cuts like "The Same One" and "Is Yours Is Mine," allied to a detached, vaguely nervous vibe unique in pop up to that point. Barring the a-go-go groove of "Elevator Operator," perhaps the track that best manages to be simultaneously engagingly upbeat and depressingly desolate is "Think I'm Gonna Feel Better."

Given Clark's lack of confidence at the time, *Gene Clark & The Gosdin Brothers* was unsurprisingly a commercial disaster. By far the best way to hear it is the original mono album version, which was reissued on Sony Music Special Products in 1991. Avoid remixed versions like the plague. (Alec Palao) (See also: Dillard & Clark)

COCK SPARRER

Cock Sparrer   (Decca, Spain, 1978)

Cock Sparrer formed in 1974 as a pub band with a bit of a Small Faces fixation. They soon caught the attention of Svengali Malcolm McLaren, who wanted to manage them but couldn't seal the deal because, legend has it, he failed to buy the band a round. McLaren did find another band to manage, and it was the release of the Sex Pistols' "Anarchy In the UK" that spawned a firestorm of signings of punk bands to major labels. Unfortunately, Cock Sparrer ended up with Decca. The band's debut was recorded at Decca's West Hampstead studio—the site of the Beatles' first ever professional recording audition; Decca passed on them in 1962. The great mystery is why on earth Decca released the full length only in Spain? Here's a clue: the label declared bankruptcy in late 1978.

Twenty-five years after the fact, this ten-song document of what could've been holds up better than almost all the early punk albums. The dual heavy metal boogie guitar wallop was captured beautifully by Nicky (Thin Lizzy) Tauber's production, and tracks like "Time for a Witness" and "Runnin' Riot" have that "bang a gong" rhythm that swings like great rock 'n' roll should. Also included was their second single, "We Love You," a metal/Oi/glam version of the Stones' track, which could have been Decca's misguided attempt to brand the band as the punk Rolling Stones. Colin McFaull's heavy cockney vocals brought up the inevitable Johnny Rotten comparisons, but Cock Sparrer's songs about strippers and other prosaic concerns lacked the Pistols' lacerating wit.

After Decca's demise the band lay dormant for several years. In 1983, Razor Records in the U.K. released *Shock Troops*, then gave the first LP a proper reissue with the title *True Grit* in 1987. (Max Hechter)

COCKNEY REBEL

The Psychomodo   (EMI, 1975)

When I would watch *At the Movies*, Gene Siskel would always bring up his tired "if only they followed this character ..." And I'd yell at the TV, "well then make yer own goddamned movie." You have to look at something on its own terms. For me, anything unique is a kind of masterpiece that raises it above general criticism with a hearty "*This* is what I wanted to do, now piss off." *The Psychomodo* falls into the glam-era summer camp—the theatre of the "crack'd actors." It was more of a one-man show, but Steve Harley doesn't seem to care if we follow him or not, a bit like music hall for the hard of hearing. Over time this album hasn't gotten the revival it deserves despite the appealing qualities of seeing a glamannerist through a broken prism. Harley's lyrics range from the incomprehensible to the offensively incomprehensible (and that's a plus) all the while accompanied by some demented cover band playing complex "classics" they heard in addled half sleep. A perfect example of the $1 record outshining the current in-favor miniscule edition "real people" missive, this one still conveys the energy of its manic attack thirty years on, something to be treasured. (Jim O'Rourke)

DAVID ALLAN COE
Once upon a Rhyme

(Columbia, 1975)

Though more infamous than famous (he's an ex-con, Mormon, masked, Outlaw Country, ventriloquist, porno-music, bigamist, biker poet) D.A.C. actually made some great recordings. With this album Coe made a mark on country (as songwriter and performer), and produced an album so strong it can stand up with the all-time classics in the genre. Opening with his million seller (for Tanya Tucker) "Would You Lay with Me (In a Field of Stone)," Coe's subtle, sublime reading really lets this song flow. The eerily pretty "Jody like a Melody," a song he'd rerecord often, follows. He ends the side with the upbeat "Sweet Vibrations (Some Folks Call It Love)," a folk-gospel number that sounds like a familiar traditional the first time you hear it. On Side 2 Coe hands the writing chores to others, and makes some wonderful choices. The album ends with perhaps his most famous number, Steve Goodman's "You Never Even Called Me by My Name." The novelty ending is what endears the song to non-country fans and frat boys (in a recitation Coe tells Goodman it isn't the perfect country song because it doesn't include mama, trains, trucks, prison, or getting drunk. Goodman adds the verse, "I was drunk the day my mom got out of prison, and I went to pick her up in the rain. But before I could get to the station in my pickup truck she got runned over by a damned old train"). The joke is funny, but the real key to the song's success is Coe's execution. Though he would later work extensively with the king of Nashville hit production, Billy Sherrill, and though he would make many LPs far different from this one and equally brilliant in their own ways, never again would Coe produce as perfect a pop country LP. Few have. (Jake Austen)

LEONARD COHEN
Death of a Ladies' Man   (Columbia, 1977)

This album reads like a mismatched-partners buddy picture with a whisper of tragedy—*One ended up in a monastery. The other went to death row!*—and it's conspicuously nonrepresented on the self-compiled *The Essential Leonard*

Cohen (though I bet it'd figure strongly on its sequel, *The Entirely Superfluous Leonard Cohen*). And yet the combination of Cohen's weary poetics and Phil Spector's sonic bombast achieves a kind of decadent grandeur, the sound of a coffee-house discotheque somewhere in Weimar-Republican America, with the sleaziest lyrics Laughin' Lenny ever wrote plopped in the middle of a self-parodic Sargasso Sea of sound. In other words, it sounds deliciously and deliriously *wrong*, and whether he'd admit it or not, fighting to be heard over Spector's oppressive Technicolor yaw gives Cohen a shot of vigor, knocking some of the cobwebs out of his morbid-unto-moribund versifying. Don't believe me? Listen to the ten-minute title track, one of the few Cohen's ever done that could be called "epic" (albeit uncomfortably intimately so once you make out what he's saying). Listen to "Fingerprints," where, believe it or not, Leonard *sings*. And above all, listen to the jaw-dropping "Don't Go Home With Your Hard-On," coupling an uncharacteristically light, though still barbed, lyric about a hairdresser (!!) with a woozily upbeat funk track and one of the best examples of Spectorian perversity on record (roping Bob Dylan and Allen Ginsberg in to sing backgrounds and then rendering them completely inaudible). I wouldn't be surprised if this album escapes oblivion soon, if only by Spector's defense team as *prima facie* evidence to support an insanity plea, but as a colorful but slightly blurred snapshot of a pair of uniquely oddball, reclusive artists meeting at a strange crossroads (whichever one is closest to the liquor store/gun mart) and for the first hints of what came to pass once Cohen morphed from melancholy acoustic poet to synth-hounded prophet of doom a decade later, it's surprisingly invaluable. (William Ham)

SAM COOKE
Night Beat (RCA, 1963)

"Sometimes I'm almost to the ground," sings Sam Cooke on "Nobody Knows the Trouble I've Seen." The first song on *Night Beat*, it sets the tone for the entire album. "Almost" is the essential part of that lyric. Few singers could deliver a line like that with the subtlety of Cooke. His candied rasp, no matter how despondent his words, carries with it the sound of perseverance and hope.

It's likely Cooke's gospel background that lends *Night Beat* that glimmer of reassurance that these blues will pass. Where Frank Sinatra and numerous country crooners tackled similarly boozy, crushed-heart material from the perspective of the guy on the next barstool, Cooke nearly preaches his tales of woe. *Night Beat* is confessional, cautionary and cleansing all at once. But don't think that Cooke's theme album doesn't give the listener plenty to cry about. As the title implies, this is music for the dark hours.

The drums pad softly and the cymbals brush like rain in "Lost and Lookin'." Cooke's own composition "Mean Old World" consists mainly of repetition of the line: "This is a mean old world to live in all by yourself." Still, the sound of recovery sneaks in. The organ work in "Please Don't Drive Me Away" recalls a Southern Baptist revival. And it ends with the loose and grinning R&B of "Shake, Rattle and Roll."

The saddest aspect of *Night Beat* is that Cooke, known primarily for his transcendent singles, had so few chances to record coherent albums like this one. *Night Beat* was out of print for years until the 2001 reissue. Inexplicably, it remains a critics' and completists' favorite only. Had Cooke lived, might he have put out more theme albums like this? All the more reason to treat *Night Beat* like the treasure it is. (Kris Kendall)

COLOURS

Colours/Atmosphere   **(Dot, 1968/1969)**

A 1968 studio group featuring Chuck Blackwell and Carl Radle, these are unashamed Beatle-sounding albums (and better by miles than Moby Grape's *Wow*). Both are brimming with compelling melodies, stylistic Mac-Len vocals and some of the tastiest arrangements ever. The inspiration for *Colours* is solely *Sgt. Pepper*, but *Atmosphere* stretches out a bit, with savory lead licks and totally sympathetic horn charts. How a song like "Angie" could go unnoticed so long is beyond me. One of the best-programmed sets I've heard.

(Gene Sculatti, *Flash* #2, June–July 1972)

COSTES
End of the Trail   (Self-released, 1992)

Costes is the ultimate DIY rocker of the French Underground. He's vile, pro-lific, poignant, crazy, unlistenable, pop. *End of the Trail* is the seventh of his releases and his third album to be recorded in English. While some would argue that *Lung Farts* is an equal masterpiece, *End* is a nineteen-song hom-age to his breakup with indie icon Lisa Suckdog Carver, and a more moving love letter has never been recorded. Splatters of filth and sonic mess hide the sentimentality, but the beauty shines through, triumphantly sad beneath lay-ers of disgust and ugly noise. A classical sonnet dissolves into layered mud-dle punctuated by overblown vocals, only to be reduced a moment later to a vulnerable whimper as a multitude of schizophrenic emotions battle for dom-inance. Costes plays, sings, manipulates, produces and destroys every track in utter solitude, shining through on borderline narcissistic tracks like "King of Rock'N Roll, Sort Of" and "I Don't Want to Be a Souvenir on a CD Player." His music is from necessity; he cannot help himself. It is a document of mod-ern humanity as representative of his era's id as Gainsbourg was of his.

Lauded by the likes of Thurston Moore and the odd rock journalist, Costes remains virtually unknown, even in his own country, a special gem without genre. (Costes has claimed Daniel Johnston and GG Allin as musi-cal kin, though he resembles neither.) He has been shunned, sued and attacked for his uncompromisingly viscous aesthetic. Still, at the time of this writing he has over thirty recordings to his credit and he shows no signs of slowing. (The Bengala) (See also: Suckdog)

JOE E. COVINGTON'S FAT FANDANGO
Joe E. Covington's Fat Fandango   (Grunt, 1973)

Around the early seventies, rock began to pastiche rock 'n' roll. Mr. Covington and his Fat Fandango (a silly Procol Harem joke, and the artiste behind "Thunk" on Jefferson Airplane's *Bark* knew from silly) certainly didn't invent this notion. Given his (low) reputation as the clumsy replacement for Spencer Dryden in late-period Jefferson Airplane and lumpy basher for early Hot Tuna, he certainly wasn't the influential genius leading the trend. Besides, those geniuses in Sha Na Na beat him by a few years. Still, "influence" is a poor standard by which to judge a record; in your room, it's down to the vinyl and your ears, not generations of progeny who may have copped an approach.

A stylistic polymathism pulling together much of what rockish pop had meant for the past fifteen years runs riot on this delightful curiosity. Some might argue that this reworking of past modes denotes a slide into decadence. But rock 'n' rollers understand that decadence beats purity most weekdays. By the nineties, it seemed every record could be described by some long list of stylistic signifiers: punk/funk/folk/jazz/metal amalgams, usually lusterless and with a low melting point. Little noted then or later, still unreleased on CD, this peculiar yet lovable record does all sorts of things, none of them perfectly, but all with a smile and infectious enthusiasm. There's yearning doo-wop (with maybe a hint of silliness), heartfelt Philly soul (with a surprisingly intense drum break), grinding organ psychedelia, rock-country ballads, and none of them sound like mere genre exercises or imitations. It's doubtful that he really wants you to think he's Hendrix as he grinds away about how hideouts are a crook's best friend. But this record spills goofy charm from its grooves, and a sense that the auteur is indulging his fullest range of personal tastes and concerns, making for an artifact of love and enthusiasm. (Brian Doherty) (See also: Jefferson Airplane, Paul Kantner)

THE COWSILLS
IIxII   (MGM, 1970)

Don't think about this record's place in rock historical memory. It has none. To the rockcrit intelligentsia, bubblegum bands like the Cowsills didn't exist, or didn't deserve to. (See the editors' *Bubblegum Music is the Naked Truth* for the only exception to this regrettable gap in cultural history.) That's the only way a record this great could have been ignored. It's beautifully crafted, sung and played pop freighted with high concept and screwy as hell. Indeed, hell and God's wrath—hell, the universe's wrath—toward a fallen humanity is one of its main concerns.

The bubblegum background helps make this record perfect—even a song as purely insane as "The Prophecy of Daniel and John the Divine" (which declares over and over that "six is the number/of a maaaan!" and with a middle-eight in which an ambisexual voice intones eerily that "finally one day she was cast back into the sea from where she came so that she would never torment ... man ... AGAIN!") is so wonderfully *wonderful* sounding that it might take a few listens for the record's dark undercurrents to stain the lovely sunshine of its singing and playing.

Every song, from the campfire-singalong pep of "IIxII" (in which the singer is prepared to joyfully take on the burden of a modern-day ark—which means, remember, that the vast majority of life on Earth gets destroyed) to the gorgeous hippie harmonizing of "Don't Look Back" (in which we are advised to "please do something as you perish") is great. It's a bottomless pleasure to sink into this record anytime and five times a day, with new details ever coming to the fore. For example, the bassist has listened carefully to a lot of Paul McCartney and seems determined to kick his thick, supple, super-imaginative bass-playing ass. A perfect record, and almost perfectly lost. (Brian Doherty)

MARSHALL CRENSHAW
Mary Jean & 9 Others　　　　　　　(Warner Brothers, 1987)
I've never talked to anybody outside of Crenshaw himself who knows that this record even came out, but it's one of my favorites. Crenshaw originally pushed the retro vibe, the story hook being that he played Lennon in *Beatlemania!* and wrote and performed like Buddy Holly. *Mary Jean & 9 Others* finds him maturing on all counts: as a songwriter, singer and guitarist. He may be one of the most underrated guitarists around, as his modesty belies his melodically smokin' ability, and longingly pretty major-seventh chording.

By the time of this album, Crenshaw's fourth, he'd lost the retro and wasn't quite yet exhibiting the rootsy, just beautiful, pop-rock love songs. Not power pop, just upbeat, pretty-ass songs with great chords and melodies. With his drummer brother Robert and the incredible Graham Maby (longtime Joe Jackson bassist), Crenshaw lovingly rips into ten tunes, all originals with the exception of "Steel Strings" (Peter Case) and "Calling out for Love" (co-written with producer Don Dixon). Most are lushly textured odes to love gone right or regret, each amazing melody framing a blistering but pretty Crenshaw guitar lead in the middle eight. Perfect examples? "This Is Easy," "Mary Jean," and the record's coolest song, "A Hundred Dollars." "Wild Abandon" is a stateside Smiths-a-billy shuffle, and "Til That Moment" is reminiscent of 1982–era Crenshaw, melding Buddy Holly and Rick Nelson.

The only drawback is Dixon's telltale 1987 overuse of reverb and "big" drum sound, but it doesn't matter much. You can still hear everything that's going on, and the songs themselves take you somewhere far, far away. You don't want the needle to lift off the record and wake you from the dream. (Doug Gillard)

D

TERENCE TRENT D'ARBY

Terence Trent D'Arby's Symphony or Damn   (Columbia, 1993)

After his debut hit "Wishing Well" in 1987, Terence Trent D'Arby seemed poised to launch a superstar career. His throwback voice rasped with Otis gravel, and his lean guitar riffs hit like shots to the body. Then with *Neither Fish nor Flesh,* Terence alienated both his audience (with his musical self-indulgence) and the press (with his outrageously egotistical claims) so completely that he's never really recovered. *Symphony or Damn* did well in the U.K. (where his duet with Des'ree, "Delicate," was a top 20 hit), but stateside he tanked. By 1993, Terence was old news, and the media's limited interest in black rockers had turned to Lenny Kravitz and Me'Shell NdégeOcello.

Ten years on, *Symphony or Damn* sounds like both a relic (after years of hip hop murk, *Symphony* rings with a too-clean digital crispness—the gated drums sound like punted dumpsters), and some magnificent folly: *James Brown Plays the Hits of XTC (and Guns N' Roses!)*. Except weirder. You've got to make a choice right at the beginning with "Welcome to My Monasteryo"—a thirty-second, spot-on Queen imitation with pompous, lush harmonies spelling out a cringe-inducing pun. If you opt in you get the whole package: ginormous guitar riffs ("She Kissed Me"), tender breakup ballads ("Let Her Down Easy"), neo-soul both epic ("Neon Messiah") and intimate ("Are You Happy?"), slinky charmers like "Delicate," power pop lifted whole from Andy Partridge's fakebook, ("Penelope Please": "You will still be home in time/to watch the 'Pops' featuring Chrissie Hynde"). These *sound* like hits. Hell, "I Still Love You" sounds like a *country* hit.

Terence tosses off at least one quirky line per song that snaps your attention back to the lyric sheet ("If Oedipus could rise/he'd probably try me on for size"). There's a surprising vulnerability in D'Arby's songwriting; though his voice recalls hard-ass soul men like Wilson Pickett, his persona here derives from Philippe Wynne (Spinners) and Eddie Levert (O'Jays). The irony of Terence's story is that he was almost as good as he said he was. (David Smay)

BLOSSOM DEARIE

Blossom Dearie (Verve, 1957)

Blossom Dearie is not underappreciated by those who've heard her perform. Johnny Mercer has written songs for her, Tony Bennett has winked an eye at her (in his album *Here's to the Ladies*), and to be truthful, she has been heard and loved by an enviably large American audience.

Unfortunately, this audience has for the most part not had the opportunity to connect Dearie's voice with her name (and yes, that is the name on her birth certificate). On the popular 1970s *Schoolhouse Rock* educational cartoons on ABC Saturday mornings, Miss Blossom sang with such grave innocence and respect about adjectives and the number eight that she forever engraved her voice somewhere between the brain and heart of Generation X. If she is remembered solely for this artistic contribution, however, this generation is doing itself a great disservice.

Her debut was the result of her garnering positive reviews during several years on the Parisian cabaret circuit. Many of the tracks have fallen into "chestnut" category after countless renditions by vocalists less skilled than Dearie, but with her clear and clean sexy little girl voice she breathes new life into such otherwise petrified standards as "I Won't Dance" and "Loverman." On the latter, particularly, she genuinely sounds like she has been staring out through the window for an unhealthy amount of time waiting for the center of her universe to come back.

Dearie never sounds disturbed, however, or disturbing, despite the "sexy little girl" tag that is impossible to avoid when describing her voice. Her voice evokes the impossible: a creature who has managed to maintain her innocence while gaining immeasurable wisdom. She is the Destroyer of Men, and she smells like fabric softener. She is Blossom Dearie; say the name twice and you won't forget. (Elizabeth Herndon)

DEERHOOF
The Man, the King, the Girl (Kill Rock Stars/5RC, 1997)

There are many reasons why I believe Deerhoof will go down in music history as one of the more important and influential bands of the '00s. Just one of them is the guy in the audience who was screaming, "DEERHOOF IS FUCKING GOD!" when I saw them live in 2003. What other band can conjure up sonic images of Sun Ra and the Spice Girls in the space of a three-minute pop song? The 'hoof is one of the few bands making modern avant-pop that shows real love for the high art *and* the low art of it all. No wonder they've managed to do a brilliant version of the Shaggs' "My Pal Foot Foot," capturing the utter creativity and total naïveté of the original.

Deerhoof's debut CD is wild and unpredictable in all the best ways. True to the band's high/low dichotomy, it presents "studio" and "live" versions of several songs, with the live recordings coming from one of the most lo-fidelity boom-box cassette tapes ever transferred to digital. The sound and performance contrast of these songs reveals a band more interested in experimentation than polish—a mark of those few artists whose influence proves lasting.

And Deerhoof isn't afraid to rock out! Drummer Greg Saunier is an incredible powerhouse, getting more organized chaos out of a bass, snare, highhat and crash cymbal than most drummers can get from five times as many drums. The juxtaposition of his playful brutality with cute Japanese singer/bassist Satomi Matsuzaki's whispery understatedness creates an amazing dynamic tension that's never less than thrilling. When I saw her perform an incredible (though poorly enunciated) solo karaoke version of the Village People's "YMCA" in 1998, I knew I was a goner for the world of Deerhoof. I still am. (Russ Forster)

Jazzbos

A generation of jazz fans cut their teeth on Basie, got spun by Monk and bent their lyrics around the changes to lay out these contentedly neurotic spiels.

Sin and Soul, Oscar Brown, Jr.: Hip lyricist for "Dat Dere" and "Afro Blue" will cut you up on "Bid Em In."

Rah, Mark Murphy: Chops, tone, taste and smarts. Sexy on "Stop the Clock" plus the definitive "Doodlin'."

King Pleasure Sings/Annie Ross Sings: The sourcebook for vocalese. "Jumping With Symphony Sid" will earworm you hard, and Annie's "Jackie" is a children's book rebopped. "Farmer's Market" digs beatnik love.

Sing a Song of Basie, Lambert, Hendricks and Ross: Hendricks's lyrics for "Jumping at the Savoy" make a jazz paradise. And when Annie comes in as the trumpet, "That's it/that's it/that's it," it's pure, undiluted joy.

Portrait of Sheila, Sheila Jordan: Cool, impeccable, swinging, plus an Oscar Brown fan.

I Don't Worry about a Thing, Mose Allison: A laid-back smartass, blue and boppish. "Your mind is on vacation, but your mouth is working overtime."

Time for Two, Anita O'Day & Cal Tjader: Anita's undeniably the coolest white woman ever, and proves it on "An Occasional Man." She rides the rhythm like nobody this side of Ella.

Travelin' Light, Shirley Horn: Right before her mom hiatus, Shirley swings it with subtle sangfroid. Classy. (David Smay)

SUGAR PIE DESANTO
Down in the Basement   **(Chess, 1989)**

You can't top Sugar Pie's soul bona fides. The peerless R&B talent scout Johnny Otis discovered her in San Francisco. Then from 1960 to 1962 she opened for James Brown, where her lightning fast footwork and backflips earned her the nickname Little Miss Dynamite. Her close childhood friend Etta James sang duets with her, and Sugar Pie wrote hits for Fontella Bass and Little Milton. Hell, she even toured with Sonny Boy Williamson and Willie

Dixon. Not bad for a tiny (4' 11") little thing born Umpeylia Marsema Balinton who grew up the child of a Filipino father and a black mother.

This record collects her work from 1959 to the mid-sixties, a funky core sample capturing R&B as it evolved into soul. Sugar Pie could do it all and did it with style and an infinite well of sass. She went toe-to-toe with Etta on scorching soul struts "Down in the Basement" and "Do I Make Myself Clear" and didn't give an inch. She co-wrote her first (and only) hit "I Want to Know" in 1959; it smolders with an insistent, hypnotic tension. "Can't Let You Go" follows in the same mode, bluesy with a taut staccato guitar, and a yakety sax turn at the bridge. By 1963 Girl Groups dominated, so she marched out "She's Got Everything" with its step-by-step rhythm and tweedly keyboard hook.

"Mama Didn't Raise No Fool," from 1965, shows a big Stax influence in the horn charts and the stinging guitar. "Soulful Dress" pairs nicely with "Slip in Mules" (an answer song to "High Heeled Sneakers"); that's Maurice White (Earth Wind and Fire founder) himself keeping the high stepping beat. Sugarpie wrote the majestic, big city blues ballad "Going Back Where I Belong," and she sings it like Dinah Washington's little sister. Though Sugar Pie DeSanto never made it big, she still tears it up live at the Boom Boom Room in San Francisco. She doesn't do backflips anymore, though; she had to quit those when she turned sixty. (David Smay)

THE DICTATORS
Go Girl Crazy!   **(Epic, 1975)**

Think of the Dictators as the *homo habillus* of punk rock. Punkers of the "Sex-Pistols-invented-everything" school never "got" them. They didn't have safety pins in their ears, had long hair, and (gasp!) their songs had guitar solos. Indeed, the Dictators never were a true punk band. But like prehistoric man, they were half human and half ape, never able to be one or the other, but a mixture of both. In many ways they were a typical early seventies heavy rock band, dressing and acting like the stoners they were. Then the Dictators recorded an album that broke free of the pack and established them in the history books.

Within these grooves the Dictators invented what would be known as PUNK ROCK. Lyrically, their songs involved cheeseburgers, pizza, professional wrestling, cars, girls, surfing, beer and enough teen angst to fill up the trunks of a thousand Camaros. Consider these nuggets of wisdom: "I'm just a clown walking down the street/I think Lou Reed is a creep/I need a girl/I need release!" There would be no songs about unicorns here. The Dictators had one element that had been missing in rock and roll since the early sixties: *humor*. Hippies hated humor and the Dictators hated hippies.

This was so left field, it wasn't even in the ballpark. In 1975 the Dictators were the only band even thinking about true rock 'n' roll—they were a beacon of light in a sea of darkness. *Go Girl Crazy* predictably tanked. But enough people (like the Ramones) heard the record that a seed was planted. Soon a thousand bands sprung up that had weaned themselves off MOR rock radio with this record. So while they themselves were never actually punks, they did invent what would come to be known as punk rock. (Deke Dickerson)

BO DIDDLEY
500% More Man (Checker, 1965)

I don't want to hear shit about "the Bo Diddley beat." Yeah, the big man rocked up the hambone rhythm and loosed it on the world. He owns that beat, no question. But that's nothing but a spoonful of black-eyed peas on a platter of pulled pork barbecue. The man made a feast, and all y'all wanna talk about is the side dish.

We're talking about one of the slyest and funniest songwriters of his generation, a signature guitar stylist, a sonic innovator and a blistering live performer. I can blind snatch any album out of his first ten years and make my case: say *500% More Man*.

Bo Diddley cut this record one year before his epic performance on *The Big TNT Show*, backed by Jerome Green on maracas and The Duchess as co-guitar slinger (impossibly soigné in a sequined evening gown). But in that one year, his whole career changed; this was his last shot at adapting to a music business that had already turned away from him. By *The Big TNT Show* he was being packaged as an oldies act.

So they put the big man out to stud, but he could still run. Drop the needle anywhere on this record and let the wampus tremolo reset you at the molecular level. You *will* vibrate in time with Bo's guitar. The maracas are just there to ease your hips into it. I bet you a bucket of crawdads, John Fogerty had this record memorized when he was still a Golliwog. It's a straight shot from Bo's guitar sound on "He's So Mad" into "Sinister Purpose." Ditto Keith Richards, because the Stones of "19th Nervous Breakdown" get their stinging attack from Bo and nobody else. (Okay, and a little Slim Harpo.) Keef must've worshipped badass rockers like "Let Me Pass." Bo's got the Cookies on backing vocals this album, and they lend real charm to the soul-styled number "Stop My Monkey" and a rare-for-Bo ballad, "Tonight Is Ours." Bo backs his bravado with vibrato on the title track, tucks in on "Soul Food" and mops up with "Corn Bread." Put down that greatest hits collection and dig into Bo's back catalogue. He's *at least* five times the rocker you think he is. (David Smay)

TIM DOG

Penicillin on Wax   (Ruffhouse, 1991)

Who set off the coastal rap battles? Biggie vs. Tupac? Suge vs. Puffy? Actually, it was probably "Fuck Compton," Bronx rapper Tim Dog's debut single. A former member of the legendary Ultramagnetic MCs, Dog grew furious watching his SoCal rivals climb the charts. In "Fuck Compton," he called Cali out, inviting N.W.A, DJ Quik and others to a Big Apple beatdown. Basically a temper tantrum set to Public Enemy period production, "Fuck Compton" is hilarious and compelling in all sorts of unintended ways. First off, there's Dog's delivery, gruff and over the top. He keeps getting madder and madder, ranting and cursing all the way through the song, but his voice is lispy, his rhymes sophomoric (more than once he rhymes a word with itself), the ultimate impact cartoonish. The effect resembles your obnoxious uncle drunkenly singing karaoke.

DILLARD & CLARK
Through the Morning, Through the Night   (A&M, 1970)
One of the very best country rock attempts. Title cut is especially haunting, and has some nice harmony stuff on it. Heads
and shoulders above the rest of this genre.

(Ed Ward, *Flash* #2, June–July 1972)

How did Dog follow up "Fuck Compton?" With an *entire album* dissing
California rappers. Actually, he only spends about a third of *PoW* on the subject, and does admit respect for Ice Cube and Ice-T. However, at any given
moment, he might make an aside about the West Coast's rhyme fakery and,
oddly enough, their penchant for wearing L.A. Raiders caps. (After all, he
reminds us more than once, the Giants—a New York team!—won the Super
Bowl that year.) Much of *PoW* is gripping in the same way "Fuck Compton"
is: ranting delivery, oft-lackluster rhymes, a few unintentional chuckles per
track. However, even Dog can't keep up this level of rage; he loses steam
toward the end of Side 2. Still, you're advised to hang in there for "Secret
Fantasies," in which he and fellow Ultramagnetic MC Kool Keith relate their
sexual daydreams with truly uncomfortable "smooth" sighing and gasping.

And the irony? Dog moved to California, where he still raps today.
(Mike Appelstein)

DOGBOWL

Flan   (Shimmy Disc, 1992)

Flan could win an award for the most
human suffering and disgusting atroc-
ities ever in an album of gorgeous pop.
Published simultaneously as an album and
a novel by Stephen "Dogbowl" Tunney, the story
begins when an ordinary guy called Flan wakes up to find his room on fire.
Something vaguely apocalyptic has happened, transforming his world into a

living hell of corpses, cannibals, and rats: also a human-headed dog, a floating eyeball, testicles that walk and a talking fish with the musical name Ginger Kang Kang.

In a world gone mad, it's nice to have an anchor, and Flan can generally be expected to react to a horrible sight with an appropriate cry of "How horrible!" At least *somebody* still has their priorities straight. Flan doesn't want to muck around with corpses or tear open their stomachs in search of undigested food. He wants to find his girlfriend, Holly, who we hope is still alive.

Dogbowl and his band do a wonderful job of creating musical personalities for the different chapters of Flan and Ginger's arduous journey up the railroad tracks to Holly's cabin. Christopher Tunney's clarinet punctuates some wild klezmer mayhem, but he plays it cool and nocturnal on "Grey Tulip." Lee Ming Tah's beautiful pedal steel guitar is a Loony Tunes sign off as well as the sound of a mind bending and being blown trying to find something to cling to in hell.

On the lovely "A Memory," Flan realizes that his memories of the pre-disaster world are dimming, lasting less than a second. "Memory" and "Mermaid in My Coffee Cup" transcend the wacky gimmicks and stand apart from the storyline as good, melancholy songwriting.

Flan is a chaotic bundle of hooks, lyrics, big themes, sadness, and fun. It sounds like nothing else, and it's a pleasure. (Kevin Carhart)

SWAMP DOGG
Cuffed, Collared, and Tagged (Cream, 1972)

Veteran Atlantic producer Jerry Williams created an outrageous persona to unleash his id on the world. Swamp Dogg's first album, *Total Destruction to Your Mind,* justly remains his calling card; it starts with the unbeatable one-two punch of the title track, a high-octane psych-soul rocker, and the bottomless cry of "Synthetic World." Despite his hilarious and scathing lyrics, fantastic voice, and a band coiled tighter than a watchspring, Swamp Dogg's albums tend to bog down in samey mid-tempo tracks. For my money, his third album, *Cuffed, Collared, and Tagged,* is his best-sequenced record, ranging from folk to funk, soul to swamp rock, and mastering them all. He writes with sharper focus; the sound hits harder.

Cuffed opens with John Prine's withering, elegiac "Sam Stone," the definitive soul portrait of a black Vietnam vet. They're such a perfect marriage of sensibilities—prickly, cynical, thoughtful, brash, wounded—that you can't help but wish the Dogg had put his voice to an entire album of Prine songs. Whether Swamp Dogg is ranting at music industry backstabbing, airing his ninety-ninth bitch session about his alimony or railing against jingoism, he backs his grievances with in-the-pocket grooves. Further in he funks up "Lady Madonna" à la Billy Preston, scatting through to the outro. He celebrates his inspiration in the funk juggernaut "If It Hadn't Been for Sly" and spouts a geyser of bile on "Your Last Dirty Trick," a vengeful little bastard of a song with a shotgun and a grudge.

If the Dogg's cranky, it's only because humanity proves a serious disappointment. Sure, he had a tendency to mistake his peeves for epic injustices, but on "You Say You Trust Your Mother" he exposes the depth of his wary, weary feelings for America, bluntly critical but still hopeful. By the time he rides out on Joe South's mournful, gospel-structured "Don't It Make You Want to Go Home," he's earned the rest that song craves so deeply. (David Smay)

JOHNNY DOWD

Wrong Side of Memphis   **(Self-released, 1997/Checkered Past, 1998)**
This strange little disc first crept into my life back in the fall of 1997. Like some Dramamine-soaked response to Johnny Cash's *American Recordings,* its stark, bleak tales of back-road behavior and questionable after-dinner practices left me dumbstruck.

Johnny Dowd, a deceptively suave character straight outta Nowhere (by way of Fort Worth), is far from your typical singer/songwriter. Johnny's much closer in spirit to Dick and Perry (*In Cold Blood*) than James Taylor. Or even Steve Earle. "If rock 'n' roll was a religion," proclaims Mr. Dowd, "I'd be a preacher in need of a church." Indeed.

Somehow equal parts Captain Beefheart, Frankie Teardrop, Muddy Waters and Luke the Drifter, Johnny bravely launched his recording career at the ripe old age of forty-nine. He scrapes his way across the underbelly of the American nightmare with these fifteen songs in one spookily sung, starkly accompanied, semi-fi fit of glory. The critics were kind if dazed and bemused. "Imagine Mr. Haney from *Green Acres* on CIA-sanctioned psychedelics," Jackson Griffith reported, upon encountering Dowd at SXSW.

"I grew up in a poor white culture, so those are the people I write about. These people need a song too. Child molesters need a song too. Losers. I just feel I got more to say on that subject." True enough, the man positively lurks down such socio-musical back alleys and fairground shortcuts, spinning often gothic, occasionally bloody tales that approach Biblical heights of redemption.

So fuss if you must over the mondo-contrived Traditionalism 101 pigeon-holing all those alternative cowboy junkies out there. But be advised that Johnny Dowd and his crack new band continue to concoct precisely that kind of music that bravely aims for the mind—by way of the neck—for those who aren't afraid to shoot *above* the waist for a change. Turns out *Wrong Side of Memphis* was only the start of this particular journey. (Gary Pig Gold)

DREAM LAKE UKULELE BAND
Dream Lake Ukulele Band   **(Crest, 1976)**

What do you get when you cross twenty-seven ukuleles, a Little Marcy record, and the Langley Schools Music Project? The result is a bizarre hybrid called the Dream Lake Ukulele Band, a Florida school group whose performances are documented on Crest Records, a New York vanity label. The back cover shows twenty-seven grade-school-aged students, all wearing white shirts and red vests, the boys also wearing neckties. Sound boring? Not when every kid is smiling and holding a ukulele.

The lead-off, "There's So Many, Many Ways," is one of the more charming Christian songs around, but I'm sure my opinion is altered by the sheer innocent joy of twenty-seven children's voices singing in harmony while strumming their ukuleles. That spirit changes a bit though, when the songs veer off into the Bicentennial patriotic songs that fill the rest of Side 1. Such lyrics as "My Sunday school teacher loves me when I am never late" preceded by "God loves when I learn to shoot the gun" makes one wish that the band director would have been cool enough to be teaching the kids David Bowie songs.

Fortunately, Side 2 has the perfect antidote, for that is where the children present and sing their own original compositions. Compiled under headings such as "Wish Songs," "Name Songs" and "Music Songs," each features a progression of five to ten kids strumming and singing solo. These aren't loud bratty kids singing "Tomorrow" at the top of their lungs, but more often small waif-like girls singing with very timid voices. My heart melts whenever I hear one girl who sings, "I am Mary, I like to play the ukulele" or another girl whose verse starts by saying her parents are always busy, and then proceeds with "Daddy is a band director, Mommy is a piano teacher, I love them." This record is listed as being volume seven, which definitely makes me wish that I also had volumes one through six. (Vern Stoltz)

DREAM WARRIORS
And Now the Legacy Begins (4th and Broadway, 1991)

Dream Warriors, a Toronto-based duo, entered the market at a time when heady, thoughtful rap was gaining ground and airtime. So it seemed that album-oriented rap might become a reality. Groups such as De La Soul and A Tribe Called Quest were delivering brainy lyrics over jazzy rhythms and winning critical praise. Dream Warriors King Lou and Capital Q also embraced that elastic side of the genre with their debut. But the legacy went virtually unnoticed. We should be ashamed.

Years before Mike Myers hijacked Quincy Jones's "Soul Bossa Nova" for *Austin Powers*, Dream Warriors recognized the song for its sample readiness. It is that now-familiar brass blast and flute flutter that power the album opener "My Definition of a Boombastic Jazz Style." The playful "Ludi" sounds like a comfortable fit for *Sesame Street's* pop aesthetics. (That's a compliment.)

Perhaps Dream Warriors misjudged their demographic, as the CD retains a childlike sense of fun and refreshing lyrical tameness. The dual MCs make the usual threats of lyrical domination via imagery swiped liberally from *Star*

Wars, superhero comics, *Dungeons and Dragons* and other mythologies. King Lou and Capital Q assure the listener that they are hard, but deliver their boasts as if they are holding back to prevent injury. Against today's chop socky rappers, this might sound wimpy. But in a genre steeped in fantasy violence, Dream Warriors, by virtue of the name alone, were up front about their imaginary action heroism. Their rubbery funk, spaced-out sound effects and hiccuppy rhythms simply add to the reverie of it all. (Kris Kendall)

DUMMY RUN

Ice Cream Headache   (Hot Air, 1997)

The British braintrust of Andrew Sharpley and Matt Wand (launching fearlessly from their initial brainchild of Stock, Hausen, and Walkman) barnstormed this album whose sleeve boasts unnaturally floppy-eared bunnies in the face of mudfucking, graceless drum 'n' bass licking windows and rotting notes. These recordings remind me of not only being a big goof but also not caring what anyone thinks—simply shouting and remembering odd mottoes, onomatopoeia, and non sequiturs. I am unabashed and ecstatic when I say that this album is now among my favorite records *ever* (up to this point, at least). There's also an attendant 7–inch from Dummy Run's equally ecstatically brilliant *Pink Pocket* CD (possibly not its actual title but a smasher anyway by proxy and double entendre, courtesy of the receipt from the record store at which it was curiously purchased). It reminds me of the way my own mind works—things leading into ideas segueing into free associations merging into other times which remind me of something else, something else, something that wends its way to another idea I had about that last time keeps on slipping into the fuchsia and it is not for nothing that a celebrity gets Parkinson's because he got a certain frank ratio of soft drink for the rest of his life. I can listen to these recordings for hours, and I have, and I do: some innate Stone Age drive to which I am duly and truly enslaved. I hear something new each time I listen to them. Jesus W. Christwads of Nazareth in a handbasket and then some plus extra! I like them more and more. They grow on me like the mange. (David Cotner)

Portions of this piece appeared previously in *Freq* and *NewCreativeMusic*.

E

THE ELECTRIC CHAIRS
The Electric Chairs (Safari, 1978)

This was the first full-length record featuring Wayne (later Jayne) County. I picked up the Canadian pressing on Attic Records, which was given the appropriate title, *Blatantly Offensive*. This disk was released into a market that was reluctantly accepting punk product and that label is as good as any to describe this snotty, hard rockin' music. The major difference between this record and the Pistols' early product is that this platter contained a campy sense of humor along with the edgy blather and tough guy swagger. While Johnny Rotten sang suggestively of his "watery love" on "Sub-Mission," Wayne spelled it all out on "Toilet Love." No imagination is needed to decipher lyrics like, "You stick your head in the toilet and I give it a flush." Wayne's voice wasn't nearly as menacing as your average pogo promoter and it was hard to resist a chuckle when he sang so eloquently about water sports, inept lovers and wife beaters, because his mock sneer never hid his tongue-in-cheek wit. While never hugely popular, the band had plenty of adolescent boys who swore by their potty-mouth power-pop. I feel safe in assuming that the Mentors, Anti Nowhere League and Pork Dukes, among many others, were all influenced to write sick absurd lyrics after grooving to Wayne. The reason I feel so strongly about the merits of the first Electric Chairs album, though, is that the songs were so strong despite the silly situations so cleverly described. "Fuck Off," "Big Black Window," and "Out of Control" are good songs done in the same style that has made much of the music of 1978 so memorable. Unfortunately, the band's subsequent releases lacked the gutsy fire that made this one so catchy and colorful. (P. Edwin Letcher)

THE EMBARRASSMENT
Heyday 1979–1983   **(Bar/None, 1995)**

This Wichita quartet's proselytizers have all but trademarked the epithet "The Best Band You've Never Heard Of." For the rest of us, this two-disc retrospective is their primary artifact. As with any "lost" band, those who were there say the recordings don't do them justice. That's difficult to believe, given *Heyday*'s lofty quality.

Disc one opens with "Sex Drive," a crunchy-guitar anthem for horndogs with Trans Ams. The deadpan lyrics carry over into "Patio Set," which explores the love of a man and his lawn chair. Things get weirder, and funnier. The band's name references Kurt Vonnegut, and they have the same curmudgeonly intelligence about them—sometimes the lyrics are mean, but they're just as often self-deprecating. Take "Celebrity Art Party" on the one hand, "(I'm a) Don Juan" on the other. It's hard to choose standouts, but "Chapter 12" is an intricately arranged earworm, "Elizabeth Montgomery's Face" a pop sensation still waiting to happen, and "Special Eyes" an ominous tale of something more (or less) than human. And there's the epic, moody "Lewis and Clark," the rollicking "Rhythm Line" and the snotty "Hip and Well Read."

Disc 2 contains unreleased and live tracks. Although "Dress Like a Man" sounds like it was recorded in a well, the band's energy comes across. They aren't all classics, but witness "Sexy Singer Girl," which encapsulates the male concert fantasy, and the grieving, confused "Casual Man." The live cover of Michael Jackson's "Don't Stop 'Til You Get Enough" is tight, relaxed, and fully cognizant of the absurd juxtaposition of a postpunk grain belt rock band invoking the king of pop.

On relistening—and you will—pay special attention to "Out of Town." It opens with a complex percussion riff, but when the guitars jump in the tempo seems off and the song disintegrates. "That was fucked," someone says, and they decide to skip it. Don't bother looking for the full version—like the band's potential, it will remain unknown to anyone but themselves. (David J. Schwartz)

ROKY ERICKSON & THE ALIENS

Roky Erickson & the Aliens/ The Evil One

(CBS, U.K., 1980/415, 1981)

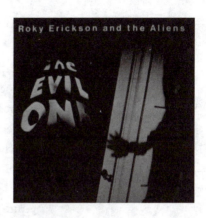

Busted for pot in 1969, Thirteenth Floor Elevators leader Roky Erickson chose to plead insanity; if he wasn't nuts then, he sure was by the time he got out of the hospital. Roky's childhood love of horror comics and films escalated to obsessional levels, and he sometimes claimed to be a Martian. Weird as he was, Roky was still a musician of great natural gifts, possessed of a sweetly emotive Texas wail and a Hollyesque melodic touch. Folks in Austin knew if he could be disciplined, coddled, coaxed, and tolerated, there was almost certainly a great record in him.

Doug Sahm produced a strong single, but it was Creedence's Stu Cook who dug in for the long haul, checking Roky out from another hospital stay, moving him to San Francisco, and recording hundreds of hours of improvisations, which were painstakingly assembled into the best songs Roky would ever "write." The sessions were split over a British and an American album, with some overlap. Backed by the Aliens, a whip-crack hard rock band anchored by Durocs' drummer Scott Mathews, Roky howled his personal mythos into existence.

Each tune is a nightmare in miniature, simple and memorable as the slavering thing that lived in your nursery closet. The Ramones didn't wanna go down in the basement, but Roky goes gleefully to meet the demon in his attic, where he conjures vampires, alligators, two-headed dogs, zombies and Lucifer himself. There's a dark, delicious poetry in these primitive horror stories, obviously so real to Roky. Every tune is a killer.

Roky has recorded intermittently since 1980, but never as successfully. If Roky's brain is like a TV set—airing nothing but old *Outer Limits*, *Hullabaloo*, and Lugosi flicks—then Stu Cook was a set of rabbit ears that briefly stopped the roll and the snow. A labor of love, and Roky's finest hour. (Kim Cooper)

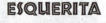

ESQUERITA
Esquerita   (Capitol, 1958)

Eskew Reeder Jr., better known by his stage name "Esquerita," is generally acknowledged as the source for the bizarre/flamboyantly gay/mega-talented/hollerin'/screamin'/rhythm and blues archetype that Little Richard would take to the bank alone. A product of the New Orleans homosexual R&B scene (which nurtured Bobby Marchan, Little Richard and many others), Esquerita played piano and sang a mixture of gospel and dirty blues that bordered on rock 'n' roll years before it was called such.

Esquerita probably would have languished in obscurity had it not been the right place at the right time. When Gene Vincent's Blue Caps suggested to Capitol Records A&R man Ken Nelson that he check out Esquerita, Nelson saw the next level of rock 'n' roll weirdness and signed him immediately. An LP and several singles followed. The buying public didn't get it, and today it seems unlikely that *Esquerita* was ever even issued. It sold so poorly upon release that original copies are rarely seen today.

Yet the album is a brilliant showcase for the man's ability. Pounding the piano so hard it sounds out of tune, shrieking and belting out the blues, tunes such as "Hey Miss Lucy," "Gettin' Plenty Lovin'," "Believe Me When I Say, Rock & Roll is Here to Stay" and "I'm Battie over Hattie" showcase his unique brand of Crescent City Rock & Roll.

Fortunately the digital age has brought about a renaissance for Esquerita, who is now openly acknowledged as one of the greats, and the original album has been reissued on CD, along with a plethora of unreleased material. Too bad Esquerita didn't live long enough to see it happen. (Deke Dickerson)

EX-GIRL

Heppoco Pou   **(Paranoiz, Japan, 1998)**

The interesting thing about eX-Girl is not that they made music light-years beyond that of the average cute nineties Japanese girl pop band; the interesting thing is that they stopped being nearly as interesting once the average cute Japanese girl left the group.

Initially the trio consisted of Kirilo the Rocker Girl (bass), Fuzuki the Art Girl (stand-up drum kit), and Chihiro the Cute Pop Girl (guitar). Upon first listen, their penchant for Japanese girl group clichés like fondness for a particular cute animal (frogs), matching costumes, and "funny" cover songs (James Brown's "Sex Machine" in this instance) seemed their weak point. They had so much going on with those classically trained voices and complex rhythms, they didn't need crutches to get an audience. Maybe somebody told them they did. If that's the case, may God damn that person to hell.

It was precisely the struggle amongst the three virtues of rock, art, and pop on their debut that made their music pull and catch on the ear. An excellent example of this is the song "Upsy Daisy Ramsy," which changes gears from art dirge to finger-snapping singalong at the precise moment listener starts thinking, "This is challenging, but I'm getting a headache."

On subsequent albums, the group seems to succumb to pop—more frogs, more poofy plastic hats, more show-offy covers for their fantastic three-part vocal harmonies. But one notices fewer writers' credits for Chihiro, and on further scrutiny, one realizes that the "pop" trappings of the group seem to be more calculated, the "art" seems more contrived and self-conscious, and the "rock" seems to have left completely. By 2001, Chihiro left the group, and while the band today is enjoying further success, the messy magic of their earlier music is gone. Never underestimate the power of the Cute Pop Girl. (Elizabeth Herndon)

THE EVERLY BROTHERS
Two Yanks in London   **(Warner Brothers, 1966)**
Eight Hollies songs, one each by Manfred Mann and the
Spencer Davis Group, and more, all done in topnotch Everly's
style, Anglicized for your greater listening pleasure.
Extremely enjoyable.

(Ken Barnes, *Flash* #2, June–July 1972)

EXUMA
Exuma   **(Mercury, 1970)**
Bahamian-born Exuma (real name: Tony McKay) gigged
around Greenwich Village in the early sixties, but his startling
debut LP of voodoo folk music, chaotic percussion and shrieking incantations only appeared in 1970. Once you become
accustomed to the fact that most of his songs are about zombies and various forms of demonic possession, you can
appreciate what a magnificent singer Exuma is. His lower
register recalls Fred Neil. On the high notes, he's a bit like
Richie Havens. But when he really starts shrieking, it's like
being face to face with Klaus Kinski. It is not surprising that
both Nina Simone and Blixa Bargeld claim Exuma as an influence.

The opening track, "Exuma, the Obeah Man," is, oddly enough, the song
Mercury pushed as a single to AM radio in the United States. It didn't get
very far. Exuma introduces himself and describes his wide range of occult
powers over steadily pounding drums, chants of "Obeah, Obeah," and at least
one heavily amplified frog. The gorgeous harmonies of "Dambala" and the
eerie "Mama Loi, Papa Loi" sound like part of a voodoo home study course.
"A Place Called Earth" goes even further out, with Exuma laying down this
Roger Corman–style zombie scenario while the Junk Band play sacred sand
and sacred foot drum through generous amounts of tape echo. The weirdness
really peaks during "Séance in the Sixth Fret," basically a seven-minute
séance, replete with a hypnotic guitar figure, voodoo harmonies, thunder, and

Exuma acting as a medium for the raving, screaming voices of dead souls. Side 2 ends with "The Vision," by which time Exuma's visions, like the painting of the zombie that stares out from the LP's front cover, are likely to haunt your dreams and nightmares. Of his later LPs, *Exuma 2, Do Wah Nanny*, and *Snake* are highly recommended. (Matthew Smith)

F

FASTBACKS
Answer the Phone, Dummy (Sub Pop, 1994)

Straight off the galloping, hook-filled song-cycle of *Zucker*, the Fastbacks followed up with the most ambitious, dynamic and sonically satisfying album of their storied existence. Packing up the captivating hopscotch vocals of Kim and Lulu, their transporting backing harmonies, and Kurt Bloch's guitar leads, they set out to open new vistas on *Answer the Phone, Dummy*.

Underlying their sixties pop sensibility and urgent seventies punk is an underdog consciousness and approachable vulnerability. Coating the racing thoughts and dashing words are astute ruminations traversing inner and outer spaces—frequently in the same song. With introspective lyrics belying the extroverted music, "Back to Nowhere" presents the band as withdrawn and reticent, but willing to take a peep out to see if the outside world has changed any for the better.

It's this constant reappraisal without oversimplification that makes the songs connect. "Old Address of the Unknown" includes the salient line, "I'll stay away from work again today and think of all the records that I want to play." What music lover hasn't had this wishful thought? The album hits top speed and peak performance in "Trumpets Are Loud." With a bass encircling a jazzy guitar solo like the monorail gliding around the Seattle Space Needle, this song perfectly combines the straightforward rush of the Ramones with the musical lane changes of Blondie's finest moments.

The album spins its way to its defining moment with the uncharacteristic "Meet the Author." Their elegant voices declare over strummy soft attack guitars, "What if we never had to sleep/Think how much better our life would be" and the song takes off musically and soars up lyrically from the introspective to the universal. The Fastbacks have always hoped for something better than the daily dreck for both themselves and their listeners. By taking this challenging course, they succeeded not by clearing every obstacle, but by knocking down some rails and galloping resiliently on as runaway dark horse favorites. (Ted Liebler)

THE FEELIES
The Good Earth   (Twin/Tone–Coyote, 1986)

Too many critics argue that *Crazy Rhythms* is the Feelies' only masterpiece. With its jumpy Raincoats percussion and sub-Television guitar interplay, let alone the odd silences and supercatchy melodies, there's good reason to rate it highly. But their second album is even better. It tosses *Crazy Rhythms'* odd components into a danceable folk-punk setting and mixes in a near-infinite number of acoustic guitars. What's not to love?

The Feelies embodied the contradictory aesthetics of punk simplicity and folk-rock songcraft. Their three-chord folk tunes are layered with gazillions of acoustic guitars and Velvet Underground–inspired lead guitar. Vocals rarely rise above a whisper, but that's no problem because the lyrics are never too smart. What kills me is the sound: carefully arranged without being fussy, complex without losing that off-the-cuff relaxed feel, simultaneously urban and earthy. This is a Hoboken pastorale.

Despite their jam-band structure (two drummers!), each song is perfectly focused; only two break the five-minute mark, and only one of those is stretched out by a long guitar solo. And "guitar solo" isn't even the right word for the fifteen-odd lead tracks that overtake "Slipping (into Something)," accelerating it from a darkly gentle ditty into a maelstrom of noise. Nothing else works up such a head of steam, but the album nevertheless manages to rock throughout. "The Last Roundup" is underpinned by a snare-heavy drum that never drops into backbeat, sounding like both drummers are just flailing away, though somehow it's *The Good Earth*'s most countryish track. "On the Roof," "Let's Go" and "The Good Earth" have the indie-pop feel of a less futzy Let's Active, while "The High Road" and "When Company Comes" are pure folk-punk goofiness. It's a delicate line that the Feelies walk, but they never waver. It's thrilling to listen to them show off. (Hayden Childs) (See also: Yung Wu)

THE FIRST TEAM
Chevrolet Sings of Safe Driving and You
(Columbia Special Products, n.d., likely c. 1965)

Avoiding the *Red Asphalt* approach to driver's ed., our corporate friends at Chevrolet decided folk-rock was the perfect medium to sell the learner's permit crowd on appropriate automotive behavior. The result was a sort of *Schoolhouse Rock* for timid auto-jocks, a catchy set of rules and prohibitions meant to instill a sense of cautious confidence in young drivers. It's delightfully catchy, and achieves all its aims.

"Grown-up Baby" (Driving Psychology) addresses those with a deadly weapon at their disposal who lack the emotional maturity to behave sensibly. Frenetic banjos build to a nervous climax as the hip parental narrators fuss about hotheads, wheel-squealers and other car-creeps. "Cities and Towns" (Driving in City and Heavy Traffic) skimps on the lyrical edumacation, but jangles like a lost Byrds track. "Nowhere Fast" (Observance and Enforcement) with its spooky, insinuating New England garage sound scans more like free verse than pop song: "there are many other THINGS THAT you will have to know/like when a sign says STOP that's what it means and not just slow."

Flip the disk for the shouldabeen hit, "Gentle Things" (Adverse Driving Conditions), a Simon and Garfunkel–style beauty with aggressively mournful harmonica. Dad guilt-trips us with the message that expert drivers let the weather be their guide, but this listener is too blissed-out on the melody to think of rain ("a gentle thing, except when you're driving") as a threat.

"The Natural Laws" (Laws of Motion) is a cool little soul shouter about what a groove it is to be subject to centrifugal force, getting raunchy when the singer pants, "they are all, UH HUH, natural laws." And "Man-Made Laws" (Common Sense Driving) is full of suggestions about rights of way, passing and distance. It's all very

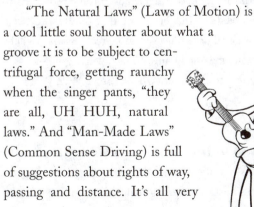

useful stuff, and I often find myself humming snippets while maneuvering around afternoon gridlock in L.A.

There are no performer credits, but the label states that Lou Adessa and Vince Benay composed the songs. This same talented pair wrote Paul Revere and the Raiders' "SS 396," also released on Columbia Special Products and given away by Chevrolet dealers around 1965. (Kim Cooper)

THE FLAMIN' GROOVIES
Jumping in the Night   (Sire, 1979)

I'm sitting on this flight to New York City, way past deadline and trying to explain in 300 words why *Jumping In the Night* by the Flamin' Groovies is my favorite obscure/forgotten record of all time. The only problems is that the record is, in fact, *so* obscure that I've never been able to find a copy on CD (I hear that a few once existed in Japan), and I can't even listen to it right now—especially as the Powers That Be at this particular airline wouldn't let me bring a turntable onto the flight. Bastards! So I'll have to resort to my memory when I tell you that when this record came out, the Flamin' Groovies were the most awesome live band around, a secret known only to the twenty or thirty people who attended their shows. The band employed 38 strings (two twelve-strings, a six-string through a chorus pedal, and an eight-string bass, if memory serves me right) to transform songs by the Byrds, Stones and Beatles (and originals that sounded as if they could have been right off those bands' records) into an apocalyptic, thundering sound that, if you closed your eyes, evoked images of giant, hairy monsters gleefully stomping in your general direction. The title track opened the record with a manic, chaotic wallop, the incredible "First Plane Home" sounded as though it was recorded from the inside of the jet engine that the lyrics evoked, and the version of "19th Nervous Breakdown" is even more reckless and twitchy than the original. Trust me—it's an amazing album. In fact, you're going to *have* to trust me, because you're not going to find it anywhere. (Steve Wynn)

FLESH EATERS
A Minute to Pray, A Second to Die   (Slash/Ruby, 1981)

After a handful of years spent slogging around the exploding Los Angeles punk rock scene circa 1977–1980 as a *Slash* magazine editor and the leader of a revolving series of Flesh Eaters lineups, Chris Desjardins (hereafter known as Chris D.) gave birth to the all-star roots/voodoo punk combo of *A Minute to Pray, A Second to Die.* In so doing, he created a schizoid masterwork of raw, netherworld blues and marimba & sax-led garage punk stomp.

Joining vocalist/howler Chris D. in this ultimate Flesh Eaters configuration were John Doe & DJ Bonebrake from the by-now nationally recognized X, Dave Alvin, and Bill Bateman from the Blasters (guitar and drums respectively) and sax player Steve Berlin, a year or two shy of joining Los Lobos. Though the "on loan" status of the musicians involved did not bode well for anything more than a one-off project, what these gentlemen created together was a landmark of brooding, often metal-tinged roots rock ramalama. Think about what you may know of the best work of X and the Blasters of the time, add Chris D. at the absolute top of his game, and some out-of-this-world arrangements that harken to some unholy trinity of the Stones, Stooges and Seeds, and you've got quite a goddamn record.

One could argue—no, I *will* argue—that this record is the premier calling card for the transformation of punk rock snottiness into a more literate, musically complex—dare I say *mature*—rock and roll beast. What reputation the Flesh Eaters still have left in the early eighties history books and with the Ameripunk cognoscenti is likely due to this album, which seems to be slowly gaining subsequent critical steam as an unequalled masterpiece. (Jay Hinman) (See also: Gun Club)

FLO & EDDIE
The World of Strawberry Shortcake
(Kid Stuff/American Greetings Corp., 1980)

This is a slightly warped, groovy, sweet, timelessly charming story-based record full of silly sound effects, fantastically energized acting, and catchy sing-a-long tunes by a bunch of consummate professionals having lots of fun on the job. Almost twenty years into their successful careers as singers, songwriters and musicians, Flo & Eddie, aka Mark Volman and Howard Kaylan, most notably of the Turtles, jumped at the opportunity to do yet another something completely different to add to their illustrious resumes.

When the animators from Frank Zappa's film *200 Motels* were given the job of bringing Strawberry Shortcake and Friends to life, they got Flo & Eddie to do the music, and presto!—magic ensued. Who could say "No" to creating soundtrack music for a brand new teleplay by Romeo Muller? That witty ingenious writer of the world-famous Rankin-Bass holiday specials (*Rudolph the Red-Nosed Reindeer*, *Frosty the Snowman*, and the animated version of *The Hobbit*) is the same man responsible for writing the stories and song lyrics to the first three Strawberry Shortcake cartoons.

The World of Strawberry Shortcake was the "berry" first of the cartoons with a soundtrack record, and a perfect introduction to the creative transcendence Flo & Eddie would eventually bring to the genre of children's music. I would also like to mention the kooky double entendres Romeo Muller subconsciously brings into the mix that are more apparent when just listening to the soundtrack record, rather than when watching the cartoon. As you listen to this record, your imagination will run wild with things revolving around stoners who grow their own, city park dope dealers, Big Brother, Merlin, the Man, war protest chants, military battle flashbacks, Hooked on Phonics, and the doomed sentiment "can't we all just get along?" being answered with an abrupt, "NO!" by the Peculiar Purple Pie Man in the next record, and the next, and the next! (Kelly Kuvo)

BRIGITTE FONTAINE
Brigitte Fontaine est folle   (Saravah, France, 1968)

Now Brigitte Fontaine is hip again. Sonic Youth claim to be influenced by her and play on her latest album. Stereolab too recorded with the queer queen. Fontaine's fanbase is growing internationally, but that has not always been the case. Fontaine began her carrier as a typical "*chanteuse rive gauche*" and soon was discovered by talent scout Jacques Canetti. Canetti was purveyor to the respected "*chanson française*": he spotted Brel, Brassens and other cabaret icons. But those artists were a bit dusty and old-fashioned for the

Five Hypothetical Sesame Street Covers

1. Beck, "Clink Clank": The veritable Fluxus anthem blossoms into a *Midnite Vultures*–style party jam.
2. Calvin Johnson, "The Ballad of Casey McPhee": Indie rock's Johnny Cash delivers this stirring tale of adversity, courage, and chocolate goo.
3. The Posies: "La, La, La": Jon Auer coos about licorice and lace. Ken Stringfellow bellows "La, la, la, LINOLEUM!" Sigh.
4. Puffy Amiyumi Featuring Iggy Pop: "Cookie Disco": Puffy's gleeful verses, Iggy's saucy spoken asides … pure gold.
5. Rufus Wainwright: "Would You Like To Buy An O?": Black-market letter pushing, with a Tin Pan Alley flair. Perfect!

(Elizabeth Ivanovich)

young generation. In 1968, Fontaine went looking for a more lysergic venture and found a new home with Pierre Barouh. Barouh could have been a mainstream pop composer; he earned fame with his soundtrack to *Un homme et une femme*. But instead of resting on laurels he created Saravah, his post–May 1968 underground label. *Brigitte Fontaine est folle* is a perfect balance between suave sophisticated pop and strange lyrical contents soaked in a feminine, witchlike hysteria. Jean-Claude Vannier did the arrangements, and boy! was he brilliant before he went senile and spat on his cool but uncommercial past. Vannier was soon to be taken under Gainsbourg's and Polnareff's wings before falling into a vortex of bitterness and uncreativity. After that stroke of genius, Fontaine recorded a quite good if dated free-jazz-meets-*chanson* album with the Art Ensemble of Chicago and the occasional cool song hidden in your typical anything-goes French agitprop album. During the eighties, the Japanese rediscovered her. Unfortunately, having signed with Virgin, she became the poor man's Björk and the fuckers from indieland gave her the college credibility she needed. Nevermind. *Brigitte Fontaine est folle* is a masterpiece with which you cannot go wrong. Furthermore, it's April March's favorite LP! (Jean-Emmanuel Deluxe)

FOOLS FACE
Tell America (Talk, 1981)

Based in Springfield, Missouri, Fools Face earned raves in the pages of *Trouser Press* and *Creem*, but remained criminally unnoticed by the general public. Even interested parties have had a hard time actually buying a damn Fools Face record. To this day, I own the only copies I've ever seen of the group's three elusive LPs, plus a bootleg CD-R of the final cassette-only release, *The Red Tape*.

Within the pop underground, however, Fools Face is renowned. For me, the moment of revelation came via the first track on the group's second album, *Tell America*. "American Guilt" is an acid-tongued critique of both gung-ho Reagan-era jingoism and mushy-headed neo-hippie naïveté, lyrically as incendiary as a testimonial from the MC5, but with a perfect pop sheen. When the chorus soars with the lines "When push comes to shove/All we need is love," the transcendent effect of the Beatles quote nails everything into place.

By turns confident and vulnerable, Fools Face was always literate, intelligent, musically accomplished, rooted in sixties songcraft but forged in the crucible of seventies punk and new wave. The individual tracks make the case: "Nothing to Say" is the best break-up song ever, encompassing casual heartache (or heartlessness?) and a matter-of-fact recognition of the need to just move on; "Land of the Hunted" and "Stand Up" compress paranoia and determination into an irresistible 1–2 punch; "L5" even manages a compelling pop tune about space colonization.

Many fans prefer the group's third album, 1983's just-as-wonderful *Public Places*, though few will speak on behalf of *Here to Observe*, the merely okay 1979 debut. As a happy postscript, the original quintet returned for a splendid reunion CD in 2002, an album that lives up to the promise of *Tell America* and *Public Places*. Tell … someone! (Carl Cafarelli)

I, BRUTE FORCE
Confections of Love (Columbia, 1967)

Brute Force is Stephen Friedland, still actively plying his trade as one of America's great linguistic tricksters. In the mid-sixties, he adopted the nom de plume Brute Force for musical activities including a long association with the Tokens, composition of the Chiffons' existential psych masterpiece

"Nobody Knows What's Goin' On (In My Mind but Me)" and this giddy treasure, inventively produced by John Simon.

Brute Force's teeming brain absorbed the clichés that fed pop's hungry maw, spun them around at 62 zillion feet per second, then spat them back out in juicy recombinant strands. No sixties rock 'n' roll freak can fail to be elated by Brute's vamp on exaggerated love-sick lyrics, "Tapeworm of Love," or "In Jim's Garage," which takes the class division subtext of the girl group genre and runs amok: "He may be greasy and dirty/But that's just a mark of his honesty/And she loves him/She loves that Jim." Brute slides all over his tonsils emoting Latin lunacy on "Tierra del Fuego," before convincingly suggesting the pinnacle of civilization might be "To Sit on a Sandwich." A year later he took direct performative action, attempting to swim the Bering Strait to unite the United States and Russia.

Friedland calls his music "heavy funny," and the wonder is how perfectly balanced the two halves are. As demented as a Brute Force song can be, there's always an underlying germ of philosophy, a point to the exercise. A couple years later, George Harrison heard Brute's sly "King of Fuh," added strings and put it out on Apple, but Capitol/EMI squashed the suggestive song, which became the rarest Apple release. Today Brute Force performs frequently at music and comedy venues in the New York area, and recently toured England in support of the reissue of his second album, *Extemporaneous.* (Kim Cooper)

FORTUNE & MALTESE AND THE PHABULOUS PALLBEARERS

Konquer Kampus   (Hillsdale, 1997)

Take a Michigan-plated Bemo potato chips delivery van and a calendar of bookings ranging from the rankest bars to the hallowed Midwest halls and you have the prime conditions for the evolution from knuckle-draggers to big men on campus. What the stuffed figures in the natural science building in 2064 may fail to capture is the sonic gala of vibrant vocals, harmonies galore and Hofner guitar playing found on this album.

Studying such arcana as *The Kingsmen on Campus* and applying action to theory, Freddy Fortune, Michael Maltese and the Phabulous Pallbearers were the only nineties garage band to give the concept album the old college try and ace it. Not only did they meld golden California harmonies to frantic Northwest stomp, but their sound showed a refreshing devotion to overlooked bands like the Gants, Music Explosion, Bruce & Terry, Fantastic Baggys and the Boys Next Door.

"Cuttin' Class" opened things up with sunny harmonic pop, perfectly capturing that feeling of waking up on a spring day and pondering why the books on the floor were even made when there are 25,000 co-eds at Michigan State to see. F&M knew that the college scene wasn't all high jinks and flowing golden brown, so they provide a timeless respite from blue books with the enchanting, tranquil instrumental "Study Break." With its typewritten intro and unhinged banjo solo, it's the centerpiece of the album that will bring a smile and a wink as an electric piano leads a fleet of instruments into the magic land of modulation. Side 2 exhibits the hard-won wisdom of "Girls Ruin Everything." And as dusk turns dark, "Cuz I Want You, Yeah I Need You" clears the book-strewn tables and fills the dance floor, foreshadowing the folk-rock tinge they would perfect on later singles.

Fortune and Maltese demonstrated that *Konquering Kampus* was not strictly academic. A well-rounded education also includes flip-flops, flip-clocks, flip-tops, flip-sides and this record to make things shake and the campus quake. (Ted Liebler)

ROOSEVELT FRANKLIN
The Year of Roosevelt Franklin (aka *My Name Is Roosevelt Franklin*)
(Columbia, 1971/CTW, 1974)

The Year of Roosevelt Franklin starts out as gently as any children's record. After a clever opening monologue courtesy of the titular *Sesame Street* character, the listener can count along from one to ten, and work on memorizing the days of the week. Standard kiddie fare, but it is all delivered atop brass-heavy soul and light funk. Then the strangest thing happens; after "Safety Boy Blues," the record takes a decidedly somber and grown-up tone.

Roosevelt croons "Just Because." The song is a piano-bar lament that rises gospel-like at the end, in the manner of David Bowie's "Rock and Roll Suicide." The lyrics question senseless violence committed "just because" that person is different. Roosevelt Franklin suddenly becomes Marvin Gaye for the preschool set, and it works perfectly. For Roosevelt, despite his purple fabric skin, plastic eyes, and tuft of fuzzy hair, is undeniably a child of the inner city. A primary target market of *Sesame Street* was the toddler from the projects. This is that child's album.

Longtime Muppet songsmith Joe Raposo and lyricist, actor and singer Matt Robinson, who originated the role of Gordon on the show, were the brains behind Roosevelt Franklin's only album. With Raposo's Fifth Dimensionesque soul groove as his backing, Robinson is able to deftly shift from kindergarten fundamentals to surprisingly deep social commentary without sacrificing the kid-friendly style.

Because children were not yet fully exploited as an economic demographic, it is difficult to know how parents reacted to *The Year of Roosevelt Franklin*. But it is refreshing to know that there was once a time when children were not spoken down to. Roosevelt tells it like it is. For some of us, his songs may be a refresher course in human relations. (Kris Kendall) (See also: Sesame Street)

FRIJID PINK

Frijid Pink   **(Parrot, 1970)**

Away down in Oz (where toilets flush backward widdershins), members *in uteri* of Radio Birdman and the Saints hadn't even begun to plan their Detroit-inspired takeover of the entire Australian rock scene when the Motor City's own Frijid Pink began an aborted charge up the American charts. Their debut LP runs off the MC5/Iggy blueprint proto-punk used to retool rock 'n' roll and it's about time someone said so.

Here we have murderous, cynical heartland rock. By the late sixties, the American Midwest was among the world's leading consumer of rock LPs, with monstrous blocks of ticket sales for every Anglophone act with plane-fare to Cleveland. F. Pink caters, with easy mastery and absolute shameless-ness, to every nuance of hearty palate and cornfed gut.

Singer Kelley Green's Morrison swagger and the blank intensity of the hustle mark *Frigid Pink* as proto-punk protoplasm. "God Gave Me You" is Mitch Ryder/Bob Seger shuck, the lyrics pure Taliban psychosis. "Tell Me Why" and "End of the Line" roar like anything off MC5's *High Times*, the latter's revolutionary preachment undercut by Green's mellifluous creepiness. "I Want to Be Your Lover" gives us a horny Charlie Manson who just wants to fuck us all to death. This 7:32 hymn of hate is kept from being the most memorable track on a great album by the meaty cover of "House of the Rising Sun," a worldwide hit peaking at #7 in the United States. Gary Ray Thompson's chainsaw guitar comes into its own here, with Green's spree-killer twisting the neck of Eric Burdon's pore country boy.

Their very name supposedly standing for "cold excellence," Frijid Pink went on to three follow-up LPs and Midwest oblivion. On this one arctic-fever dream of a record, they measured up to the boast. (Ron Garmon)

FUGU

Fugu EP   (Semantic, 1996)

Fugu is Mehdi Zannad, a classically trained French pianist who discovered he could compose only three-minute songs. Don't be fooled by the indie world that tries to "Hello Kitty-ize" him. However pretentious Zannad's titles, his music could be taken seriously by the sternest scholars.

This self-released EP, which predates debut full-length *Fugu 1* by four years, is as despicably rare as it is charming. I was able to obtain a copy directly from Zannad after a Boston performance. His jaw-dropping post-modern Beach Boys deconstructions (complete with four-part harmonies) combined with skillful power pop spelunking led me to confront his timid frame after the set and proclaim, "you are my new favorite band!"

More consistent and battier than *Fugu 1*, the EP is one of the least bor-ing and most rococo recordings you are ever likely to hear. "F29" is a trip into a cavern of multicolored rock candy stalagmites triggered by swift piano arpeggios, skronky Vox organ hits, sweeping cello melodramas and Zannad's own incoherent trilling. Complete with sighing violins, "F4" evokes a mythological place where the Beatles are composed of two French Paul McCartneys, the Velvet Underground's Sterling Morrison plays his ultra simplistic "non-rock" leads, and Ringo pats on the muted snare, like on *Abbey Road*'s "Something."

On "Untitled" and "Interlude," a cacophony of voices and bubbling machines intermingle with gurgling horns and myriad symphonic cutting-room floor clippings before returning to Earth. "F26" pits the thrush of strummed guitars, frowning horns, and cotton candy organ against Zannad's voice on the odd-canticle chorus. Although it's possible to be swept up in the obvious magical mystery of his production, or the fractured-ness of his arranging sensibility, there is always at the core an essential song, a framework to shake you of your every sun-baked boredom with pop music. Orgiastic, steeped in utter coherence. (Jonathan Donaldson)

LEWIS FUREY
Lewis Furey (A&M, 1974)

Montréal's answer to Lou Reed, Lewis Furey had played violin on Leonard Cohen's *New Skin for the Old Ceremony*, but asserted his own rough-edged, pansexual identity on this eponymous debut with the help of Cohen's producer John Lissauer. The result, roundly ignored at the time except by French audiences, was idiosyncratic cabaret music, very much out-of-step with the glam agenda of the period. Furey peopled his songs with characters culled from his hometown's sleaziest neighborhood. Indeed Furey's songs comprised the soundtrack for Frank Vitale's film *Montréal Main*; one of the film's stars, painter/actor Stephen Lack, provided the faux-Warhol sleeve art for Furey's album.

The songs are steeped in cynicism and wounded pride, with the singer invariably cast as protagonist (and tireless bisexual adventurer) in each. Bitterness never sounded so appealing as when set to the updated Weimar Republic strip club tunes heard here, with banjos, trombones and castanets forming an armature of duplicity and sorrow. Furey oils his way from one louche setting to another: on "Feelin' Shy" he (and backup singer Cat Stevens!) take on all comers during a night on the town, then he crashes to earth describing "Louise" ("Everyone's talkin' 'bout the girl/Who left my heart a mess of tracks"). Lissauer frames these mediations on dissolute behavior with the glossy patina of a Broadway cast recording; his engineer, Leanne Unger, would go on to produce Leonard Cohen, Laurie Anderson and other artists of a similarly confessional bent.

Lewis Furey never found the North American audience he deserved, even with Queen's producer Roy Thomas Baker helming his sophomore A&M release, *Rubber Gun Show*. Furey would eventually decamp to France, where he continued to record and graduated to film directing. He married Quebecois film star Carole Laure, whose own RCA solo album was produced by Furey and featured several rewritten versions of songs first heard on *Lewis Furey*. (Richard Henderson) (See also: Lou Reed)

G

SLIM GAILLARD & BAM BROWN
Opera in Vout (Groove Juice Symphony)
(Verve, 1946)

From its David Stone Martin cover to the snobby jazz label that issued it, *Opera in Vout* may appear to be a great, obscure jazz album. But although Slim Gaillard is highly revered in some jazz circles, the jive-talking, fast-living Gaillard was really a forties version of a rock and roll hip-hop star. His bluesy guitar licks, boogie woogie piano playing, and comic vocal improvisations were highly influential building blocks for the first generation of rock 'n' rollers—Chuck Berry comes to mind as a Slim disciple. Slim is best known as the inventor of the "Vout" language, an alternate-universe hipster lingo with which he peppered his records.

This two-disc 78–rpm album recorded live at the Embassy Theater in Los Angeles is absolutely brilliant in every aspect, and to many is Slim's crowning achievement. Slim and his bassist Bam Brown absolutely kill the audience with their back and forth jive-talk patter. They take the Nat "King" Cole tune "Hit That Jive, Jack" and turn it into a fierce rap battle that must be heard to be believed. Simply one of the most exciting live albums ever recorded, this album can be heard in its entirety on the essential Slim compilation CD *Laughing in Rhythm—Best of the Verve Years*. Slim Gaillard's incredible life story can be read in the liner notes—it's too long and twisted of a tale to reproduce here. (Deke Dickerson)

DIAMANDA GALAS
Saint of the Pit   **(Mute, 1986)**

After knocking the avant-garde on its ass with two jarring early eighties releases, Diamanda Galas dedicated the latter half of the greed decade to recording and releasing the three albums that comprise her magnum opus *The Plague Mass*. The plague in question is AIDS, and the trilogy was sparked by the death of Philip-Dimitri Galas, her brother. *Saint of the Pit* is part two of the trilogy.

The lyrics are in French, taken from the poetry of Baudelaire, Nerval, and Corbiere. They could just as easily be in tongues, as Galas croons, howls, whispers, spits, barks, shrieks, and sustains long, seemingly inhuman operatic melismata. She backs herself on grand piano, synths, chains beating on concrete, and on the opener "La Treizieme Revient," a horror show organ that would creep out the Phantom of the Opera. Societal and artistic considerations aside, however, this album strikes a bit deeper under the skin than one might imagine by merely reading about it. It scratches right at the point where the blood runs cold and the chills methodically rush up the spine. Put another way, this is the goddamned scariest record ever made. Whether or not this was Galas's intention as she released her rage and anguish over her brother's sad passing, who knows? Nonetheless, turn out the lights, light a single candle, sit right in the middle of the stereo speakers, turn it up, and see if you don't have an experience similar to the first time you saw *The Exorcist*. The sleeve instructs, "Correct playback possible at maximum volume only." Why not? I tried it once and some troublesome neighbors suddenly became very aloof and non-present. Perhaps this is a more multipurposed album than even Galas imagined. (SL Duff)

GAME THEORY
Real Nighttime
(Rational/Enigma, 1985)

Up until this point, it was hard to get a handle on Game Theory. Scott Miller had already proven himself capable of brilliant tunesmithing on the level of "Metal and Glass Exact" and "Nine Lives to Rigel Five." But this was the group responsible for "I Wanna Get Hit by a Car," which was as pretentious as its title. On one album and two EPs, Game Theory soared toward the power pop heights, but sometimes settled for a thin, cheesy Casio rhythm. Through it all, they displayed a sense of ambition and high concept they weren't yet capable of reaching. The next step was critical.

Luckily, that step was *Real Nighttime*, the album that introduced Game Theory to the college-radio audience. From its Joycean liner notes and opening track, the band walks a fine line between pretension and genius; genius wins out heartily. Produced by the extremely in-vogue Mitch Easter, *Nighttime* is full of chiming guitars and great pop melodies. Here, the band prove themselves the equal of any of their Paisley Underground cousins, and very nearly up there with Big Star.

There's a certain poignancy propelling these breathtaking melodies. Recurring themes involve growing into your own skin, finding a specific life direction, and sorting out what your peers and family assume to be true. Indeed, *Nighttime* is a virtual concept album about life after college. The sunny-sounding "I Mean It This Time" asks us to give the singer "all the gin I need/Because I may not be this strong/When I phone my parents and tell them they've been wrong." "Curse of the Frontierland" bitterly recalls how "a year ago we called this a good time." Most of all, there's "24," which finds Miller on the cusp of his mid-twenties pondering opposite signs, parallel lines, and the eternal question: "coffee or beer?"

With Game Theory and the Loud Family, Scott Miller would equal and even surpass *Nighttime's* achievements. However, this one remains my favorite, the unrepeatable product of a very specific place and time in the songwriter's life. (Mike Appelstein) (See also: The Loud Family)

Songs for Word Geeks

In alphabetical order by title, natch.

"Aeiou Sometimes Y," Ebn-Ozn: For the chorus, of course.

"All My Little Words," The Magnetic Fields: It's good to be reminded that sometimes words aren't enough. Especially with this much pretty melancholy.

"Bad Word for a Good Thing," Friggs: There are no bad words, only bad things.

"Dictionary," Muckafurgason: Possibly the only pop song, ever, to mention the OED.

"Girls," Dictionaraoke: Didn't think synthesized dictionary pronunciations could be distilled into great cover versions of rap songs? Think again.

"Miss Teen Wordpower," The New Pornographers: With any luck putting this song on this list will keep people from asking me if I've heard this song. Yes. Yes, I have. Yes, I like it.

"O Is the One That Is Real," My Morning Jacket: Everybody has a favorite letter of the alphabet, right?

"Three Little Words," Mel Tormé: Which three little words, of course, make all the difference.

"Verb: That's What's Happening," Moby: The best of the *Schoolhouse Rock* covers.

"Word on a Wing," David Bowie: One of the most cerebral gospel songs ever.

"Word Unspoken, Sight Unseen," Richard Thompson: Words are often conspicuously—even ostentatiously—passed over in love songs ("Words Get in the Way," "No More Words," etc.), but RT, as usual, does it darker and better.

"Word Up," Cameo: Gets the lexicographers out on the dance floor. If lexicographers were ever near the dance floor, that is.

"Words Are Like," The Crummer Family (They Might Be Giants): Ineffable? That's what words *are* like. (Erin McKean)

JESSE GARON & THE DESPERADOES

A Cabinet of Curiosities   (Velocity, 1989)

Ask any discerning indiepop historian about Scotland in the eighties and you'll probably hear about the Pastels, Shop Assistants and Vaselines. But there were other, no less worthy, Scottish indie bands like the Fizzbombs, whose EP captured a band equally transfixed by the Ramones and surf music, and Rote Kapelle, who released some engaging (if spotty) EPs and singles. Most significantly, there was Jesse Garon & the Desperadoes, a sextet with a deceptively American-sounding name. All three bands existed in Edinburgh and shared members, but somehow they've fallen off the radar, forgotten by even the most ardent students of C86-era British pop.

This is particularly unfortunate when considering the Desperadoes. Between 1986 and 1988 they recorded a series of singles on the Narodnik and Velocity labels. *A Cabinet of Curiosities* collects a dozen of these never-were-hits. They are of such uniformly high quality that you could call it a pop *Singles Going Steady*. Most of these songs are powered by jangly guitar and Fran Schoppler's plaintive, low-key vocals. The melodies are instantly memorable, performances ebullient and slightly naïve, the mood bittersweet and dark around the edges. Tracks such as "I'm Up Here," "Laughing & Smiling," and "Just for a While (If Ever)" recall the quieter moments of Talulah Gosh or the Flatmates, but with a certain added composure. "The Rain Fell Down" is simply stellar, lulling you with its evocative description of "Glasgow town, asleep in the hills/Like the Legoland you had as a kid." When Schoppler gets to the chorus of "this town is mine tonight," it's as if she's paving the way for Belle & Sebastian's odes to shy people, trains and rainy cities.

The Desperadoes followed *A Cabinet of Curiosities* with one CD, *Nixon*. It's got its moments, but the singles collection is what you want. Your best chance of finding it is at Edinburgh's Avalanche Records, where you can occasionally find an ex-Desperado or two working behind the counter. (Mike Appelstein)

MORT GARSON & JACQUES WILSON

The Wozard of Iz: An Electronic Odyssey (A&M, 1968)

Hitherto mainstream producer-arranger Mort Garson fell hard for the Moog, and found his own outré voice amidst its visceral soundscapes. Over a series of high-concept discs (1967–1976), Garson riffed on the zodiac, satanism, sexuality and plants, but his masterpiece is this tripped-out reinvention of Baum's classic fantasy.

Wozard is simply a gas, with wild lyrics (by narrator Jacques Wilson), inventive use of Moog effects, and a period McLuhanesque message that isn't *too* embarrassing. Lee Hazlewood associate Suzi Jane Hokum makes a terrific Dorothy, her voice at once jaded, naive and adorably congested. As the disc opens, she's stuck in Kansas City with tube-addled relatives. A frenetic sound collage indicts the media, deteriorating into a delirious repetition of the phrase "Isn't it funny that Dino drinks?" which maybe sums up the sixties all by itself. Escaping coastward by bus, Dot muses: "Kansas City isn't where it's at/It's a place where people throw rocks at dreams/And the dream shouldn't be stoned, only the dreamer."

Spat out onto the swirling human show of the Upset Strip, Dorothy meets a good witch who says the Strip is old news, but the Wozard can help her. Joined by the consumption-mad Thing-A-Ling, hyper-analytical In Man and the gutless Lyin' Coward, Dorothy eases on down the road to a psychedelic madrigal: "As sure as phosphate fizzes … the wise old Wozard of Iz is!" On Side 2, the adventurers visit a therapy happening and Big Sur, but never do find the Wozard, because, dig, each of the characters always had what they lacked, and never needed a guru at all. Too quickly, the record ends in a witch-killing ceremony in which the four mind-travelers destroy the destructive forces in themselves, emerging free and clean as newborn souls, ready to join an anarchist commune, take up macramé or write a hit record.

The novelty of producing a Moog record structured like a pop album, with wit, melody, and electronic squawks kept to an effective minimum, makes this the pinnacle of the rather small genre of psychedelic *Wizard of Oz*–themed albums (see also: Capitol's *The Wizard of Oz and Other Trans Love Trips*). (Kim Cooper)

MARVIN GAYE

Here, My Dear (Motown, 1978)

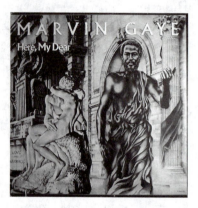

The music sounds like it's holding everything barely in check: at the same time blissfully static and nervously funky. Marvin talk/sings through barely composed repetitive art-funk, his voice eerily multitracked at times, sounding tranquilized to keep some burst of temper from exploding, driven to a soporific mellowness by a grief and anger that sounds this far from madness. It's the most complete and detailed pop concept album about divorce—a topic pop songwriters are doubtless quite familiar with. The cover says it all: the front features Marvin as a Greco-Roman statue, while to his right is a fascist-looking eagle on a pedestal reading "love and marriage." On the back cover facing it across the courtyard is another eagle, identified as "pain and divorce."

This rich man's anguished lament—"someone tell me please/why do I have to pay attorneys' fees?"—is a buppie version of Sly and the Family Stone's *There's a Riot Goin' On*'s street-crazed angst. It's a double album, but "When Did You Stop Loving Me, When Did I Stop Loving You" sums most of it up. It has occasional shocking screeches into falsetto, smooth jazz trumpets, and begins with a spooky recitation: "When you say your marriage vows it's supposed to be for real … if you don't honor what you said, you lied to God." Marvin has a lot of questions for his ex-wife: "If you ever loved me with all of your heart/Then you wouldn't take a million dollars to part." "If you loved me, how could you turn me in to the police?"

It wraps up brilliantly with "Falling in Love Again" which *maybe* is supposed to be optimistic, but with all the pain that precedes it comes on like a horror movie conclusion in which we get sinister hints that all the bad things we have just lived through are going to happen all over again. Start over on Side 1.... (Brian Doherty)

Trouble Man Soundtrack (Motown, 1972)

A superb actor nearing middle age stuck in junk TV like *Hogan's Heroes*, Ivan Dixon's directorial ambitions briefly coincided with the so-called "blaxploitation" movie boom. Herbie Hancock scored the director's *The Spook Who Sat by the Door* (a 1973 LSD-drenched, bluntly Americanized *Battle of Algiers* that blew managerial holes in United Artists and sank Dixon's feature career), but the music of this effectively paranoid gangster's nightmare is the sole property of one Marvin Gaye.

The plot tells of Mr. T (Robert Hooks), an icy Watts private detective administering an *ex parte* foot to the ass of an ofay gambling ring. To illustrate this claustrophobicically familiar plot, Gaye wraps a series of tricky-tickly variations around a muscular main theme, making excursions into hateful soul streets and after 4 A.M. jazz rooms ripe with burning reefer. "Poor Abbey Walsh" laments the gangster whose ugly erasure puts T into a syndicate civil war. Gaye lilts lyrics sparsely explanatory of the truly deep shit our antihero is in. Ghosts of "What's Goin' On" raised in "Trouble Man" dissolve in the dread and violent discords of Trevor Lawrence's sax and Dale Oehler's arrangement. "Life Is a Gamble" is all sad shimmer and ecstatic nihilism taking us all the way down to "Deep-In-It," with the main theme battling for reemergence in the last two tracks. T winds up a bloody night's work by smoking the main honky pig (a greasy Ralph Waite, known to you as upright Pa on *The Waltons*), and the composer ends the movie with a final, abrupt smash.

The album sold well, peaking at #3 on the R&B charts, but is still left off conventional accounts of Gaye's discography. Coming as it does between masterpieces *What's Goin' On* and *Let's Get It On*, this mean-ass symphony doesn't fit the general meme of Marvin as lover and optimist so beloved of music commentators. Along with Willie Hutch's evil freehand cartoon drawings for *The Mack* and *Foxy Brown* and Sam Waymond's chill brilliance on *Ganja & Hess*, this is soundtrack soul at its bleakest. (Ron Garmon)

BOBBIE GENTRY
The Delta Sweete   (Capitol, 1968)

If all you know of Bobbie Gentry is "Ode to Billie Joe," you're likely to be gob-smacked by the lady's sure and striking amalgam of country, soul and subtle psychedelia. Gentry was raised in Mississippi, studied philosophy at UCLA and worked as a Vegas showgirl, and these apparently contradictory experiences prove surprisingly cohesive in her art. Her second album is an utterly original dip into rich, conflicted pools of sophistication and simplicity, each of the twelve songs offering one facet of Southern experience. Kicking off with the swampy, seductive "Okolona River Bottom Band," Gentry hoots and giggles with her group, telling the listener to strip off city inhibitions and just *enjoy*. The regional portraiture is imbued with a rich psychological understanding and a streak of dark humor, her voice is warm and knowing, and the arrangements—ostensibly by Jimmie Haskel and Shorty Rogers, though Gentry claimed in interviews that she actually produced and arranged all her Capitol recordings—are terrific. From the erotic maternalism of "Jessye' Lisabeth" to the eerie orchestral dream-psych of "Refractions" to the actorly familial collage of "Reunion," Gentry forges a strong, strange persona that's more akin to Southern literary tradition than to anyone else on the pop charts. *The Delta Sweete* ends with "Courtyard," a Southern belle's dream gone sourly existential. None of her original albums is available on CD, but if you want a digital collection, look for Raven's *An American Quilt*, which highlights Gentry's originals and goes a long way towards restoring the reputation of this mysteriously neglected singer-songwriter. (Kim Cooper) (See also: Glen Campbell)

ROBIN GIBB
Robin's Reign   (Polydor, 1970)

Does it make sense to be a devotee of a record one is sometimes certain one doesn't like? To start with, it's *no fun*—not even a little bit. This sad, drear little record is, well, usually too sad and drear for listening pleasure. It doesn't even achieve that wonderful effect of many a classically depressing record, of making something burningly lovely and stirring from sadness. This one is mostly just a *stone drag*. So why am I proselytizing for it?

I ... I ... don't know! I'm a Bee Gees fanatic, so I was willing to keep listening past an initial instinct to bury the damn thing like a bone chewed clear of all juicy flesh—not a bad metaphor for this record full of dry little mini-symphonic swells with the occasional lockstep synthesized drum beat and slow, sour melodies framing glum, mysterious lyrics. Recorded during an interregnum in the Bee Gees' hit-making in which Robin quit (Barry and Maurice made the cleaner, only slightly saner-sounding, *Cucumber Castle* without him), it has fallen into the critical chasm yawning expressly for long out-of-print solo albums from bands rock critics don't like to begin with.

But if you are willing to listen past the point where you think it's boring you to death or it's just too hard to get a grip on its languorous haze, *Robin's Reign* will conquer you. Robin is taking you somewhere you've never been—perhaps, to go with the title and cover conceit, a petty kingdom for him to lord over. There's not really a standout track. Sometimes it's positively painful, in a mysteriously impersonal way. But I keep returning, a confused but worshipful peasant, to Robin's kingdom. Perhaps it's a sinister mind control experiment—Robin does claim here to be "an evil man who sings a new song/but all the same/I'm still to blame"—an existential despotism from which there is no escape. (Brian Doherty) (See also: Bee Gees)

GIBSON BROS

Big Pine Boogie   (Okra, 1987/Homestead, 1988)

The debut from Columbus, Ohio, blues and country archivists the Gibson Bros arrived at the height of indie rock's fascination with noise, "scumrock" and SST/homestead/Touch & Go heavy punk rock. Somehow this roots-reverent band was quickly grasped to the bosom of budding—mostly East Coast—scenesters, likely due to *Big Pine Boogie*'s loose-limbed Cramps-style primitivism and heavily reverbed, cranked-up guitars.

The record has been seemingly lost to time, and criminally remains out of print and unavailable on CD. *Big Pine Boogie* has a fantastic front porch feel to it, like no one's taking the whole thing particularly seriously, and there's a big bucket of beers beckoning nearby for consumption when the set's wrapped up. Guitarists Don Howland, Jeff Evans and Dan Dow and drummer Ellen Hoover took their cues from the pantheon of rough-hewn

American genius, from shambling Bo Diddley thumping, deep-South country à la Charlie Feathers and pre–WWII delta blues giants like Skip James and Charley Patton.

The thoroughly reworked cover of Furry Lewis's "Kassie Jones" that kicks off the record is worth the admission price alone—in the grand tradition of their forebears, the band borrowed admirably and liberally from the aforementioned pantheon, and reworked it for a 1980s punk rock mentality. There's also a muted sense of cornpone comedy in all this, from Evans' ludicrously faux hillbilly accent to forced "rhyming" couplets like "He's the cat that wrote 'I'm A Man'/Ate a whole bucket of Kentucky Fried Chicken" (from "Bo Diddley Pulled a Boner").

Trouser Press generously called it "intentional amateurism," which perhaps bestows musical abilities on the band they hadn't yet earned. But you won't care. There hasn't been a muted roar quite like *Big Pine Boogie* since, and it's high time this bandwagon got rolling again. (Jay Hinman)

HARRY "THE HIPSTER" GIBSON
Boogie Woogie in Blue   (Musicraft, 1944)

Imagine a jazzy Jerry Lee Lewis or an epileptic Esquerita, and you might begin to understand what Harry "The Hipster" Gibson was all about. Popular with the druggie crowd for his tune "Who Put the Benzedrine (in Mrs. Murphy's Ovaltine)," Gibson was much more than a novelty artist. Trained classically at Julliard, he was a pianist of immense talent, but eventually the life of boogie woogie, fast women and hard drugs took him to the dark side, where he would stay the rest of his life. His recordings were infrequent and sporadic over a nearly forty-year career, but often brilliant. Such was the case with his first album released on the obscure Musicraft label. It contained several of his signature pieces, including the autobiographical "Handsome Harry, the Hipster," the ode to late night revelry "Stop That Dancin' up There," and several show-stopping piano instrumentals, including "Riot in Boogie" and "The Hipster's Blues, Opus 6 7/8." Best of all, on the inside cover is a jive-talk dictionary explaining the weird hipster language used on the album. *Boogie Woogie in Blue* can be found easily, reissued on a budget CD that seems to be perpetually for sale on eBay. If your tastes run to drug-addled genius with manic highs and incomprehensible lows, check it out. Harry "The Hipster" ended his own life in a lonely trailer on a farm road in Brawley, California in the late eighties. (Deke Dickerson)

THE GO-BETWEENS
16 Lovers Lane
(Beggars Banquet, 1988)

Like *Pet Sounds* or *Forever Changes*, the Go-Betweens' sixth album is a perfect refutation of that dirty word "overproduction." The Go-Betweens built their records smarter and more grown-up: bitter, sentimental (but not nostalgic) lyrics; lush, symphonic arrangements; soaring melodies; elements of postpunk woven inextricably into perfectly produced pop. Their best songs are cathedrals of melody, instrumentation and wordplay. This album is as exhilarating as taking a drag on the first cigarette you've had in years, and as tinged with regret as the thought of how your ex-wife hated smoking so damn much.

16 Lovers Lane dissects heartbreak with care and grace. It's an effortless listen, despite the difficult themes and odd chord changes. "Love Goes On!" is either a literal story of obsession or a metaphor for the transitory nature of love, driven by a cheery electric guitar line and a Spanish guitar break over strings, synths and God knows how many other instruments. "Quiet Heart" is an epic of regret over constant heartbeat drums, equal parts Wilson, Cohen and Big Star. "Streets of Your Town," the least successful song on the album—ironically, one of their only U.K. hits—still has lyrics incisive enough to draw blood ("This town is full of battered wives"). And "Dive for Your Memory" is a lovely almost-suicide note ("If the cliffs were any closer/if the water wasn't so bad/I'd dive for your memory/on the rocks and the sand") that balances the immediate emotional resonance of the threat with the distance in the opening lines. As bad as the singer feels, it's not bad enough to quit living.

That song was the Go-Betweens' last for twelve years. Thankfully, the distance between band members wasn't bad enough to prevent principal songwriters Robert Forster and Grant McLennan from reuniting in 2000. Idiosyncratic to the end, they have avoided the typical crappiness of reunited bands. 2003's *Bright Yellow Bright Orange* is as good as anything they ever did. (Hayden Childs)

GODZ

Contact High with the Godz   (ESP, 1966)

The Godz fell from the sky into an East Village populated by Fugs and hippie degenerates. The sound of impact was singular, an arrhythmic folkish freakout that seemed lumpy and broken even by psychedelic standards. Clearly this band had been dropped on its head. From this simple and innocent place, this first album's opener, "Turn On," states all they ask of their new earthly neighbors, the message sung with few words and less harmony. In fact, a lone guitar chord marches drunkenly to the beat of elephantine drums and maracas, as a gentle waft of lyrics and hobo harmonica slip through the monotony.

In their heyday, the Godz were called brilliantly inept and compared to such luminaries as the Mothers, Holy Modal Rounders and the aforementioned Fugs (the latter two label mates on the legendary ESP imprint). Thing is, the Godz were even more plodding and primitive, belonging more to the proto-punk world of the Monks than the strict longhair set. Even now, the record sounds strange, both hopelessly amateur and sublime, even mystical. This dichotomy between the fun-loving musician and the obscure audio mystic played out not only on songs (the inanity of "White Cat Heat" versus the numerological intentions behind "Eleven") but on album covers. Two were issued for the record's initial release: one featuring the "fun-loving" Godz bearing smiles and good tidings, while a second hid behind an abstract collage portraying the players in a more deific manner. The choice was left to the fans. (The Bengala)

GRAHAM GOULDMAN

The Graham Gouldman Thing (RCA, 1968)

Graham Gouldman was the British Invasion's very own pop Chekhov. His pocket dramas turned on commonplace details—a note left to a milkman, queuing up for the bus, the concession stand at a Saturday matinee—and he scored each scene with his distinctively lush, pensive, minor-key melodies. He recorded *The Graham Gouldman Thing* between his stints as hitmaker *par excellence* and 10cc member, with assistance from a pre-Zep John Paul Jones. Graham's voice was too light to do absolute justice to his own tunes, but this really only affected "For Your Love," which can't escape comparison to the Yardbirds. We do miss the Hollies' harmonies on "Bus Stop," but Jones' string arrangement dramatically cossets the melody. It's not the remakes that make this record so memorable, though; it's the glittering cache of lesser-known gems.

Throughout, Graham identified unfashionably with parents and pawn-brokers, girls pawed at by loutish lads, and loners forever on the outside look-ing in. Not for Graham the typical cave-stomping, garage rock misogyny of the sixties. He was a sensitive lad, who'd inspire fellow Mancunian Morrissey (who covered "East West"), and presaged all manner of indie-pop kids with his plaintive, wistful melancholy.

On track after track, Graham balances the closely observed detail of his lyrics against the poignancy of the music. With delicate backing by what sounds improbably like an electric bouzouki, "The Pawnbroker" sketches a portrait of loss with a soulful Russian air. Gouldman's impeccable pop hooks charted "No Milk Today" for Herman's Hermits and "Pamela, Pamela" for the Mindbenders. On "The Impossible Years," Graham spins yet another haunting melody while portraying a young girl's fraught teens with rare empathy. John Paul Jones' string arrangement on "My Father" anticipates his more famous work on R.E.M.'s "Nightswimming." Few composers can rival the sheer ravishing beauty of Graham Gouldman's songs—among his sixties peers, perhaps only Brian Wilson and the Left Banke's Michael Brown. As the curtain came down on the sixties, Graham staged his masterpiece. (David Smay) (See also: 10cc)

GRAFFITI
Graffiti   (ABC, 1968)
Of all the 1969 Springfield-Grape "West Coast influenced"
groups (Bodine, Stained Glass, now Cochise too), my favorites,
from D.C. I think. This LP hit me over the head years ago and
still does: the band's composing depth and breadth is awesome,
and the arrangements (mucho segues and brief instrumental
interludes) and production (Bob Thiele, Eddie Kramer) are
superb. Caught 'em once on Dick Clark, but don't know whatever became of them. Search this one out.

(Gene Sculatti, *Flash* #2, June–July 1972)

THE GUN CLUB
Fire of Love   (Ruby, 1981)
This isn't southern gothic, it's feral white trash. Jeffrey Lee Pierce is Jack
White's charming older brother until the Wild Turkey comes on; then he's an
arrogant prick swathed in a cloud of Aqua-Net.

The Gun Club had a long career after this album and never hit this mark
again. The rhythm section of Rob Ritter and Terry Graham hounds Jeffrey
Lee through the scrub pine, chasing down the hollow keen of his voice. Ward
Dotson's slide guitar slashes wildly at Pierce, coming after him from the
shadows like a trucklot whore with her pimp's buck knife.

The lyrics whip past your head until you catch one in the face: "I've been
a real good tombstone/but now I'm blown away." Gun Club cofounder (but
absent from this first record) Kid Congo later covered "She's Like Heroin to
Me" with Sally Norvell, where it loomed in the half-light with an eerie, nar-
cotic allure. "We sit together drunk/like our fathers used to be/I'm looking up
and God is saying, 'What are you gonna do?'/I'm looking up and I'm crying,
'I thought it was up to you.'" Pierce sends murderous, adoring valentines to
Ivy Rorschach ("For the Love of Ivy") and gets at a piece of Robert Johnson
on "Preaching the Blues" that nobody else ever touched.

Then there's the "Sex Beat," which isn't sexy or erotic but base, urgent, murderous, nothing more than a criminal motive as unconsidered as the reflex at the base of a dog's hunched spine. The sex beat hammers away like an all-day speed freak. It's dry hump sex; it's a black pubic hair caught in a crust of blood on polyblend panties. It's just a fact, a part of the mosquito landscape.

This record forges the earliest link between punk and blues. For hippies the blues represented a base truth and authenticity. For Pierce it's raw, repetitive, hypnotic, clangorous, syphilitic. Ultimately, Jeffrey Lee drugged and drank and fucked himself into the grave, but don't get this record because he lived out his blues cliché. Get it because he knew his special rider in the dark, and he had a band that could preach the blues in hell. (David Smay) (See also: Flesh Eaters)

H

HACKAMORE BRICK
One Kiss Leads to Another (Kama Sutra, 1970)

A straight-up classic rock 'n' roll album, so honest and direct and fun that peculiarity can't be any reason for its disappearing into an historical black hole. Okay, the band's verbal wit and imagination might raise a few eyebrows among rock 'n' roll dullards. The one about loving the song on the radio so much you don't notice that your girl has fallen out the window of your car when she leans out to flip a bird to the dude you're drag-racing with might be considered peculiar, yes, but it's really more cheery-melancholic and play-that-one-again than weirdo. And you'll be surprised how often you need to hear the stirring choral couplet on another song that goes: "Oh I miss that Mary Anna/O those sweet bananas!"

While praising this pretty much forgotten band (as far as I know, none of them ever did anything before or since) in *Rolling Stone* when the record came out, Richard Meltzer somehow pinned the Zombies on them, which I don't hear at all. This record wins you not on originality, but just for sounding so damn good. From Brooklyn-not-Manhattan, these guys are clearly devotees of late-period Velvet Underground all the way. This is the companion album or follow-up to *Loaded* that Lou and Doug never got around to. It's brimming with New York wit, love of rock 'n' roll and trashy city life, humorous cynicism, and firm-not-hard rock 'n' roll that is solid and satisfying without any obviously flashy gestures. Sometimes it drives on piano, sometimes organ, sometimes acoustic guitar, sometimes clean electric, sometimes even tambourine. There's lots of empty space and room to move and groove and it's like discovering the characters from the Velvets' "Rock & Roll" grew up to make it—pure spunk, pure fun, soulful and light and delightful. (Brian Doherty)

BUTCH HANCOCK
West Texas Waltzes and Dust Blown
Tractor Tunes   (Rainlight, 1978)

With notable exceptions like Townes van Zandt and Willie Nelson, the mid-1970s weren't kind to real country music. There just wasn't room for songwriting in the Williams/Guthrie/Rodgers tradition, a patch of ground no one had worked more convincingly than the Flatlanders for a good, long time. But after cutting one now-legendary record (which wouldn't see the light of day for a decade), Butch Hancock, Jimmie Dale Gilmore and Joe Ely split up, with Hancock settling in Austin to open a gallery, paint and write songs. During that time he applied his modernist's lyrical eye to the arid landscape around him. The results, released on his own label, boast as breathtaking a range of pure American music as any debut I've ever heard.

Just skipping down the song list: "Dry Land Farm" is a tractor driver's lament, a rage against nature; "You've Never Seen Me Cry," also on the Flatlanders' record, sports some fine Hancock wordplay in service of a modern West Texas love story. Hancock is a devoted naturalist (and sometime river guide) and many of his songs focus on nature and our responsibility to the land, as in "Texas Air" and "They Say It's a Good Land," counterbalancing "Dry Land Farm" by offering thanks for a good life lived off the soil. But if I had to point out two reasons to seek out an obscure 26-year-old country record, just give a listen to "I Grew to Be a Stranger," about trying to reconcile a developing political and social consciousness with the expectations of your family and home town, and "Just One Thunderstorm," a tone poem about the damage left in the wake of a storm.

Hancock has gone on to write some classic tunes like "She Never Spoke Spanish to Me," but this record is a starting place for a body of work—a crazy-ass, testifying-in-the-desert-at-High-Noon song of devotion to a place most of us will never know. (Ken Rudman)

THE HANDSOME FAMILY
Through the Trees   **(Carrot Top, 1998)**

It seems odd for an album that initiates a new lineup and a new sound for a band to take as its central themes death, decay, and loss, but then again "odd" has always been an appropriate adjective for the Handsome Family. Working without a drummer for the first time on their third album, the husband and wife team of Brett and Rennie Sparks made a quiet masterpiece.

Death and loss are everywhere on this album, random and sad and even darkly funny. A giant dies from a blister on his toe. Lovers share a suicide pact. Boys throw stones at a swan. The lyrics combine a fantasist's imagination with a Carveresque eye for the telling detail: in "The Woman Downstairs," the dead woman's boyfriend weeps, the cops steal her TV, and the singer dreams of lying down on the El tracks as "Lake Michigan rose and fell like a bird."

Brett Sparks' music matches Rennie's lyrics with a sound that hovers between the past and the present. The album's instrumentation includes autoharp, banjo, Dobro, violin, bass, melodica, washboard, piano, tuba and a drum machine. The result is both spacious and delicate, a musical latticework around Brett's baritone. When he sings, "This is why people OD on pills/And jump from the Golden Gate Bridge/Anything to feel weightless again," the song soars with him, exhilarating and annihilating all at once. That the lyric is obliquely comparing the sensation of jumping to the terror of falling in love doesn't flatten it out to cliché: the song is so full of rich detail, both invented and lived-in, that it makes both love and death seem like even deeper mysteries. (Michele Tepper)

ROY HARPER
Born in Captivity   (Awareness, 1985)

Roy Harper has released over thirty albums since 1966. I don't claim to have heard even half of them, nor is *Born in Captivity* his most famous album, but I have to proselytize: this is great stuff. Critics tend to like *Stormcock* best, but the one with the most fans is probably *Flat Baroque and Berserk*, containing "Another Day" (covered by Kate Bush and Peter Gabriel, This Mortal Coil, etc.) and the oft-compiled "Tom Tiddler's Ground." Oh, what the hell, go buy that one too.

Born in Captivity was the acoustic demo Harper cut in preparation for *Work of Heart,* but I prefer it to the overproduced finished product. I appreciate the album's bare nakedness, which allows the poetry, the unsentimental emotion and the music to which they're wedded to emerge. He's somewhere between early Pink Floyd and Donovan, only better—and I say this as the proud owner of in excess of twenty Donovan albums.

One of my all-time favorite songs is "Stan." Of course, as a Man. U. supporter, I'm a tad biased, but nonetheless, it conjures up the magic of it all on what Harper calls "planet football." "Drawn to the Flames" is a wondrous love song complete with mushrooms, Eden and anarchy. Nobody writes more truly about passionate love. "I Am a Child" is about coping with everyday realities, and the six-part "Work of Heart" starts with "No-One Ever Gets out Alive" (but you knew that…) and works its way through love and a denunciation of "politics of slime" back to the *memento mori.*

As a final ringing endorsement, I used to play this in the used bookstore where I worked. Every time I popped it on, people asked me what it was and how to get it. You can find it in a double CD with *Work of Heart* on the Science Friction label. (Brooke Alberts)

MICHAEL HEAD & THE STRANDS
The Magical World of the Strands   (Megaphone, 1997)

I have seen this record only once, the day I bought it in 1997 or early 1998. Just looking at the sleeve, I could tell it was something special. The cover shows a small, old wooden door right next to a brick wall. It looks like the type of door you would have seen Nick Drake walking past had you been hanging out in London in the late sixties.

The magic of this record was the work of one Michael "Mick" Head. This was after he'd led the Pale Fountains to some fame and notoriety in the fickle U.K. press and just before his comeback with Shack. Apparently Strand was in the throes of heroin addiction; this record was him exorcising his demons.

The record begins quietly with "Queen Matilda" as Head whispers, "What would you do if the sun hit the ground, and the trees poked through beneath the sea...." And he trails off and lets his acoustic guitar do the talking. At one point it sounds as if he's saying "apple juice," but he couldn't be possibly be saying that ... could he? "And Luna" sports a climbing guitar hook and Head's thick brogue telling the listener every secret he's ever heard. "The Prize" sports the loudest guitar heard on the record (but it's not AC/DC or anything) while "It's Harvest Time" sounds like the ghost of the very-much-alive Neil Young sporting the most beautiful acoustic strum I've heard in ages.

I don't know whatever became of the Strands, but I sure wish they had more than eleven songs lying around in the vaults. Magical? Indeed. (Tim Hinely)

HEARTS & FLOWERS
Now Is the Time for Hearts & Flowers/
Of Horses—Kids—and Forgotten Women   (Capitol, 1967/1968)

Lodged somewhere between the early sixties acoustic folk boom and the twilight of country rock, this trio released two albums of equal import, then vanished as thoroughly as the Sunset Strip freedom movement that beget them. Fronted by Larry Murray with David Dawson and Rick Cuhna, Hearts & Flowers signed to the short-lived Capitol subsidiary Folk World, also home to Linda Ronstadt's Stone Poneys.

"Rock 'n' Roll Gypsies," Hearts & Flowers' only hit, was, like the Buffalo Springfield's "For What It's Worth," an anthem for disenfranchised striplings thrown out of L.A.'s banned teenage nightclubs. The debut album countered Sunset Strip optimism ("Try for the Sun," Kaleidoscope's "Please") with a shameless spiritual philosophy ("10,000 Sunsets") soon lost with the coming cynicism of the late sixties. Such lost innocence was resplendent within their second long player, on which Bernie Leadon (later to become the Eagles' significant Brian Jones entity) replaced Cuhna. The trio morphed into a brilliant songwriting team, yet their interpretations remain the highlight: forgotten Rising Sons guitarist Jesse Lee Kincaid's "She Sang Hymns out of Tune," the carnivalesque "Colour Your Daytime" (the pop synonym of Buffalo Springfield's "Merry Go Round") and an orchestrated take on Arlo Guthrie's "Highway in the Wind" that foretold of Poco's "Rose of Cimarron" a decade later. Bespectacled and Lennonesque, "Ode to a Tin Angel" is psychedelic gobbledygook at its best. And yes, Mike Nesmith once quoted Hearts & Flowers at the end of a *Monkees* episode. (Domenic Priore)

HERMAN'S HERMITS
Blaze   (MGM, 1967)

The British Invasion's friendliest group resorting to psychedelia? Their 1964 debut "I'm into Something Good" was cheerful and clean. Subsequent singles and album tracks were equally spotless. Though the Stones evolved and Beatles revolved, the Hermits strayed nary a foot from their original happy course. In 1966 that could cost a career.

Their first 1967 LP, *There's a Kind of Hush All over the World*, presented admirable steps down more mature avenues, including their fine reading of the Seekers' "Rattler." In October, four months after the world was *Pepper* sprayed, *Blaze* crept into record stores.

The Hermits built *Blaze* from reliable parts: songwriters Graham Gouldman, John Carter, and Geoff Stephens all penned previous "Hermhits." As insurance, the band even tackled "Museum" by thoroughly hip Donovan, who shared producer Mickie Most. Of the ten songs, only "Ace King Queen Jack" sounds misguided, a rocker giving way to Herman discussing garbage trucks. But almost everything else delights. "Green Street Green" mirrored "Penny Lane," and "Moonshine Man" had an admirable darkness. Even songs echoing their pure-pop days, like the wonderful "Busy Line" or bouncy "Don't Go out into the Rain" (a Swinging Blue Jeans flop), kept ears listening. The end result proved even Herman's Hermits capable of moving forward without selling out.

All in vain. By 1967, fans of cheerful pop had turned to the Monkees, while more progressive fans had long written the band off. *Blaze* only reached #75 in America, while Britain passed altogether. The minor success of singles "Don't Go out into the Rain" (#19) and "Museum" (#37) suggested America would henceforth only consume the Hermits in smaller doses. Excepting a soundtrack, America saw no further Hermits studio albums.

In subsequent years, *Blaze* has been reassessed, appreciated, and even regarded as their magnum opus. But for all the attention it received in 1967, a more fitting title would have been *Blasé*. (Michael Lynch)

Deeply Wrong Big-Eye Pop-Psych

West Coast Pop Art Experimental Band, "I Won't Hurt You": Yeah, right. Creepy hippie come-on as outsider art.

Ballroom, "Love's Fatal Way": We'll be together one fine day—in the morgue.

Move, "(Here We Go Round) The Lemon Tree": Taking advantage of your mentally ill teenage neighbor.

Timon, "The Bitter Thoughts of Little Jane": She'll find a head to pound on. Someday.

Free Design, "Kites Are Fun": So are lobotomies.

Harpers Bizarre, "Happyland": The Banana Splits on Ecstasy.

Pink Floyd, "Bike": Careful with that axe, Syd.

Beach Boys, "I'd Love Just Once to See You": Reclusive millionaire seeks ladies for nude pie-baking.

Hollies, "Lullaby to Tim": Proto-Jacko pedo-psychosis.

Jan & Dean, "Yellow Balloon": Perfect for: trepanation, disembowelment. (Andrew Hultkrans)

DAN HICKS & HIS HOT LICKS
Where's the Money   **(Blue Thumb, 1971)**
The world is waiting for this group—and here they are. '40s
showmanship, 1950s lyrics, 1960s instrumental expertise,
1970s recording job. Soul music for the very drunk.

(Ed Ward, *Flash* #2, June–July 1972)

THE HOLLIES
Evolution   **(Epic U.S./Parlophone U.K., 1967)**
I came across this one rather late in life (like just a few years ago), and much
to my chagrin, since it's a doozy. I knew the hit song from it, of course
("Carrie Anne"), but I was amazed at how strong the rest of the LP was,
given how self-indulgent and trippy-hippy rock albums from 1967 tended to
be. Several songs—especially "Games We Play" and "Have You Ever Loved
Somebody"—are not only great examples of the Graham Nash–era Hollies
at their absolute best, but would have been hit singles themselves if they had
bothered to release them as such (a fact that their former bass player bemoans
in the liner notes of the recent CD reissue).

One maddening thing about buying Brit pop LPs that date from before
1968 is that although the U.K. releases usually had more tracks on them
(fourteen as opposed to eleven or twelve in the United States), the Brits also
had an odd habit of *not* including any songs that had already been released
on a 45. Thus, while the U.K. version of *Evolution* may have had *more* songs
on it, it didn't have what is arguably its *best* song, "Carrie Anne," which the
U.S. version *opens* with. Fortunately for us twenty-first-century dwellers, the
reissue has all of the above plus some excellent "bonus tracks," including such
orphaned singles as "When Your Lights Turned On" and "Jennifer Eccles"—
neither of which had ever been included on an LP in *either* country.
Inconceivable! (Peter Bagge)

THE HONEYCOMBS

The Honeycombs (Vee Jay 1964)

Joe Meek was the ultimate sixties British producer, outsider, and, of course, murderer. He was everything a boy of nine would love. At that age I discovered the Honeycombs' "Have I the Right?" and was immediately struck by the emotional chorus with the stomping feet recorded on the staircase of Meek's North London flat. There was also this stinging sweetness of the lead guitar that sounded like it was fighting something frightful in some dark corner … which was maybe the case, since Meek held séances seeking musical advice from Buddy Holly. The record struck me then, as today, as 100% emotion with a suggestion of violence and madness.

The otherworldly echo of *The Honeycombs* seemed odd compared to other sounds of 1964, and the record teemed with emotional breakdowns and romantic obsessions. The titles spoke volumes to me: "Without You It Is Night," "How the Mighty Have Fallen," and the fatalistic "Nice While It Lasted."

Lead singer Dennis D'ell was always on the cliff of hysterics, just about to jump off into the whirlwind of despair and loneliness. The one comfort was female drummer Honey, whose vocals express a tender sweetness, and in duet with D'ell convey a yin and yang duality. "Color Slide," which is about watching a loved one's image on a projected photographic slide, is a remarkable *visual* commentary on romantic obsession.

The Honeycombs is a series of songs dealing with total romantic failure. Meek was a genius not only at making space age sounds, but also at capturing a certain emotional strain that fitted so perfectly in his personal life. In the end, Meek, in either a drug-induced frenzy or deep mental stress, shot and killed his landlady on the very steps that were used in the recording of "Have I the Right?". He then shot himself and that was the end of the Honeycombs. (Tosh Berman)

THE HOT DOGS
Say What You Mean   (Ardent, 1973)

There were thousands of ways to process a wondering adoration of the Beatles (more the Harrison end, with McCartney's early solo high-on-life-and-pot country boy persona shining as well), or even merely Beatlesque artists like Todd Rundgren. Not all of them were going to stick in pop lore, not all were going to change the world. But they could still be pretty great.

This came out in 1973, and sounds it—suffused with that slightly doped, sunny even when fretful, back-to-the-country feel with occasional light boogie tendencies. The elements of the time infected such obscurities as McGuiness Flint and stars like America. It's in no way unique but still doesn't sound precisely like anyone else. Rock had become the demotic language of its time, with thousands speaking their own little dialects, and the conversation was so full of riches even history's hungry maw couldn't swallow it all—hence, lost gems like this.

It's possible the Hot Dogs could have been an alternative universe Big Star, except we never got to find out what their second or third records might have accomplished. They were from Big Star's hometown of Memphis and on their label—the Stax pop offshoot Ardent—and had former Chris Bell bandmate Terry Manning on production and guitar and Richard Rosebrough (veteran of many Alex Chilton sessions) on drums, though neither was an official band member.

As full of mellow pleasures as it is, there is not a hell of a lot of unique personality on this record. But it is perhaps all the more worthy of mention for that, standing as an example of how inexhaustible the pleasures of loping, melodic pop rock could be once the template was invented. It's the kind of everyday treasure that makes stepping outside the paved roads of rock history a continuing pleasure. (Brian Doherty)

THE HOUSEMARTINS
London 0 Hull 4/The People Who
Grinned Themselves to Death   (Go!, 1986/Elektra, 1987)

With one foot balanced in gospel music and sixties American soul, England's Housemartins steadied their other foot on the back of Elvis Costello. They harmonized like a barbershop quartet and wrote funny and cynical lyrics set to catchy jangle-pop melodies. Yet few people outside of the United Kingdom have ever heard them.

The Housemartins forged a radio-friendly guitar-pop sound akin to their postpunk peers the Smiths and Aztec Camera. But the Housemartins' hook was a strange combination. Swinging further left than the anti-Thatcher Labor Party, they openly encouraged Marxism. Then in the same breath they embraced Christianity. Their manifesto in the liner notes of *London 0 Hull 4* was "Take Jesus—Take Marx—Take Hope."

That incongruous match did not keep them from cracking the British charts with the spiffy pub mockery of "Happy Hour." Their *a cappella* "Caravan of Love" reached #1 over Christmas of 1986. In England, the band was hugely popular, but in the US "Happy Hour" played only on college radio and MTV's *120 Minutes*. By the time the sophomore album arrived in 1987, American Top 40 radio was sliding into a pop-metal and teen fluff wasteland. There was no room for a band like the Housemartins.

With a new drummer, the group enjoyed a couple more English hits and seemed to be expanding their sound and perfecting songwriting abilities. But in 1988 the Housemartins called it quits, claiming the band's popularity had eclipsed all expectations and intentions. All four members moved on to different projects. Guitarist Stan Cullimore produced records for the Farm, singer Paul Heaton and drummer Dave Hemmingway formed The Beautiful South, and bassist Norman Cook founded Beats International before adopting the stage name Fatboy Slim. Most of these offshoot projects garnered more success than the Housemartins ever did. (Kris Kendall)

I

THE INCREDIBLE MOSES LEROY
Electric Pocket Radio   (Ultimatum Music, 2001)

Genre-bending songs that are a pastiche of new wave, soul, hip-hop and rock? Check. Positive press in *The New Yorker* and *Los Angeles Times*, *Harper's* and numerous music magazines? Check. Airplay on college radio? Check.

Stardom seemed to be destined for The Incredible Moses Leroy with *Electric Pocket Radio*. What should have been a sparkling entry into mainstream success instead became one of the best pop secrets of 2001. Those who discovered Moses Leroy's sophomore album cherish it. If you missed it, it's time to rectify that.

Ron Fountenberry, the musician who is, more or less, The Incredible Moses Leroy, challenges music career expectations. He didn't even play an instrument until college. His day job is substitute teaching. He cites eighties radio, comic books, and his great-grandfather—the Moses Leroy of the band moniker—as influences. With that knowledge, how can you not love *Electric Pocket Radio*?

There is great comedy in "Fuzzy" ("Let's paint the town red/just like Carrie"), and "Tomato Soup" is an instrumental that pays homage to light jazz without a trace of irony. "Our One Millionth Customer" transmutes Beach Boys harmonies into spastic drum and bass beats before settling into twinkling techno. *Electric Pocket Radio* opens with a winning cover of Gruppo Sportivo's "Beep Beep Love." Yet the album was generally passed over by the record-buying public. Missing out on the fun stuff in life really stinks; don't miss *Electric Pocket Radio*. (Kris Kendall)

THE IDLE RACE
The Birthday Party   (Liberty, 1968)

This is black, sweetly hallucinogenic fruit that once bent a spindly tree at some barren grove in Pepperland. The band that grew it started in late-fifties Birmingham, mutating into Mike Sheridan & the Nightriders before shaking off Roy Wood for the Move and taking on teenage Jeff Lynne, and a new name, the Idle Race. A Lynne-penned single, "Impostors Of Life's Magazine," was silly and loud enough to draw favorable notice in 1966 London and eventually led to *The Birthday Party*.

Here are thirteen stopovers on a tour of a cheery, post-imperial England, often overcast with black gusts of acidhead Thackeray. The sunny whimsy of the early singles is splotched over with depression ("The Birthday"), infantilism ("I Like My Toys"), and dementia ("Sitting in My Tree"). Then there's Side 2, opening with belches and tinny music before settling into a nice prechewed morsel of proto-ELO. There are more vignettes and snatches of groaning tune. Bad luck and explosions predominate. A mother signs over her sons to distant slaughter, as a music hall chorus croaks "Don't put your boys in the Army, Mrs. Ward!" "The Lady Who Said She Could Fly," is a rose-gold cameo of a pale woman gone to heaven, and probably the best song Lynne will ever write. The chirpy, Kinky finale rolls by like a filigreed hearse, and you are let off far from home.

The Race held onto Lynne for one more try. *The Idle Race* (1969) is perfectly respectable Brit psych-pop: not so good as Blossom Toes' *If Only for a Moment*, better than *The Small Faces*. Sales and group career advancement registered a tick but little north of *bupkes*. Lynne decamped for the Move, which, in turn, became ELO, later to lose Roy Wood and gain world superstardom. The Idle Race did one more album and had two hits in South America before reentering the pubs as the Steve Gibbons Band. (Ron Garmon)

THE INDIVIDUALS

Fields   (Plexus, 1982)

It is a truth universally acknowledged that art students like to put on funny costumes and dance at parties. Historically, American art pop bands like Talking Heads and Pylon have catered to young aesthetes by sinking a ropy bassline and backbeat under their skittery guitars and gnomic yelps. The Individuals were just such an art school party band.

They emerged from the same Hoboken scene that produced the Bongos and the dBs, but owe more to the Feelies. Their entire discography amounts to one single, one lesser EP, and this entirely perfect LP. Their sound reflects the early eighties college-rock era and would not sound unprecedented to fans of *Crazy Rhythms* or *Stands for Decibels* or *More Songs about Buildings and Food*: astringent harmonies, call and response vocals so casual they sound like two people holding a conversation in different rooms, the danceable groove, the jittery, jangly, angular guitars. Glenn Morrow's lyrics function in a dead-pan dreamlogic ("My three sons revolve around the earth/They've been doing it since the day of their birth/My three sons are young and able/See them sitting around the kitchen table"), floating along the top of simply skewed structures of tension and release. Janet Wygal's more modest songs take twilight walks past empty lots and closed storefronts. She just wants her boyfriend to grow his hair a little bit longer.

The Individuals rigged smart, offhand arrangements—loose, grooving, sharp and distinctive. Janet Wygal locked up a meaty bass groove with her brother Doug on drums, Glenn chopped up the rhythm, and Jon Klages blistered the whole thing with shimmers and shards of guitar. (Klages's surgical solo on his "Johnny's in the Mines" illustrates why Richard Lloyd later worked with him.)

They all went on to other bands: Glenn with Rage to Live; Janet to the Wygals, Splendora and even the theme to *Daria* on MTV. Klages recorded a solo album backed by not-quite-yet Yo La Tengo. But *Fields* was their best work: your good, smart friend of twenty years who never got boring. (David Smay)

J

THE JACKSONS
Triumph   (Epic/CBS, 1980)
Although this album sold extremely well and spawned several hit singles ("Lovely One," "Can You Feel It," "Heartbreak Hotel"), it remains sorely overlooked. This is largely because the Jacksons released *Triumph* shortly after brother Michael's phenomenally successful *Off the Wall*, and just before his *insanely* successful *Thriller*. Hey, I like those two Michael solo classics as much as anyone, but the shame of it is that I think *Triumph* is better. It's more consistent; it doesn't have any of the gimmicky, cult-of-personality moments

that make for both the most inspired and most *embarrassing* moments (which can be interchangeable, depending on your point of view) of Michael's solo efforts.

Triumph has it all: great songs, flawless production and beautiful harmonies—all provided by the Bros themselves. It *grooves so* relentlessly and effortlessly that a casual listener would hardly be aware of the eccentric arrangements on tracks like "Walk Right Now" and "Give it Up." Michael was clearly at his creative peak when this record was made—his singing is incredible. It's remarkable how seamlessly he collaborated with his brothers before his own fame reached stratospheric proportions.

This divide in their collective destiny is all the more tragic to anyone who saw the Jacksons perform together as a group for the first time in ages in that 2001 *Tribute to Michael Jackson* TV special. Not only because they were so fantastic, but because Michael has become such a shell of his former self that his brothers were carrying *him* for a change! (Peter Bagge)

HENRY JACOBS' MUSIC & FOLKLORE
Radio Programme #1 **(Folkways, 1954/Locust, 2003)**
Henry Jacobs was an important member of the Bay Area experimental community of the fifties, collaborating with filmmaker Jordan Belson on the seminal "Vortex" electronic music Planetarium shows as well as hosting a long-running and very eclectic radio program on KPFA in Berkeley. The Locust CD is a condensed version of that program, originally released on Moe Asch's idiosyncratic Folkways label.

The record stands as one of the strangest aural concoctions ever, veering wildly between collaged sound effects, early electronic noise, tape loop composition, proto-hippie percussion jams (remember, this was the year Elvis first walked into Sun Records!) and public radio–style interviews ranging from real to patently fake. These include a deadpan interrogation of a schizophrenic about his association with Al Capone, a mini-lecture on the various forms of Indian raga and the jive mutterings of a highly influential faux-hipster named Shorty Petterstein. It was as if cacophonous novelty purveyor Spike Jones had been torn into his constituent parts and sprinkled liberally with herbs—postmodernism in all its indeterminate glory, decades before anyone bothered to lay out a formula.

Of course the response was almost nil, but Shorty Petterstein took on a life of his own: Ralph Gleason adopted the persona in his syndicated music column and the Petterstein routines were reissued as a comedy single by Fantasy Records to wide acclaim. Jacobs moved on, to five years of sitar study under Ali Akbar Khan, among other adventures.

Jacobs is alive and kicking and enduring a resurgence of interest in his work, including a number of other reissues and compilations of unreleased material. Here's hoping they're half as mind-boggling as this weird pastiche of avant-garde humor and experimental composition. (Doug Harvey)

THE JAMES GANG
Yer' Album   (MCA, 1969)

With unique, inspired production by an obviously excited producer, Bill Szymcyk, and the psyched attitude of a live performance by the band, this record is a classic example of things yet to come in the decade of Album Rock. This easygoing debut by a trio of phenomenally talented Ohio dudes from Kent State is unpredictably smokin', unpretentiously eclectic and solidly rockin'. This was a band that not only created beautifully crafted, unforgettable, captivating gems of their own, but also paid homage to their musical contemporaries with cover songs that still managed to sound original instead of redundant. They played kick-ass solos without sounding like annoying showy wank-offs, and that is a rare gift that could only have been a blessing from heaven. Speaking of heaven, Jim Fox' mind-boggling percussive performance on this record is so goddamned astounding that if a CD release became available consisting of just his drum tracks, I would buy it. Best of all, Joe Walsh's puzzlingly sexy vocal range at certain points makes him sound exquisitely female, without sounding like a drag queen. (Kelly Kuvo)

JAN AND DEAN
Jan and Dean Meet Batman   **(Liberty, 1966)**

The year was 1966. Rock and roll, not to mention society in general, was undergoing a radical conniption which would forever wipe clean, and then redraw, boundaries both artistic and altruistic. Jan Berry and Dean O. Torrence commemorated these psycho-seismic upheavals by producing *the* most subversively potent statement during the hallowed year of *Revolver*, *Pet Sounds* and *Blonde on Blonde*. Taken at the time as little more than a cash-in on the craze for all things Bat, *Jan and Dean Meet Batman* reveals itself today as a dense, multilayered uber-production which couldn't help but be misunderstood upon its initial release, having entered unsuspecting record stores years before long-players from Monty Python and the Firesign Theatre.

This largely spoken-word tour-de-farce owes more to the surrealism of vintage *Goon Show* radioplays than to the audio antics of Beach Boy side-fillers like "Bull Session with the Big Daddy." An intricately tiered weave of comedy and crime-fighting, with surf-rock thrown in to break the bizarrity, *Jan and Dean Meet Batman* is the crazed culmination of their laff-riddled career.

Knowing the strained dynamic between "Captain" Jan and his hapless cohort Dean ("the Boy Blunder") only enhances the biting satire lurking beneath the pair's seemingly innocuous hang-ten humor. Within weeks of the *Batman* album's release, Jan, just like the hero of his million-selling "Dead Man's Curve," would plow his Corvette under a parked truck at 65 mph, sustaining massive head injuries that effectively brought the duo's career to a screeching halt—including their planned move to television.

We can only speculate how much even more whacked 1966 would've been with Jan and Dean appearing weekly, in living color, on small screens across North America. With that stupefying thought in mind, let us instead repair to our collective BatPlayers to cue up *Jan and Dean Meet Batman* with newfound appreciation, as brought to you by the only Dynamic Duo that ever really mattered. (Gary Pig Gold)

JANDEK

Blue Corpse   (Corwood Industries, 1987)

Jandek is a flat-out weirdo. No one knows who he is, and the guy is either making up his own chords or just doesn't care how his guitar is tuned. Jandek is like an alien trying to play music after hearing it described to him once. *Blue Corpse* is his masterpiece.

By the third song, Jandek has made it clear that he's in no mood for women, sunlight, or a second chord. Some cite Dylan's *Blood on the Tracks* as the most harrowing break-up album ever, but even a happy Jandek could redefine the word "harrowing." This, my friends, is not the work of a happy Jandek.

His lyrics reveal a man suffering from a pain so oblique that the listener must simply allow him to revel in his misery. Jandek doesn't need us for comfort. Hell, he doesn't even care if we're there. However, *Blue Corpse* shows Jandek at his most reflective and strangely accessible. Over the course of this song cycle (I think this is the appropriate term), Jandek howls about a lost love over a single discordant chord ("I Passed by the Building"), moans his psychotic blues ("C F," "Down at the Ball Park," "House of the Rising Sun"), and sometimes even comes up with surprisingly conventional strummed guitar tracks ("Part II," "Your Other Man").

The centerpiece of the album is "Harmonica," which starts with solo harmonica for three solid minutes, but is joined by guitar and unholy yelps for the remainder. The relatively smooth guitar through the middle section ends defiantly in "Quinn Boys," where Jandek interrupts the two notes he's been playing to tune behind the vocal track. The final song, "One Minute," eschews the guitar altogether for raucous inept drumming while Jandek demands that the listener just relax and listen to the music. You should listen to him; you may never hear music the same way again. (Hayden Childs)

JAN DUKES DE GRAY

Mice and Rats in the Loft   (Transatlantic, 1971)

These days the creation of many classics would be impossible; Van Dyke Parks' *Song Cycle* immediately springs to mind, and this belongs alongside it in the pantheon of big budgets for the small audience. Maybe it was the same man who opened the gate on Ken Russell's *Lisztomania* who allowed three possible lunatics—twelve-string guitar, sax (with wah wah), and a drummer—to bring us new meaning to the word "enthusiasm." These guys are trying so hard to do things outside their "technical ability," but it doesn't matter to them. They're gonna go for it anyway; and what the hell, let's add an orchestra. (It took one hell of a conductor to follow the best beats this side of John French.) This is the sound of getting what's in their heads *out*, and flailing with absolute joy in the attempt. The sidelong "sun symphony" is a super-sized underdog, taking on the scope more of "Supper's Ready" than "Inna Gadda Da Vida." It spirals through themes shot forth as if their eyes were on the studio clock, inspiring them to peaks of true inspiration. Released on Transatlantic, it doesn't fit in with the likes of Bert Jansch, but nor is it bedfellows with the progressive scene of the time. Or any time! This one looks to the hazy future on the horizon, throwing aside its crutches, because they *believe*, and they're *free*. When you see it in the store, check out the back cover: there they are in all their glory, some kind of pajama-wearing hippie-pirates, with bonus muskets, pistols, and a sound that kills. (Jim O'Rourke)

JEANETTE

Porque te Vas, Soy Rebelde (Hispavox, 1976)

In summer 1976, the hottest dog days Europe ever knew, "Porque te Vas" ("Because You've Gone") blows right out of Franco's Spain, delicate breezy pop with one of those super-suave catchy tunes, transubstantiated by Jeanette's sultry, angelic voice. Born in fifties London, Jeanette (after stops in Chicago and California) heads back to her parental hometown of Barcelona. Slowly but steadily, the Franquist regime loosens its hold (at least for urbanites) and the local scenes crave Brit and Yankee pop sounds. Our teenybopper begins as frontgirl for the clean-cut band Pic-Nic. It is a time of innocence, but a subversive filmmaker will change the girl's destiny. Carlos Saura discovers "Porque te Vas" on the radio. He's hooked, and instantly wants to integrate it into his new film, over star Geraldine Chaplin's objections. (Actually, "Porque te Vas" broke out in 1975, just before Franco's death—quite symbolic.) Saura's film, *Cria Cuervos*, is a journey into the dark, deranged side of infancy mixed with a metaphoric comment on Franco's gray Spain. It's forever coupled with Jeanette's song. *Porque te Vas* instantly surfed on the wave of the movie's worldwide success. Jeanette's album had some stylistic connections with Claudine Longet's finest hours, but the Iberic siren was one of a kind. "Que le Han Hecho a Mi Canción" reaches places where Melanie's original "What Have They Done to My Song" never went. Existential and erotic in a David Hamiltonesque Lolita way, the LP, sung in French and Spanish, is tender, perverse, full of youthful hope. And it's more subversive than John Lydon when he was called Rotten, though Jeanette probably had no idea. Its strong yet restrained emotional power will change your life, believe me. (Jean-Emmanuel Deluxe)

JEFFERSON AIRPLANE
Bark   (Grunt, 1971)

The sound was thick, muddy, muffled, rumbling, like it's projecting from the bowels of the hollow earth that sci-fi fanatic and band leader by default (this is their first effort after founder Marty Balin jettisoned himself) Paul Kantner doubtless believes in. Kantner's lyrics are increasingly frantic with escapist fantasies of rock 'n' roll islands and fighting the Man's armies in the far-flung future year of 1975 with battalions of mind raiders, master computer killers, and "sunfighters."

Especially for fans of the Airplane qua Airplane, and not just a handful of their hits, this is the album where they are most quintessentially themselves in all the absurdity and distance and teetering toward madness that implied. Jorma Kaukonen chugs in, out, and around with his purest bluesy-boogie in "Feel So Good" and his most tenderly melodic acoustic folk in "Third Week in the Chelsea" (mostly about how he desperately wants to quit the band); Grace freaks out the squares with the incomprehensibly absurd "Never Argue with a German When You're Tired or European Song" (sung in a portmanteau language not quite German and barely human); new drummer Joey Covington *a cappellas* about how he's "thunk and thunk/couldn't think of anything better."

While the momentum of their growing reputation and cultural prominence as the major radical "movement" band of any pop success led this queer record, their next-to-last, to chart as high as 11, you certainly aren't going to be hearing the eerily prescient "Law Man"—in which Grace predicted a scenario that came true over two decades later, a home invasion by busybody cops repelled by her gun-waving—on a classic rock electric lunch. At the time, the *Village Voice*'s Robert Christgau damned it as "a collection of weirdnesses rather than an album," but that's exactly what's so fascinating and endearing about it. (Brian Doherty) (See also: Joe E. Covington's Fat Fandango, Paul Kantner)

JOHNNY JENKINS

Ton-Ton Macoute! (Capricorn, 1970)

There's an old photo of Johnny Jenkins and the Pinetoppers, the Macon, Georgia, R&B revue that gave Otis Redding his start. Johnny, with his rockabilly pompadour, is playing guitar left-handed and doing a split. The sax player and the other guitarist (there is no bass player) are also crouched down on the floor, scuffing up their suits. Even the drummer is striking a pose. Otis, for his part, is standing flat-footed, mic in hand, holding up the wall. No one knew it, but within a few years it would be Johnny Jenkins and the Pinetoppers who would be upstaged. Otis became the star.

This was partially Jenkins' doing. Music was strictly a part-time love for this legendary guitarist who influenced Jimi Hendrix but still continued to work day jobs. Prior to recording this album, his discography consisted of a few scant 45s. Out of nowhere, he emerged with *Ton-Ton Macoute!*, which crossed the Delta blues with Dr. John's New Orleans swamp rock and Hendrix's psychedelia. Slide guitars and cryptic background vocals slithered all over the record. On top of that, he showed off his acoustic guitar chops on Muddy Waters' "Rolling Stone." This album shoots off into so many genres and subgenres it's ridiculous, hinting at hard rock and Funkadelic while maintaining its own character. Jenkins was still relatively young when this was recorded (31) and could have been a major black rock guitar star (in the Jimi Hendrix/Ernie Isley mode) if the stars had been aligned right. Apparently the galaxy had other plans; after this album's release, Jenkins went underground for over twenty years. He returned in the mid-nineties when a revived Capricorn not only reissued *Ton-Ton Macoute!* but released an album of all-new material, *Blessed Blues*. He was a lot more earthbound this time out—no psychedelic swamp music, just basic Southern blues.

Apparently back to stay, he's lately been self-releasing his own material. But the otherworldly sound of *Ton-Ton Macoute!* remains a gas after all this time. (James Porter)

JOSEFUS

Dead Man   (Hookah, 1970)

Derided by ignoranti as a Led Zeppelin knockoff, this is one of the two or three early metal LPs as shot the load for a decade of nitwit progeny. Black Sabbath operated best in a welter of terror and preachment, Blue Cheer was louder than God and said less than Leviticus, but Josefus spoke with the flat contempt of a plain American watching his neighbor die.

The heaviest blues rock in Houston, Josefus was a fabled free-show monster that toured with Grand Funk Railroad and ZZ Top within a few months of their first gig. A 1969 demo album went begging, but *Dead Man* was self-released on the flyspeck Hookah label, winding up in Texas record shops the same day as *Let It Be* and outselling it.

All seven tracks are snotty and casually punk as only Southern boys are and Iggy Pop can only dream of being. "Crazy Man," "I Need a Woman" and the villainous "Country Boy" are built on equal parts Dave Mitchell's guitar hammer and Pete Bailey's vulpine bawl. No one or nothing appears sacred to these evil narcissistic bastards until "Dead Man," a 17:29 meditation on a victim by his murderer. A dry clatter, then an ancient bass line walks the corpse while the guitar shrieks like Howlin' Wolf in a desert wind. Then come the stagy taunts, "Dead man, I only hear a rattle when you breathe." The rest is *Stagger v. Billy* as an extended psych-blues universe of terror finally shrinking to a crust of resignation and a bullet. The song is enough like "Marquee Moon" to make you wonder if Tom Verlaine scored a copy of this album sometime in 1971.

Josefus made another album of no account, which can be found, along with *Dead Man*, in Akarma's *Dead Box* set. Sundazed's Josefus release features *Dead Man* along with the unreleased *Get off My Case*. All sport the incomparable "Dead Man." (Ron Garmon)

JUICY GROOVE
First Taste (Payola, 1978)

I was flipping through albums, midsummer 1978. Attracted to a colorful picture disc, I looked closer. It had no sleeve, just the disc in a plastic bag. Something about it said "take me home." The guy behind the register looked down his glasses and said, "You don't want this crap."

But this record would've been worth $8 for the graphics alone: the band, solarized, acidized … maybe even psychedelicized. Freaks all, they appear to be glowing from some evil inner fire, framed by a sick red sky. The players are mostly named as aliases. Imagine my growing sense of wonder when I discovered their true identities:

Mercury Flyer, guitar (Elliott Ingber, aka Winged Eel Fingerling, from the Mothers, Little Feat, Fraternity of Man, the Factory, Beefheart's Magic Band, Mallard)

Magic Marker, bass (Gary Marker, Magic Band, Rising Sons)

World Peace, drums (Ed Cassidy, Spirit, and his son Mike "Thundercloud Heartbeat" Cassidy)

Mars Bonfire (Steppenwolf)

Rainbow Neal, vocals (Michael Neal, later lineup of the Seeds)

Guest artists included drummer Ron Bushy (Iron Butterfly) and "Victoria Reid" (who I think is really Grace Slick) on backing vocals.

The disc includes a couple of all-time great rock songs ("Secret Lover," "Drums Guitars Stars"), others that simply provide solid offbeat groovination, and a couple that sound like they were left unfinished, probably due to chemically induced departure from the world of ideas. These the alert listener can easily deselect, while playing the really great ones over and over. The musicianship is raw and edgy but consistently outstanding, a perfect framework for Rainbow Neal's innocent protopunk vocals. Neal might have sounded amateurish if not for his supremely unselfconscious delivery, at best eclipsing Reg Presley of the Troggs for pure lack of pretension.

Lyrically they never stray from three concepts: sex, rock and money. The sex is as obvious and basic as a sidewalk proposition at closing time, but the main theme is wanting money. The writers are obviously suffering from having had brief flashes of fame and being "ripped off by the Man." This time they'll not only gain world fame but "make damn sure the band gets paid." Normally it sucks when bands get autobiographical, but here it's so honest it's endearing. This record was so anachronistic in 1978 that the only way to explain it was that the band must have been placed in cryo around 1971 and thawed out right there in the studio.

Juicy Groove died quietly without having been noticed by anyone or even making a ripple in the incoming tide of overproduced eighties "rock." (Deniz Tek)

K

PAUL KANTNER
Planet Earth Rock and Roll Orchestra　　　　　　　　　(RCA, 1983)

However camouflaged in history and theory, criticism comes down to arguing preferences. Nothing is more a matter of passionate preference than science fiction. It means everything to its devotees; it is as understood and welcome as an oozy rash to those opposed.

One of Jefferson Airplane/Starship singer-guitarist Paul Kantner's enduring peculiarities as songwriter is that he's *the science fiction guy*. Many remember his first SF rock opera, 1970's (Hugo Award nominated! The only rock album thusly honored!) *Blows Against the Empire*. *Blows* had some sleepy merits, but musically and melodically it was so thinly arty-druggy-acoustic that it was transparent.

By 1983, Kantner junked up and pop-rocked his science fiction with this barely noted sequel, allegedly a soundtrack to a novel that never surfaced. In so doing, he made the ultimate science fiction record—this one should have *won* a Hugo. Like the genre at its most fun and funky (not necessarily its most serious and literary), this album is fanatical, crass, over the top, direct, visionary and delightful.

If "she is a telepath," how does the rhyming couplet end? "I want her autograph," natch. With help from Ron Nagle and his Durocs partner Scott Matthews—and the crew of his Starship—Kantner delivers a geeky gotterdammerung, full of flashy pop sci-metal and gorgeous Tamalpais campfire singalongs: "somebody's gonna have to sleep with the machines/If you want to make the sky be home."

If you've ever despaired of humanity's future, the closers "The Sky Is No Limit" and "Let's Go" should be genuinely inspirational. This record's joys may appeal only to people for whom fantasies of technological escape from the bounds of Earth resonate strongly. But for those who do, this will be a beloved treat—a special record just for you. (Brian Doherty) (See also: Joe E. Covington's Fat Fandango, Jefferson Airplane)

KAS PRODUCT
Try Out   (RCA, France, 1982)

When KaS Product released *Try Out*, its debut album (following a pair of EPs) in 1982, it joined a fertile French postpunk scene that included bands like Marquis de Sade, Taxi Girl, Orchestre Rouge and Edith Nylon. But KaS Product got even less mainstream recognition than its peers and never outgrew its status as a footnote, albeit a rather fascinating one.

Coproduced by the band and Gérard Nguyen, who also ran the influential Nancy label Disques du Soleil et de l'Acier, *Try Out* is both minimal and expansive. Minimal because the arrangements boil down to a drum machine, cheapo synths à la Suicide and occasional shards of guitar; expansive because singer Mona Soyoc unleashed some of the most mannered, theatrical singing this side of Siouxsie Sioux.

A lot of early-eighties singers tried to sound as cold and detached as possible, but Soyoc sounded as if she could barely contain herself. On *Try Out* her vocals are all over the map, furiously hysterical one second, dangerously seductive the next. Sighs, hisses, and moans punctuate the urgent singing on "Never Come Back" (one of the duo's signature galloping tracks) while the album closer, "Pussy X," is still as sexily abrasive as it once was, with Soyoc basically singing a duet with herself. While all this drama unraveled in the forefront, Spatsz kept the machines percolating wildly in the back. (Live, he stood expressionless, half-hidden behind his asymmetrical, Phil Oakey-like haircut.)

Though hindsight would lead to classification of KaS Product as pioneers of synthetic noir, the duo was above all an unclassifiable entity. *Try Out* isn't so much ahead of its time as outside of time, a musical UFO now and for-ever. (Elisabeth Vincentelli)

ANDY KIM
How'd We Ever Get This Way   (Steed, 1968)

Andy Kim was surely designed to put out an awesome solo LP, especially a debut. Brill Building alumnus and Jeff Barry's partner in the Archies recipe, Kim was a preeminent gear in the Bubblegum machine and a killer song-writer who didn't let cutting-room floor flotsam clog up his own efforts. The number of self-proclaimed sixties pop heads that I have turned on to this album is scary. It really seems to have missed the past two (almost three) decades of sixties revivals, having not been reissued or touted roundly by the tastemakers. Cram together the first four Bee Gees LPs, select moments of later Beach Boys (*Friends* through *Sunflower*), early Neil Diamond, a touch of Scott Walker when his albums didn't shudder away from a guitar, and we would have one badass LP that, being admittedly generous, could be compa-rable to *How'd We Ever Get This Way*.

More pensive and glum than any Bubblegum LP, Kim's debut can be lyrically backhanded (title track) and full-on suffocating ("Resurrection") ... in a good way: not a reactionary crooner like Walker, but more of a six-string friendly place for folks who would dig Scott Walker recordings if they weren't so damned Scott Walker. This is a Jeff Barry Production released on Barry's label; both playful warnings of the lush sound maze in store after you get past the ridiculous (even for the times) album art. Kim poses as a pensive dandy in the park, rocking a collapsible stool and giant, esoteric breed of dog! All in all, *How'd We Ever Get This Way* is still a very affordable and locatable zenith of late-sixties pop. (Andrew Earles)

JUNIOR KIMBROUGH
Sad Days, Lonely Nights   (Fat Possum, 1994)

Sad Days, Lonely Nights is my all-time favorite blues LP. When I first heard it playing in a record shop, I couldn't tell if it was the Stooges, Canned Heat, Funkadelic or Ash Ra Tempel. Turns out it was a 63-year-old black man from

Mississippi named Junior Kimbrough. There's nothing ordinary about this LP. The hypnotic, distorted guitar lines and steady, funky rhythms don't recall any particular era of electric or acoustic blues. Junior's riffs are repetitive alien mantras inhabited by the ghosts of Africa. He sings like a shaman muttering magical spells under his breath. When I heard this in 1994, I couldn't believe it was actually a new recording. There's an ancient, haunted quality to this music, a primal electric drone that gives it more of an affinity with La Monte Young's minimalism and seventies German art rock than it has with most contemporary blues. It's juke joint party music that gets all the way down. It'll make you dance. It'll put you in a trance. (Matthew Smith)

KING CRIMSON
Lizard (Atlantic, 1970)

1969 was a whirlwind year for Robert Fripp and King Crimson. Forming in January, by summer they played their first show at Hyde Park opening for the Stones, soon after their debut hit Top 30 on both sides of the Atlantic. They had no place to go but down. Indeed, by the end of the year all key members except guitarist Fripp had bailed. Instead of opting to take the easy way out, Fripp assembled a new Crimson with Gordon Haskell replacing Greg Lake, Mel Collins on horns, and drummer Andy McCulloch. This core group was augmented by a full horn section, free jazz madman Keith Tippet on piano, and even Yes' Jon Anderson on one song. The result was the uniquely unusual and forward-looking *Lizard*.

This is one nasty trip. Nightmarish, claustrophobic, and unpredictable, the album is conceptual in that several of the songs seem to be about collapse, either internal or societal. The album is book-ended by a repeated theme: "Cirkus" is the opening freak show bad dream; the finale "Big Top" is an audio fun house mirror of calliope malevolence. In between, the album snakes through "Indoor Games," an oddity about trouble at home, further extrapolated by the tense, straight-jacket madness of "Happy Family," which has been interpreted to be about the Beatles' break-up. Side 2 gets proggy as you wanna be with the side-long epic "Lizard," broken into various sections like a proper art rock suite. The horns seem to have escaped straight from Miles' then-fresh *Bitches Brew* sessions, and composer Fripp recapitulates themes

throughout the piece with varying instrumentation. One can find new surprises with every listen, no matter how often you visit. This version of the
band never toured, and *Lizard* largely became the forgotten Crimson album.
For fans of the crazier side of experimental rock, from kraut to Branca and
back, this album could be a hidden treasure in your collection. (SL Duff)

THE KINKS
Muswell Hillbillies   **(RCA, 1971)**

November, 1971, and the freshly revitalized Kinks have just signed a new
contract in the wake of their worldwide smash "Lola." Who on Earth would
have ever expected the band would—or *could*—deliver such an inscrutable li'l
gem as *Muswell Hillbillies* as a follow-up?

Defiantly out-of-step in its time, *Muswell* remains remarkable today not
only for its sound but for its weird and utterly wonderful undercurrent of
deceit, deception, and conspiracies set against the seedy backdrop of post-
WWII Britain. For in those dank times, inner city London's bombing victims
were coldly up-ended and up-rooted into the bleak, government "new-
towns." Not coincidentally, the Kinks spent their ignoble childhoods amid
such prefab rabble.

Many of *Muswell's* best songs confront this sad, sorry state of affairs
("Here Come the People in Grey," "Acute Schizophrenia Paranoia Blues")
and how the once-proud victims cope with their sordid new lives and neigh-
borhoods ("Alcohol," and the early ode to anorexia, "Skin and Bone"). To
augment the Kinks' sound, Ray set up an extra microphone in the bathroom,
hired three players to approximate the luridly liquid New Orleans horn
stylings of the twenties and thirties, and turned "Alcohol" and "A.S.P. Blues"
into slippery, slidey blues-ups of the lowest odor (like Dr. John directing Side
1 of *Blonde on Blonde*). Just when you're ready to slit your eardrums over the
cacophony of despair and perfectly bum notes, a shimmering beauty like
"Oklahoma USA" comes drifting through the underbrush.

Muswell Hillbillies sank without much of a trace on its arrival, and char-
acteristically, the band self-sabotaged the entire proceedings by mounting a
drunken and debauched world tour. But as joyously misguided as all this

tomfoolery may have appeared to many circa "Rocket Man," make no mistake that future alt hillbillies like Steve Earle, Paul Westerberg and most certainly Ryan Adams were paying extremely close notice indeed. "God Save the Kinks," as I believe the olde saying still goes. (Gary Pig Gold) (See also: The Leopards)

KLAATU
Klaatu (aka *3:47 EST*)   (Capitol, 1976)
Despite *Chunklet* magazine's pronouncement that Klaatu is a band "that will never be considered retro-hip," I believe this odd collection of songs recorded over a three-year period by a trio of faceless Canadian session musicians is a truly memorable classic. Not just because one of the songs was recorded by the Carpenters at Karen's most anorexic moment, making for one of the most frightening and bizarre music videos of all time. Not just because they are one of the only bands (Hawkwind being the only other one that comes to mind) that sings songs about subatomic particles. Not just because a well-placed rumor in a prominent magazine started months of wild speculation that Klaatu was really a secretly re-formed Beatles in disguise. I love all these tidbits, but what I love most is how the Great White Northern goofs behind this sterling slab of sugary pleasure manage to compress a brilliant history of pop music into forty minutes or less, filling it with humor, obscure references, backwards masking, and even a Morse code solo.

As the true identities of the band members surfaced, Klaatu suffered the same fate another Beatles conjurer called the Knack was about to suffer: a massive, relentless backlash. And with punk bringing rock music back to its roots, overblown pop productions went out of style. Klaatu would never recover, despite an effort to follow the musical trends of the time (read: "new wave") with their next several records. But their first LP is a testament to the beauty of naïveté and unfashionability, made by talented musicians hopelessly out of the loop. And "Little Neutrino" stands out as the oddball masterpiece that having three years to anonymously create a record can produce. (Russ Forster)

KLYMAXX

Meeting in the Ladies Room   **(Constellation, 1984)**

I admit it: I have fantasized about Eminem covering Klymaxx. It's just ..., "I had my Kenneth Cole shoes on/My Gianni Versace blue leather suit/My nails were done and my hair looked fierce/The men all pause when I walk into the room/The men all pause and the brides hold their grooms" ... there's a pleasing rightness to it, don't you think? I don't know, maybe Greg Dulli.

Indisputably the greatest all-woman electro-funk band of the early eighties, Klymaxx brought audacious attitude to the dance floor. They got over on personality, smarts, and hooks. Electro-funk arrived as the last innovation in black dance rhythms before hip-hop loops became the chassis of choice for Urban Contemporary. For a brief period, funk spliced in new wave synthesizers and spewed out a mutant music ideal for freakin' strange on the neutron dance floor while atomic dog bombs dropped on you. The era was funky but geek: Prince rocked the drum machine, Larry Blackmon strapped on his codpiece, and even George Clinton played *Computer Games*.

This record threw off three hits, two dance club classics, and one early quiet storm ballad. "Meeting in the Ladies Room" stretched out in an irresistibly spiky groove and Lorena "Lungs" Hardimon warned off any skank who tried to step up on her man. The chorus spawned an earworm so potent that women still mutter it as they exit for a bathroom break twenty years later. "The Men All Pause" worked a stop-start, sex-bot rhythm triggering off an enfilade of synthdrums. Bernadette Cooper flashed the full array of her formidable diva quips here. It's hard to imagine "I Miss You" on the R&B charts now; it unfolded like an earnest prom slow dance without a trace of the handwaving, diva ululations that typify soul ballads today. The other tracks were fun but less essential. "Video Kid" took its conceit right down to the obvious joystick entendres and "Love Bandit" could've been an early Madonna B-side. Get it for the hits; it's worth it. (David Smay)

L

THE LEE HARVEY OSWALD BAND
Blastronaut **(Touch & Go, 1996)**

After issuing two collections of Butthole Surfer/Scratch Acid–inspired, guitar-based noisy art rock, the Lee Harvey Oswald Band surprised the handful of people paying attention by releasing a bona fide glitter rock masterpiece. There was no set up, no hype and no turning back. Henceforth *Blastronaut* sat alongside *Ziggy Stardust* and *Slider*, seemingly self-assured that the calendar would never turn past 1975.

That's not totally fair, though, for although the band plays with seventies glitz as cunningly as a cat toys with its wounded prey, the presence of late-seventies and eighties punk and metal is undeniable. Mostly though, it's the trio's confident wordplay, the world-class instrumental and vocal performances and the clear but potent production that would make this timeless collection a keeper in any era.

Never playing live, the band has long been presumed to be a side project of other Chicago-based Touch & Go artists (a careful listen to guitarist Zowie Fenderblast's vocals will clue you in). His ripping tenor drives "The Scorpio Letter," a doom metal scorcher that would have been at home on *Sabotoge*. It's bassist Dredge's low, sinister vocals that up the swagger level of tunes like "Rocket 69" and "Morphodite," on which he sings "Gotta bomb in my britches and it's ready to blow/I'm not your morphodite, I'm not your silly 'ho." The pair's vocals complement wonderfully, as on the majestic "Green Like the Color of Blood," or "Panic in Hanoi" ("Mama, I'm a soldier, Jehovah with a gun/Mama you'd die if I told you what I've done.") Their choice of covers, interestingly, come from the *Nuggets* era: the Move's "Brontosaurus" and the Amboy Dukes' "You Talk Sunshine ... I Breath Fire."

Rumors abound of a new LHO release, but as of yet all's quiet on the Midwest front. Nonetheless, they left us with the second-best rock album of the nineties, better than *Nevermind* but not as good as TurboNegro's *Apocalypse Dudes*. (SL Duff)

THE LEOPARDS
Kansas City Slickers   (Moon, 1977)

One of my favorite aberrations in the world of music is the phony Beatles bands. There were plenty of these poor man's versions shortly after John, Paul, George, and Ringo struck pay dirt in the mid-sixties. This album is the closest thing I've heard to what might be called Kinks-mania. As far as I know, this is the only band that tried its hand at being an alternative universe Kinks. This is the first album the Leopards put out and I would imagine Moon was a vanity label. It was definitely a small independent. The ad that convinced me to pick up this album when it came out claimed that you could easily trick your friends into believing this was a rarity along the lines of Ray Davies and crew's *Great Lost Kinks Album*. The band made nary a ripple in the rock world with this debut and fared little better with their 1987 Voxx release, *Magic Still Exists*. The band that recorded the late seventies material contained two songwriters with a flair for capturing the essence of Ray's particular brand of music hall–inspired, happy feet songs. Like the Beatles-patterned Rutles, the Leopards used short phrases from some of their idols' more memorable tunes to jazz up their homespun material. Lead vocalist Dennis Pash also had a voice that was a dead ringer for the head Kink's. There are some fine moments on the later album, but *Kansas City Slickers* is a gem from the opening notes of "Road to Jamaica" to the final strains of "Summer's Gone." It's a tad stilted, highly derivative, and none of the material quite matches the genius it strove to mimic, but the LP is still a charming curiosity and a delightful listen. (P. Edwin Letcher) (See also: The Kinks)

BOB LIND
Don't Be Concerned   (World Pacific, 1966)

Folk-rock's best kept secret is hidden behind a bad, radio-worn irritant ("Elusive Butterfly"). This is a record that should be seen on par with Tim Hardin's debut and the first two Byrds albums, and one that is better than (but not as self-consciously whacked as) any by Tim Buckley. Lind's perversely self-deprecating liner notes to the LP's only digital rebirth, 1993's *You Might Have Heard My Footsteps*, would have you believe that this music is an "embarrassing" and "shameless" (words he uses in describing the arresting

Imitation Is the Highest Form of Flattery

Success in the music industry breeds copycat artists. It isn't surprising that the Beatles chose a name that echoed that of Buddy Holly's Crickets. Things get more derivative when there are more elements involved, especially if the elements are unrelated to each other. If a band chooses the name Large Marge after some other outfit had success using the name Big Bertha, it is pretty likely that the new group is jumping on a band wagon. If Granite Pickle Inundation followed Marble Cucumber Submersion, the likelihood of name borrowing goes way up. Which of the following are just coincidentally similar?

    Fats Domino—Chubby Checker
    Ohio Express—Chicago Transit Authority
    Jefferson Airplane—Hamilton Streetcar
    Lightnin' Hopkins—Thunderclap Newman
    Loudest Whisper—Quiet Riot
    Chocolate Watch Band—Strawberry Alarm Clock
    Iron Butterfly—Led Zeppelin
    Contemporary Music Unit—Modern Jazz Quartet
    Juicy Lucy—Wet Willie
    Bill Haley & the Comets—Rory Storm & the Hurricanes
    Sons of Adam—Daughters of Eve
    Neurotic Sheep—Crazy Horse
    The Artist Formerly Known as Prince—The Artist Formally Known as Vince
    Angry Samoans—Violent Femmes
    Luke & the Apostles—Neil Christian & the Crusaders
    Johnny Kidd & the Pirates—Paul Revere & the Raiders (P. Edwin Letcher)

jewel, "You Should Have Seen It") exercise and should be brushed off to languish in a thrift shop purgatory. Well, the listening public hasn't done a bad job of doing just that. As much a Jack Nitzsche affair as it is Bob's (whatever Lind did without Nitzsche failed on every level), the late super hero of orchestrated pop did on *Don't Be Concerned* exactly what he is rightfully remembered for.

There are three ultimate convincers, tracks that, even standing alone, could lift any album out of the margins. "You Should Have Seen It" is the first killer, with two monster hooks (verse and chorus) and a prescient take on the man/woman fiasco with more guts than any bedroom whiner has mustered over the past fifteen years. "Unlock the Door" is a wordy heartripper that you won't be humming for less than a lifetime. Finally, "Truly Julie's Blues (I'll Be There)" celebrates another inhuman hook and lover lyrics shiny with gilded fatalism. Under the umbrella of these three are seven slightly inferior but nonetheless remarkable numbers, one complete misfire ("The World Is Just a 'B' Movie"), and the unfortunate hit. Prone to drunken self-pity record sessions at four in the morning? Meet your new star. (Andrew Earles)

THE LIPSTICK KILLERS
Mesmerizer   **(Citadel, Australia, 1984)**

On the strength of a Deniz Tek–produced 45 issued by Bomp subsidiary Voxx in 1979, Sydney's Lipstick Killers decamped for Los Angeles and dreams of Northern hemisphere success. They lasted a year in the cozy grime of the Tropicana Motel and a bug-infested Silverlake apartment, playing about a dozen gigs, including a Brian Jones memorial at the Whisky and at Madame Wong's with the Plimsouls. *Mesmerizer* is the document of one of these shows, recorded on cassette by Flesh Eater Chris D., cleaned up nicely and released posthumously on Radio Birdman crony "Brother" John Needham's Citadel imprint. In the absence of an official studio album, this high-energy set stands as slightly sloppy but irresistible evidence of the band's magic.

Over twelve songs, including terrific covers of the Chocolate Watchband's "Let's Talk about Girls" and the Elevators' "I've Got

Levitation," the Lipstick Killers swagger like the Hindu gods of their signature song, all power chords, tribal drums and perfectly controlled frenzy. The band's originals come across like unknown frat rock standards gene-spliced with a finely honed blend of psychedelia and DIY punk energy. Insinuation was their strong suit: "Dying Boy's Crawl" and "Strange Flash" get right under your skin and pull you bodily towards the music. Maybe a band this tight and moody was nothing special on the Sydney scene, but they must have blown their L.A. competition sideways. Unfortunately, the usual band problems intruded—mental illness, money, the singer getting a day job to pay rent on the communal flat—and the Killers called it quits. The members eventually wound their way back to Australia, where they still occasionally play as the Lipstick Killers. When I saw them open for Radio Birdman in 2002 they fulfilled every promise of *Mesmerizer* and more. (Kim Cooper)

LOS LOCOS DEL RITMO
ROCK! (Maya-Dimsa, 1960)

The recordings produced during Mexico's *grande época del rock* (1960–1965) were primarily *refritos* (as in *frijoles*), Spanish-language renditions of U.S. chart hits. However, one of Mexican rock and roll's most original statements happens to have been one of its first full-length testaments. *ROCK!* features six band compositions, four vocal *refritos*, and two instrumental covers: since a preposterously demented version of "La Cucaracha" full of "banda borracha"–style false endings is one of the instro covers (the other: "Pedro Pistolas," aka "Peter Gunn"), the disc is tipped firmly on the side of national content and is an early (and, alas, rather lonely) victory over the egghead bugaboo of rock as cultural imperialism.

Tono de Villa's spirited vocals and the band's enthusiastically raw accompaniment stamp their versions of Jack Scott's "Geraldine" and two songs made famous by Elvis, "Baby I Don't Care" and "A Big Hunk of Love," as more than novelties, but it's the original material by guitarist Jesus Gonzalez that makes *ROCK!* essential. Three Gonzalez contributions are instrumentals featuring brittle guitar attacks over frantically loping backing. "Un Vasito de Agua" is especially remarkable, a genuine hunk of primitive mambo garage-rock; proof of God's nonexistence (or unconcern with human welfare) is that

Santana's later forays into noodly mambo rock, rather than this, became the archetype for Latin rock fusion.

"Yo No Soy Rebelde," is Gonzalez' answer to the Mexican media's anti-rock panic. While the band gloriously grinds the Loco beat, Tono sings that he's not a rebel without a cause or a wild one; he just wants to wear cowboy pants (jeans, I reckon), dance without rhyme or reason, and brandish a stiletto (well who doesn't?). Rounding out the disc are two ballads: "Old Enough to Love" (made famous by Ricky Nelson) and drummer Rafael Acosta's lovely "Tus Ojos," the latter as enduring a hit as "Rebelde," both still renowned in Mexico.

Los Locos Del Ritmo subsequently produced many fine albums (although only two more with Tono, who died at twenty-one, reportedly of larynx cancer), but never as completely visionary an album as *ROCK!* If only their vision had come to pass. (Michael Lucas)

LOS MACHUCAMBOS
Percussive Latin Trio   (London Phase 4, 1962)

Percussive Latin Trio is an album early in the career of Los Machucambos. Founded in Paris in 1959 and virtually unknown in the United States, the group includes Romano Zanotti, Julia Cortes and Rafael Gayoso. Recorded in the London label's quirky "Phase 4 Stereo," *Percussive Latin Trio* is an album that lives up to its title. It is a candy store of beats from worlds old and new, both pre- and post-Columbian.

Classics like "Granada" and "Amor" come to life under Zanotti's direction, which brings a warmth and sensitivity to every arrangement. Standouts include "Perfidia," the Latin jazz classic (sung beautifully here by Julia Cortes) and the cheerfully seductive "Pepito," which reached number two on the German Top 40.

The music of Veracruz known as *Jarocho* is characterized by a variety of stringed instruments. Harpist Ignacio Alderette lends an authenticity to the most famous of all *Jarocho* standards, "La Bamba." Artists as diverse as the Mormon Tabernacle Choir, Ritchie Valens, and the Plugz have recorded "La Bamba," but Los Machucambos define it here in its traditional form.

"El Otorinolaringologo" ("The Ear, Nose, and Throat Doctor"), a whimsical cha-cha written for this album, reveals their true genius. It is as witty as a Noel Coward lyric, as catchy as a Cole Porter melody and as charming as Mrs. Kennedy speaking Spanish on her husband's tour of Latin America.

Unfortunately, this album has never been re-released since its original pressing, so if you ever see one at a secondhand shop, grab it! Even if you don't understand a word, don't be surprised if after one listen you find yourself singing along. (Sean Carrillo)

THE LOUD FAMILY
Interbabe Concern (Alias, 1996)

If Loud Family paterfamilias Scott Miller is the true heir to Alex Chilton's cult-pop throne (and you'll get no argument from me) then *Interbabe Concern* is his *Sister Lovers*—a harsh, difficult album drawn from a dark period in the songwriter's life. Unlike Big Star's infamous supernova, the third album from Miller's post-Game Theory combo is no drug-besotted flameout; Miller's a touch too wholesome for that. But, in the face of estrangement—the departures of his wife, Shalini Chatterjee, and longtime producer/collaborator, Mitch Easter (and since Chatterjee is now married to Easter, we can assume that the two events were not mutually exclusive)—Miller proved as adept at fashioning a jagged sonic mosaic from the shattered pieces around him as his hero. Unbuffered by the baroque flourishes Easter used to cushion his experiments in structure and oblique, lit-major lyrics, *Interbabe* is filled with dizzying mood-swings and mid-song digressions that rival even his masterpiece *Lolita Nation* for pure bizarro-pop overload—the song titles alone show more concentrated inventiveness than some artists' entire careers. And the songs themselves are chock full of surprises—rolling coin percussion, a quiet acoustic plaint blemished by steady bursts of atonal noise, even Miller's close approximation of an arena-rock scream. It's a lot to take in, to say the least; unlike the instant gratification one expects from pop music, it takes several spins for the hooks to snag on something. But once they do, and you go from smiling at the cleverness in songs named after shampoo ingredients and the high- and low-culture references throughout (this is surely the only album ever to namecheck Aubrey Beardsley, Alexander the Great, *and* L. Ron Hubbard) to being bowled over by the sadness and resignation packed into a couplet like "I'm not expecting that I'll end up with you just because I need to/I shouldn't count on having air around me just because I breathe," you'll find yourself a friend of the Family for life. (William Ham) (See also: Game Theory)

M

THE MAGIC FINGERS OF MERLIN & HIS TRIO
The Swinging HI-FI Organ
(Pickwick International, The Grand Prix Series, 1961)

The Swinging HI-FI Organ evokes the swanky lounges and nightclubs that populate fifties B movies and dime-store crime novels. It is a place that exists exclusively in fiction and nostalgia, but you can visit when this record is playing.

With just drums, saxophone, and a Hammond B3, Merlin and his trio bop and grind through twelve cuts of jazzy rhythm and blues. There is burlesque and boozy romance and nearly every song wiggles and giggles like a tipsy cigarette girl, pulling even reluctant feet onto the dance floor. Original compositions like "Number 33 Wickpick Lane" and "Blues for Rafe" share the same triplet-happy attack and sweat just a bit more than the straight reading of "Blue Moon." The thick swirl of "Dilemma at Dusk" shows that Merlin and his players could do more than boogie.

Pickwick's Grand Prix imprint was bargain-bin music. The liner notes don't offer a clue about the identity of Merlin & His Trio. The players' names are not listed. No release date is provided. There is no photograph of the band. But *HI-FI Organ* actually benefits from the faceless nature of this sort of no-name pop product.

Without the expectations that come with a known group, Merlin's slinky keyboard work and the respective honk and slap of the sax and drums have room enough to impress. If Merlin was a session player, he or she deserves a spot next to Jack McDuff, Jimmy McGriff and other B3 magicians whose skills were overshadowed by organ wizard Jimmy Smith. (Kris Kendall)

MICHEL MAGNE
Moshe Mouse Crucifixion
(Spot/Sonopresse, France, 1975)

The U.S. audience probably listened to many a seventies pop landmark, unaware that it had been recorded at Michel Magne's Hérouville studios, located in a magnificent castle in the Val-d'Oise, near Paris. The odyssey of Hérouville is one of the most magnificent, heartbreaking rock stories, from Bowie to Iggy Pop's *The Idiot* to Visconti, Marc Bolan, and Elton John's *Honky Château* and *Goodbye Yellow Brick Road*. From *Saturday Night Fever* to the Grateful Dead playing in front of bedazzled French locals, Hérouville was one of a kind.

Michel Magne was unique too: a successful arranger and composer of movie soundtracks, he wrote a number of popular scores starring French pop icons (Belmondo, Bardot) and some international films too. But Magne, a man endowed with a great sense of creativity and humor, wasn't satisfied. He decided to use his knowledge and hospitality to create the most avant-garde recording studio of its time. It became the home of some incredible sound research.

With all these facilities at hand, the maestro was ready to fulfill his personal artistic ambition with *Moshe Mouse Crucifixion*. Moses (Moshe) is turned into a Jewish tailor mouse wandering into heavy-duty metaphoric "Dismayland" as well as the grooves of this conceptual extravaganza. The sleeve says it all: it depicts a Mickey Mouse look-alike (underground comix-style) crucified, draped in an American flag while tiny G.I.s shout and shake their rifles. The music can be described as a mix of Eastern Funk, Gregorian plainchant on acid and seventies French-flavored lunacy. This fairy tale for adults is really too weird to be true and will puzzle many. What are they thinking of? Free creativity, I answer. Sadly, Michel Magne went broke, and in 1983 committed suicide Kurt Cobain–style. This is a record and a composer craving rediscovery. (Jean-Emmanuel Deluxe)

MICHAEL MANTLER
The Hapless Child and Other Inscrutable Stories

(Watt Works, 1976)

This record made all kinds of sense to me when it first wormed its way into the artsy jazz section of hip record stores. I was just getting into the artwork of Edward Gorey and the music of several of the musicians involved with this project at the very time everything came together. I don't remember seeing this album on display racks when it came out and can't imagine it was even known except by fans of one or another of the avant-garde players involved. It has certainly never been a work that enjoyed a large audience, though I would think most any Gorey aficionado would deem this required listening. Robert Wyatt is the perfect voice for this project. His uncanny control, thick British accent, and dark, mysterious mood are very evocative of the anachronistic, mondo gothic word etchings of "The Insect God," "The Sinking Spell," the title track and the other three peculiar poetic pieces from *Amphigorey* (1972). Michael Mantler's music does an equally eloquent job of conveying an atmosphere of twisted intrigue, frantic desperation, chilling unease and a host of other theatrical mind pictures. Carla Bley on piano, clavinet and string synthesizer, Steve Swallow on bass, Terje Rypdal on gui-

Top 10 Non-Goth Albums Goths Listen To

American IV: The Man Comes Around, Johnny Cash
Lateralus, Tool
Little Earthquakes, Tori Amos
Bloodletting, Concrete Blonde
Dummy, Portishead
Changes, David Bowie
Post, Björk
Rio, Duran Duran
Bone Machine, Tom Waits
Floodland, Sisters of Mercy (Since Andrew Eldritch keeps saying the Sisters aren't goth ...) (Jillian Venters, The Gothic Miss Manners)

tar and Jack Dejohnette on drums and percussion are musicians' musicians. Without their impeccable performances the experience of this album would not have been so richly rewarding. Some of the other recordings of these talented envelope pushers are so esoteric it is not surprising how small a body of adventurous souls swear by them. However, Edward Gorey's unique imagery, the otherworldly beauty of the tunes and their flawless execution make this a work that transcends most musical barriers. (P. Edwin Letcher)

MARIANO & THE UNBELIEVABLES
Mariano & the Unbelievables
(Capitol, 1967)

After the fuzz guitar of "Satisfaction" infected airwaves in 1965, it took American teenagers a year to respond with their primitive garage music. However, artifacts excavated at thrift stores today hint that a less rock-us revolution was also raging by 1967. Though this is pure speculation, this detritus suggests a subset of boomers instead ingested the Beatles' "In My Life" with their pot, then jonesed to hear and form old-timey chamber ensembles, which inundated the market with harpsichord-heavy hits. "Groups" spouting such quaint, antiquated names as the Carmel Strings, the 18th Century Concept and Mason Williams were issued powdered wigs and frilly neckwear and set forth to bring the classics to mass audiences.

But the heir to the baroque 'n' roll throne was Mariano Moreno, a dandified Don Juan who was equal parts Elvis Presley and Liberace. The Argentinean piano prodigy was set up with a band of young, cool classicals christened the Unbelievables and these dukes of doily rock were dispatched to tour with Donovan.

Graced with all the visual trappings of a budget release or standard "Switched On" swill, a listen to Mariano's debut disc proves its superiority over the usual chamber chum churned out to exploit the psychedelic crowd and its parents, who were invited in by the sunshine pop and images of stringed civility. A gaggle of grumps in itchy wigs are pictured on the cover, while the flipside's hyperbolic liner notes seem pseudo-serious, so much so that "Mariano" sounds fictitious—perhaps the concoction of a Capitol bean counter. But gorgeous versions of "Up, Up & Away," "Windy" and "Georgy Girl" suggest otherwise. (So do band members, who insist Mariano was their leader and have the anecdotes to prove it.) While an exploito album at heart, Mariano's arrangements are nothing less than brilliant, as witnessed by the interchanging harpsichord and violin leads on "Wendy"; musicianship is also top notch (several Unbelievables graduated to the L.A. Philharmonic).

The group's second LP, *The 25th Hour*, is also a gem, containing covers of "Hello Goodbye," the requisite "Sunny," and "Love is Blue," on which Mariano's maneuvers could make Paul Mauriat weep in his escargot. The Upper Crust would be proud. (Becky Ebenkamp)

CURTIS MAYFIELD
Back to the World
(Curtom, 1973)

CURTIS MAYFIELD   BACK TO THE WORLD

Coming on the heels of his high-profile masterwork, *Superfly*, Curtis Mayfield's next album was bound to receive muted applause upon its release. Yet in many ways it is an equal achievement. A song cycle about a Vietnam veteran's return to a changed America, *Back to the World* is Mayfield exploding with realized ambition and prodigious talent. The title track, the lead cut off Side 1, announces the artist's intent with sound collage, symphonics, unusual horn charts, percussion and Mayfield's trademark guitar, instantly recognizable and never duplicated, setting the tone. Its lyrics are a singular mix of protest and uplift, another Mayfield signature. Who in '73 could not relate to the following, and who can deny that little has changed, thirty years after he wrote these words: "In these city streets—Everywhere/You got to be careful/Where you move your feet, and how you part your hair/Do you really think God could ever forgive, this life we live/Back in the World." Next is "Future Shock," a thick slab of angry funk and a comment on the misrepresentation of the man's own work ("Our worldly figures/Playin' on niggers/Oh see them dancin'/See how they're dancin' to the superfly"), followed by the straight-up classic, "Right on for the Darkness," with its simple rhythm guitar-and-string arrangement accompanied by one of Mayfield's most beautiful vocal performances. Side 2 highlights include "If I Were Only a Child Again" (shades of the Impressions), "Can't Say Nothin'" (with its long, driving, instrumental intro), and "Keep on Trippin'," an herb-and-love anthem that manages to be both cautionary and celebratory. The sub-par mix of the original LP and the import CD will put some off, but that doesn't stop this from being an essential seventies funk collection, and one of the highlights (and last truly great record) of Mayfield's career. Plus, the cover and inner sleeve art tell a time-evocative story, from an era when album art really mattered. Robert Christgau gave this a "C." Another reason, in my opinion, to check it out. (George Pelecanos)

Sweet Exorcist   (Curtom, 1974)

We all know Robert Christgau is "the dean of American rock criticism." His web site tells us so. This suggests some pompous figure of fun out of Nabokov or Trotsky: a careful, mannered old fusspot sourly grading stacks of indie discs by the fire while his young wife's panties come off at an OutKast show. Sad and near-graven, the dean stamped a C mark on this album, flabbergasting the vulgar. "No," the great man cautioned us, "Curtis hasn't latched on to another lucrative soundtrack."

Well, it's a blind frog indeed that snatches a Superfly. *Sweet Exorcist*, a subtle, demanding work of album art, is probably best approached as, yes, the soundtrack to a movie that existed only in Curtis' skull. That the dean couldn't wrap his tongue around this concept without injury probably says more about rock *Kritizismus* at the end of the Nixon era than about any "incoherence" imputable to the artist.

It's not like the very *cover* isn't rejected art from an unreleased AIP hybrid horror-gangster-martial arts extravaganza. The version currently screening in my cranial octaplex stars Pam Grier, Jim "The Dragon" Kelly, Ji-Tu Cumbuka, Brenda Sykes and Robert Quarry as The Man. Except for the sparsely anthemic "Power to the People," the songs are moody character pieces with "Ain't Got the Time" going in for sass and sex and "Suffer" caressing with sophisticated grief. "Sweet Exorcist" is dope and star booty in 35mm Eastman color. Two of Curtis' best-ever songs, "To Be Invisible" and "Kung Fu," centerpiece sides A and B. The former is Ralph Ellison's *Invisible Man* tossed off with dreaminess and pain in 4:19. The latter is a long mystic groove invoking ghetto stoicism, discipline and wariness, prelude to the film's 45 silver bullet finale.

The music-buying public ignored Christgau and made *Sweet Exorcist* #2 on the R&B charts. Rebuked, the dean rolled another sheet into the typewriter and resumed his lonely Emersonian duty. (Ron Garmon)

PAUL McCARTNEY
McCartney II   (Columbia, 1980)

It's 1979. Paul McCartney has spent the better part of the decade with Wings, experiencing near-Beatles levels of success. But it's been a bad year. *Back to the Egg* suffered mixed reviews and lackluster sales. McCartney foolishly attempted to smuggle drugs into Japan. Shortly after, Wings imploded.

McCartney's response was to hole up at home and make solo four-track recordings. The result, *McCartney II*, was even more ignored than *Back to the Egg*. The consensus was that McCartney was being self-indulgent, killing time between "real" releases. Yet, listening to *McCartney II* now, it's obvious that it's the neglected jewel of his solo career. Judging from the title, it's meant to be a sequel to 1970's *McCartney*, home recordings released during the Beatles' waning days. Both albums find McCartney reacting to stress with solitude, and are rewarding in low-key ways.

One of the joys of *McCartney II* is its sheer unpredictability. There's mutant rockabilly ("Nobody Knows"), Kraftwerkian instrumentals ("Front Parlour," "Frozen Jap"), and cartoonish children's music ("Bogey Music"). "Temporary Secretary" takes a throwaway lyric about temp workers and sets it to a ping-ponging sequencer, while "Darkroom" has Devo keyboards and clipped vocals that make an amorous advance seem downright threatening.

Sandwiched between the experiments, you'll hear some of McCartney's best songs. "Coming Up," for all its Chipmunked vocal manipulations, is a great radio hit that doesn't sound so strange anymore. "Summer's Day Song" is simple and majestic, with cathedral-like organ evoking sunrise over an English garden. Best of all is "One of These Days," an echoey ode to appreciating what you have. It wouldn't be so out of place on *The Beatles* next to "I Will" or "Martha My Dear."

McCartney II deserves to be held in the same high esteem as other superstar-outré works like the Beach Boys' *Love You* and Neil Young's *Trans*. There's a nicely homespun quality lacking in McCartney's later experiments with electronic and classical music. Here's hoping for a *McCartney III* someday. (Mike Appelstein)

BARRY McGUIRE
This Precious Time (Dunhill, 1966)

P.F. SLOAN
Songs of Our Times/Twelve More Times
(Dunhill, 1965/1966)

Shell out 50¢ and bring it all back home to 1965 with these dandy gems of unadulterated folk-rock, L.A. version. Wow! Dig the pix and Andy Wickham-hype on *Precious Time's* backside; it was all happening then—the Strip, Cher's flared bells, the Child of Our Times, harmonicas and granny glasses, and any of these sets document the age with super accuracy. McGuire's bombastic style murders the Dylan stuff and "Let Me Be" and it's a joy to watch! Lou Adler and the Dunhill family are lurking throughout all this. Sloan's LPs are too much: from Jan & Dean to leather fringe and protest in one summer is beautiful! Unquestionably one of the greatest commercial pop hacks, the man who saw the Eve and lived to write about it. His later stuff, on *Measure of Pleasure – P.F. Sloan* (Atco), demonstrated more sophistication and put him in Memphis for some respectable singer-songwriter stuff, but it isn't nearly as much fun.

(Gene Sculatti, *Flash* #2, June–July 1972)

K. MCCARTY
Dead Dog's Eyeball: Songs of Daniel Johnston   (Bar None, 1994)

Your robot tour guide trundles up to you, takes your hand gently in its metal grip and leads you on a tour of the "Museum of Love," bleeping on about Mott the Hopple [sic] and Doris Day. You've had days like that, right? Or perhaps you're out walking your cow, and you're struck into dumb ecstasy by the nighttime sky. Oh, when K. McCarty croons "Lucky stars in your eyes" her rich, unadorned alto can spin your heart like a top.

Kathy McCarty roots through Daniel Johnston's strange emotional landscapes and affectingly broken metaphors knowledgeably, intimately. Her love and respect for his work lets her husk the rinky-dink production of his own recordings, and extract these sweet kernels. *Dead Dog's Eyeball* has distant familial relations with the Beach Boys' *Love You* and the first Os Mutantes record. It's homemade, and slightly cracked, and the kitchen sink production (literally— one backing track is simply a running faucet) produces perfectly apt settings for each song, whether it's drum loops or string quartets or big rock guitar.

Richard Linklater ran "Living Life" over the end credits of his movie *Before Sunrise*. Emotionally this works, though lyrically the song attempts a more elusive subject than passing romance. The song is about adjusting to the heavy medications that controlled Johnston's manic depression, trading in the wider spectrum of feeling that he could never stabilize for a balance that costs him the ecstasy and romantic flight that had defined him.

In song after song, K. McCarty unearths both the melody and the naked, smart, defiant, rapt lyrics of Daniel Johnston. It's hard to know what's more moving about this minor masterpiece: her voice, the splendid arrangements she created for his songs, his lyrics, or the act of friendship the whole enterprise represents. (David Smay)

MEGADETH
Rust in Peace   (Capitol, 1990)

Rust in Peace is a breathtakingly sophisticated, intensely constructed, jaw dropping, mature thrash metal experience that transcended the hard rock genre and raised the bar to a whole new level. After five years of creating songs in a drug-induced haze, Dave Mustaine and David Ellefson bravely managed to get their shit together with what brain cells they still had left and produce this sizzling record. With impeccable skill and talents, newly recruited guitarist Marty Friedman and drummer Nick Menza (son of famed jazz saxophonist Don Menza) didn't merely resuscitate the potential of the band—they brought it kicking and screaming back to life.

Rust in Peace is a masterpiece aimed at intelligent human beings who refuse to bury their heads in the sand when confronted with the unsavory political, sociological and psychological events that happen in our world. Although the album was praised by the mainstream press upon release, the overwhelming media hype over grunge buried thrash and the whole metal scene. Unbelievably, the fine art of this historically significant, beautifully crafted record is still ignored and unappreciated by both the snooty record-collecting music geeks and the clueless mainstream music journalists of today. You're not one of those awful people, now are you? (Kelly Kuvo)

THE MEKONS
The Quality of Mercy Is Not Strnen/OOOH!
(Out Of Our Heads!) (Virgin, 1979/Quarterstick, 2002)

Less a band than the greatest (and most long-winded) drinking club ever, the Mekons are a collective roughly centered on a few consistent personalities. They've had several distinct stylistic periods, a few hiatuses, a handful of stinker albums and another handful so brilliant as to make you reconsider your entire stance on rock music. *The Quality of Mercy …* is the Mekons' debut, a funk- and football-chant-inspired punk classic with the best combination of title and cover art of any album in this writer's memory. *OOOH!* is their most recent album as of this writing, but the anger and passion belie the twenty-three years between.

Quality's cover features a chimp before a typewriter, presumably typing the garbled Shakespeare of the title. The music is pure DIY funk-punk: every track is propelled by Jon Langford's herky-jerky, somewhat arrhythmic drumming; most feature two chords max. Some critics call this "rank amateurism," but they seem to miss the brilliance in the songs. Like their pals in Gang of Four, the Mekons' lyrics were highly political leftist rants, but tending to eschew agitprop in favor of a more literary approach. Standout tracks include "After 6," "Lonely and Wet" and the sublime "Dan Dare." If you plan to hunt down a copy, try to find Caroline's 1990 re-release with six additional tracks.

OOOH! is the finest Mekons album since *Mekons Rock & Roll* (1989) and their third-best overall. Twenty-five years into their career, they've blended genres so many times that the music is nearly impossible to categorize: elements of punk, country, folk, reggae, pop and choral singing run through every tune. Lyrically, the Mekons have crafted *the* answer album to September 11th, although the event is never mentioned. The theme of losing one's head (first explored in 1996's "Orpheus") takes on the extra significance in the context of mass hysteria and loss plaguing the Western world. Lyrically, the songs explore topics like historian E. P. Thompson's theories about the creation of the working class ("Thee Olde Trip to Jerusalem"), nuclear winter ("Winter"), renouncing one's faith ("Take His Name in Vain"), regicide ("Stonehead") and a lovely meditation on war without end ("Hate Is the New Love"). But the dire subject matter doesn't stop the music from rocking harder than the now-middle-aged Mekons have in ages, proving that a band can age gracefully while carrying the same DIY seed from its beginnings. (Hayden Childs)

The Edge of the World   **(Sin, 1986)**

Innovations and breakthroughs get the headlines, but consolidations and refinements can be just as important. *Fear and Whiskey* was the album on which the Mekons first defined their postpunk sound, and it helped inspire a whole generation of musicians to explore the porous boundaries between country and punk. Their next album, *The Edge of the World*, is another tour de force, and one that's perhaps even more important, because it's the first album on which the Mekons are recognizably the band that is still playing today.

A large part of that is the inclusion of vocalist Sally Timms. Timms' remarkable voice, clear and disenchanted, adds a new element to the Mekons' sound, and when she takes the lead vocal for the first time on "Oblivion" she turns what could be a dismissive singalong into something almost regal in its disdain. Another part is that the band had coalesced around a core group of musicians, and their increased fluency in their new idiom shows, helped along by improved production.

But perhaps most importantly, it's here that the band's ethos really emerges. The songs speak of isolation and anger even in their titles: "Big Zombie," "Bastards" and a cover of "Alone & Forsaken." "Down in the basement the ugly band plays," as one song puts it, "pushed into the corner like some creeping little thing." Yet the album meets its doom with a smile on its face: the first song is called "Hello Cruel World." Things are terrible, the songs say, but they're not hopeless. In the middle of the ruins, the band forms its own community of the lost and forgotten. "There's one thing I know, we're not in the same boat at all," they sing on "Shanty," but when everyone joins on the chorus, it sure sounds like we are. (Michele Tepper)

MIDDLE OF THE ROAD

Acceleration   **(RCA Germany, 1972)**

Hands downs, the bubblepop prom queen to Ron Dante/Joey Levine's split guy-crown would be Sally Carr of Middle of the Road. She's also the *only* female pop voice/look to ever automatically qualify as the real-life Betty (of the Archies, next Saturday live at the Fillmore West). Verily, a more lethal high-pitched air raid siren of an up-tempo pop voice has never been heard on the airwaves—and yet, on the best slow album tracks, it is also a positively gorgeous neo-girlgroup layered-femme-vocal-group sound.

Out of many European hit singles and eight albums, these are the greatest cuts: hits "Chirpy Chirpy Cheep Cheep," "Tweedle Dee Tweedle Dum," "Sacramento," "Talk of All the USA," and "Yellow Boomerang"; album tracks "On This Land," "Love Sweet Love," "Then You'll Know What Love Is For," and "Eve." Check any *Best of* digital comp against those tracks—otherwise, *Acceleration* is their best original LP (except on its wanky American "Dynaflex" pressing) and easily found.

The thumbnail history of MOTR is not unlike Slade or Hawkind or any former sixties beatgroup vets who persevered into the seventies and eventual chart success. Drummer Ken Andrew and brothers Ian and Eric McCredie had served time in Glasgow beat groups the Talismen Beat Unit, the Dominos and the Electrons, which evolved into a more loungy 1967 act the Part 3, renamed Part Four when Sally joined, renamed yet again Los Caracas to match the popularity of their half-dozen Latin Pop numbers (and with new stage costumes to match).

Okay then, 1970: an upcoming booking in Argentina necessitated another name change (to Middle of the Road), with five weeks of work in Italy scheduled first. The big casino gig in South America didn't happen, because the month in Italy turned into a Top 40 hit career when producer Giacomo Tosti redirected MOTR into becoming Europe's all-time #1 bubblegum act ... who were also really a performing band.

By sheer volume of strong tracks (and worldwide hits except in America) I hereby deem MOTR the #2 pre-Leif bubblepop act, and of course the real-life Archies band that only Sally Carr could have fronted. Oh, and their taped *TOTP* appearances? I wouldn't recommend being on acid, or even too much booze, if you ever get a chance to see them ... . (Metal Mike Saunders)

KYLIE MINOGUE

Impossible Princess   **(Mushroom, Australia, 1997)**

Life was weird for Kylie Minogue in the mid- to late nineties. The Australian "singing budgie" had scored many Euro hits with her Stock, Aitken & Waterman–produced songs in the eighties. But at the end of her contract with SAW, Kylie was restless, so she signed with the British dance label deConstruction and went to work on the second phase of her career.

Recorded during her relationship with video director Stephane Sednaoui, *Impossible Princess* is an unsettled piece of work. Her label was in disarray and left her free to do whatever she wanted; that newfound freedom translated into an album imbued with a sense of restlessness (even relatively straightforward dance tracks like "Too Far" and "Breathe" feel antsy). But it also makes the record completely gripping because you never know what the hell is going through Kylie's head. The semi-autobiographical lyrics (she wrote or cowrote them all) feel penned by someone who doesn't know who or what she is. In any case, she's obviously not sure where she fits in the pop landscape; the producers include the Brothers in Rhythm dance team, ex-Soft Cell synth man Dave Ball, and Manic Street Preachers frontman James Dean Bradfield. The results can be as frustratingly uneven as they can be absolutely brilliant. "I Don't Need Anyone" remains one of the best pop songs of the nineties, a driving, intoxicating paean to the never-ending quest for something, someone. As if the project wasn't enough of a tough sell, Princess Diana was killed a few weeks before *Impossible Princess* was scheduled to come out, so the album was retitled *Kylie Minogue* and its UK release was delayed by a few months.

To this day, this is Kylie's worst-selling record, the album maudit that encapsulates the transition from pop nymphet to pop empress. After *Impossible Princess* bombed, the singer figured out that existential dread just wasn't her ticket to world domination and she promptly returned to hot pants and disco. The result was 2000's *Light Years*, one of the best, most hedonistic albums of the new century. But that's another story. (Elisabeth Vincentelli)

MIRACLE LEGION

Me and Mr. Ray   **(Rough Trade, 1989)**

Personal canons can be built on pure coincidence. Miracle Legion never meant much to me before or since this record, which is somewhat anomalous in their R.E.Mitating career. This is usually thought of as their "acoustic duet" album, perhaps because only the singer and guitarist are listed on the back. But the record has plenty of uncredited piano, strings, drums, and electric bass as well.

This was a favorite from my college years, and what I loved about it was that it was a soothing pile of—completely convincing, compelling, and winning—romantic goo. But studying it afresh today, I realized that those were just the parts I wanted to connect with when I was a (rather consistently) lovestruck youngster who really wanted to sing to somebody, "My queen/Where have you been … I meant it when I said that yours are the only hands that ever felt right … I feel like Apollo and you could be my Venus." If you can't imagine ever not thinking those lyrics are icky, this record's potential warmth will probably evade you.

But returning to it when older and more jaded, I found more that is wonderful and compelling and still forms a queer sort of conceptual unified whole—something about summer life in the south, though that subject is never explicitly mentioned. The romantic parts are redolent of a warm morning, full of promise and with some receding-into-smoke memories of the sultry night before. Other tracks, though, are like a mysterious and almost scary reverie that can sink over you late in the afternoon on a hot, thick afternoon, especially "Pull the Wagon" and "Sailors and Animals." And jaunty tracks like "If She Could Cry" and "Even Better" are town square singalong material where all the people you've ever known gather to celebrate away doldrums. And it all sounds sweet and mysterious and nostalgic right from the start. (Brian Doherty)

MR. FOX

Mr. Fox   **(Transatlantic, 1970)**

Mr. Fox was a Yorkshire-based folk-rock band formed by the husband-and-wife team of Bob and Carole Pegg. Rather than prowling through the Child Ballads and old broadsheets for material from the misty mists of time, they concocted originals inspired by local folklore. With their dramatic arrangements, the band aimed to evoke the sounds of rural traditional Englishness (brass bands, Morris dance music), woven in with medieval and baroque elements and instrumentation. The resulting concoction is pleasantly psychedelic.

Starting with "Join Us in Our Game," the debut lets the listener know what sorts of songs lay in store. These include a cover of "Little Woman," a Dave Mason song, and Carole Pegg's setting of "Salisbury Plain," with lyrics by Ashley Hutchings, a founding member of Fairport Convention, Steeleye Span, and the Albion Band who was responsible for the electrification of the Morris dance. A high point is the deliciously creepy, gothic tale of "Mr. Fox," a take on the traditional tale of Reynardine (a Bluebeardesque were-fox) delivered menacingly by Carole over a droning melodeon. Another is a magical transformation tale, "The Gay Goshawk." These are two of the best original songs of the genre.

Mr. Fox was known for either blowing people away with their shows (of which this album—essentially a taped performance—is a good example) or bombing completely. The critical juncture for the band's career was at the

1971 Loughborough Folk Festival, where they went head to head with Steeleye Span. Unfortunately for Mr. Fox, they crashed and burned while Steeleye Span pulled out a truly impressive performance. Thus did the trajectory of English folk-rock follow off Steeleyeward and Fairport Conventionally into the future.

After their second album, *The Gipsy*, the band splintered. Bob Pegg recorded a few solo albums and now does storytelling and songwriting workshops for children. Carole Pegg recorded one album and briefly joined Graham Bond in the band Magus. She went on to become an ethnomusicologist. (Brooke Alberts)

MONITOR

Monitor   **(World Imitation, 1981)**

Monitor got together in the seventies as an art project called "World Imitation." Initially restricting their output to a series of handmade collage zines, they eventually got the performance bug. Mastering a rudimentary skill on their instruments, they developed a sound one could describe as Devo meets Martin Denny and the Manson Family in Disney's Haunted Mansion.

Though their live performances were full of nervous (even paranoid) energy, their self-released album was comparatively sedate. A paean to "the irresistibleness of things that neither threaten nor jeer" (as Charles Fort is paraphrased on the back cover), *Monitor* vacillates between moody pop songs and atmospheric instrumentals, never displaying any of the sadomasochistic avant-garde edginess one would assume from a group that spent much of their time thrift shopping with their friend Boyd Rice. Monitor's approach is wide-eyed and affectionate, displaying a most untrendy fascination with their subjects: pet weddings, spontaneous combustion, evolution and communication with the spirit world.

Naturally, their album sank without a trace. If you were lucky, you might have found it in the punk section of your favorite record store. But the world has caught up with them somewhat by now. One could easily classify Monitor as retro or loungecore. They have that cartoony, non-rock, informed-by-easy-listening vibe that our ears have since been trained to accept. But Monitor was too dark for the cocktail hour. With its slow, deliberate tempos and eerie muttered vocals, the album sounds more like a series of incantations than a collection of pop tunes. At times, the band sounds as if it's attempting nothing less than to raise the dead.

Within a year, Monitor themselves were gone. Like so many before and since, they joined the ranks of bands that, to again paraphrase Charles Fort, "pass and keep on passing." (Derrick Bostrom)

MONTY PYTHON

Monty Python Sings (Virgin, 1989)

If you ever spent a spring afternoon in late high school sitting on a low stone wall while a cadre of theater kids recited the "Knights Who Say 'Ni!'" word for word until you wished they would stop, you'll be happy to know that the collection *Monty Python Sings* contains lots of music from the *rest* of Python that will make you laugh and that hasn't yet been jackhammered into the ground like so much Spam.

Take Kissinger. The plummy colonialism of "Henry Kissinger, how I'm missin' ya" reminded me of Neil Innes and the Bonzos playing twenties trad-jazz. But that's Eric Idle singing: "With your funny clothes/and your squishy nose/you're like a German Par-o-quet."

Idle dominates the disc as singer and writer or cowriter of such ditties as the grandiose "Galaxy Song" and the less grandiose "Penis Song." Since most of the songs on the disc have one lead singer mixed high, you can often feel the personality of an individual Python coming through, especially compared to the cacophony of sketches. Terry Jones is sad and frumpy on "I'm So Worried." John Cleese narrates and sings the twitchy Idle composition "Eric the Half a Bee," in which "semi-carnally" gets mistaken for Cyril Connolly. Some of the less funny songs, like "Christmas in Heaven," redeem themselves by being one big hummable hook.

Shortly before the release of the disc, Graham Chapman died, which brings home the glum point that in 1989 the group had pretty well run its course. That big mouth on the front cover looks like a Gilliam—but it's not. *C'est la vie.* Taken as a retrospective, *Sings* is a good one with a lot of funny moments. The Spam and the lumberjacks are here too, in case you never did find yourself on that low stone wall. (Kevin Carhart)

The following is an excerpt from the review that appeared

in the September 1972 issue of *Creem*.

BOB MOSLEY

Bob Mosley   (Reprise, 1972)

Save for one major flaw, *Bob Mosley* could've been the best
Moby Grape-derived album ever, and that includes the legendary Grape debut album. A majority of the music on *Bob
Mosley* dates right back to the style of the first Moby album:
"The Joker" opens the LP with a burst of energy that is the
equal of anything Mosley ever did with the Grape. Mosley's
backup group sets up that familiar kinetic Moby Grape drone,
only this time bass-dominated and tense.

On the very second cut, "Gypsy Wedding," *Mosley's*
Achilles heel stares you right in the face—someone has added
horns on three cuts in a way that, if not outright stupid, is at
least irritating. Soul horns on a pure rock 'n' roll album??? I
can't believe it.

The opening of "1245 Kearny" has a sound that reminds
instantly of 1967 rock and roll, and "Squaw Valley Nils" is a
pure early Moby Grape song. Gorgeous falsetto singing!
"Where Do The Birds Go," "Hand In Hand," "The Joker " are all
driving, powerhouse *up-tempo* rock and roll. For my money,
Mosley has to be one of the most impressive shouting rockers
ever.

Mosley's music is so distinctive and unique I can't think of
anyone (save the early Grape) who sounds even remotely like
him. So much of the music on *Bob Mosley* has the urgency that
is absolutely essential to first-rate rock and roll: it's the type of
music that, once you hear it, seems as if it *had* to get out. The
best music on this album has an edge that few rock artists ever
achieve. It could've been a magnificent, near-perfect album; as
it is, it's still as good as a flawed album can be. Coming as it
does five whole years after the first Grape LP, *Bob Mosley* has
to be the surprise album of the year. (Metal Mike Saunders)

THE MUGWUMPS

The Mugwumps   **(Warner Brothers, 1967)**

I detested the Mamas & Papas, yet this album is almost fascinating in its weirdness. In some respects it's almost mouldy
1963 rock and roll because of the sparse instrumentation and
crude production, but Zally Yanovsky's influence and some
primeval folk-rock touches are mixed in. For the first time, I
have to admit that Cass Elliot was an excellent harmony
singer. Fact is, this album has a lot of great group-singing.
Don't let the nine songs and 21 minutes of playing time scare
you off: the neanderthal production techniques and so-crappy-
it's-good instrumental backing almost give this LP the charm
of 1950s rocknroll. In an early folk-rock sort of way. Or something.

    (Metal Mike Saunders, *Flash* #2, June–July 1972) (See also: Zalman Yanovsky)

PAMELO MOUNK'A

Pamelo Mounk'a   **(Eddy-son, France, 1981)**

In the post-war years, the Congo and Zaire spawned a Latinate dance music
that's come to be known as rumba-rock or *soukous*. Like disco in mid-seventies America, *soukous* ran amuck throughout Africa, trampling local dance
music. The movement spawned huge stars, notably Franco and Tabu Ley
Rochereau, respectively the Stones and Beatles of the form. Among
Rochereau's backing singers was Pamelo Mounk'a, built like a quarterback
but equipped with a gentle, nuanced tenor. Mounk'a began as a solo artist in
the seventies, hitting his stride as the eighties began, when he partnered with
the French producer Eddy Gustave.

Surrounding Mounk'a was the cream of expatriate Zairois musicians
then residing in Paris. Additionally, Gustave fabricated the perfect reverber-
ant sheen for Pamelo's keening voice. Their premier collaboration, simply
titled *Pamelo Mounk'a,* distills all that is catchy and endearing about *soukous*
in that era. The lyrics, sung in a creole of Lingala and French, provide wry

MARTIN MULL

Martin Mull   (Capricorn, 1972)

There are only a few songwriters around these days who could
be said to have a truly distinctive vision, a world-view that sets
them considerably aside from their fellows. There is Randy
Newman, of course, and Ron Nagle, who is currently prevented
from recording by contractual hassles. The weird New York
school is represented by Loudon Wainwright III and Georges
Gerdes, both of whom are currently recording and Andy
Zwerling, currently unsigned, brings a whole new meaning to
the word "teenage."

And then there is Martin Mull. Mull, like Nagle, is also an
artist, and, like Nagle again, his art is about as crazy as his
songwriting. Mull's latest attempt was a number of famous
paintings executed entirely in hors d'oeuvres. At the close of
the show, viewers were allowed to eat their favorite painting.
And Mull did his own airbrush album cover.

But the songs, the songs! How about "Ventriloquist Love"
("it ain't such a groove/Whenever I kiss you/your lips never
move."); Or "(I Made Love To You) In A Former Life?" The
words are just as good as the titles lead you to believe, for
once. And the music! The only way I could describe it would be
"hard electric swing music," sort of Dan Hicks on speed or
something.

The whole thing gets summed up in "Dancing In the
Nude," which one Mull fan I know describes as "the best version of 'Moondance' I've ever heard." It swings, it's hilarious,
and the band (made up mostly of unknowns, but with Levon
Helm drumming) is tight, tight, tight.

Mull, it appears, is headed for stardom whether you go out
and buy his album or not. He'll be on *Laugh-In* this fall, and I
may watch just to see him. There are those who think he
sounds a little too much like Randy Newman, but if you listen
to the words, you will see that Martin Mull is far more dangerously neurotic. Will fame spoil Martin Mull? Buy the album
before you find out!

(Ed Ward, *Phonograph Record Magazine*, November 1972)

social commentary on money, jealousy, and competition. Gustave's all-star band featured drummer Domingo Salsero, bassist/guitarist Pablo Lubadika Porthos, and, best of all, spiraling lead guitar played by "Master" Mwela Congo. If the latter's sound had an American counterpart, it might be the signature timbre and phrasing of Al Green's guitarist Teeny Hodges; both possess the sound of a guitar telling itself a dirty joke.

All four songs on *Pamelo Mounk'a* (therein lies the template for *soukous* of the period: if the album's got four songs, buy it!) sparkle with exuberant performances and insouciance. Best of all is the seben, a standard feature of rumba-rock, when the band suddenly shifts from a languid 3+2 rhythm into high gear for the final two-thirds of a given song. Pamelo chants the song's title over and over, the horn section jabs like a prizefighter, and "Master" tears off minimalist guitar figures as vivacious as the flick of a sperm cell's tail. You don't want these songs to stop, and the wonderful thing is, they don't. (Richard Henderson)

N

RON NAGLE

Bad Rice   **(Warner Brothers, 1970)**

Nagle's history is as curious as this great Jack Nitzsche–produced record. He started as a member of *Nuggets*-sanctified sixties art-school pop band the Mystery Trend, and this was his only solo pop record. But he went on to form the duo the Durocs (with one 1979 album on Capitol), write songs for artists ranging from Leo Kottke to Barbara Streisand, and do sound-effect manipulation on movie soundtracks, with the famously spooky sound crafting on *The Exorcist* (said to include animals being sent to slaughter and the buzzing of angry bees) to his credit. Today he's better known in the world of ceramics, making artsy-craftsy cups that are considered hot shit in the world of, um, artsy-craftsy cups.

Bad Rice is a true original of Americana pop, sometimes vaguely bluesy, sometimes sounding like mutated ragtime, not sounding exactly like anybody, although the contemporaneous work of Randy Newman is the best touchstone for those who need to compare. Like Newman on *12 Songs*,

Nagle's piano dominates many of the tracks, and he brings in Ry Cooder for some bloody-fingered blues action. Nagle has a brilliant writer's eye for the details of strange people's lives and times, like the family disrupted by sonny accidentally stepping on mom's parakeet or poor sucker Frank who lets Eddie watch his corner store and lives to regret it. The string coda on that one, with Nagle keening "cry, cry, cry," will induce waves of sympathy for small business owners in trouble that you might not have known you had in you. And "Party in L.A." is, of course, about a worried dad who fathered a son with a hardcore commie only to have her abscond with the kid to the west coast on May 1 because she is "needed by the [Communist] Party in L.A." It's that kind of album. (Brian Doherty)

BUCK NAKED AND THE BARE BOTTOM BOYS
Buck Naked and the Bare Bottom Boys   (Heyday, 1993)

Lordy, he was a vision. I remember Buck stepping up to the mic at Raji's wearing pink cowboy boots, an orange feathered boa, aviator shades, bright red lipstick and the kind of cowboy hat you'd typically see on a bitter divorcée from Santa Fe. And that was all he wore. Except for the Fozzie Bear muppet strapped across his crotch in a crucifix posture—Fozzie's face a rictus of surprise as he took it up the muppet hole.

This was entirely appropriate for the only band I know that did a medley of songs about anal sex. If you weren't grinning ear to ear at a Buck show while chanting the chorus, "Up Up/Up Your Butt!" then you just didn't love rock and roll. It's that simple. They were very jolly about their kinky sex, and it was … well, infectious. Of course, there's a tendency to dismiss Buck and the Boys' pornobilly as a cheap novelty. And while it was cheap, and it was certainly novel, I want to tell you it rocked with urgent, lewd authority.

The Boys plugged in and rolled that throbbing beat down to the nearest motel. They dialed the reverb to "Grotto" and erected mighty oscillations of bayou swamp twang. Buck sang "Enema Party" with such insane glee, he made the entire prospect sound like the ideal Saturday night. That's an impressive bit of salesmanship, you've got to admit.

Everything on this record is a Buck Naked original, except the Billy Childish cover "Sometimes (I Want'cha for Your Money)." There's not a duff cut here, and it moves like a silicone dildo display in a 5.4 temblor. Pearl Harbor did Buck's "Trouble," and it's very probably the ultimate post-rockabilly bad-girl-with-big-hair anthem. Certainly up there with Ben Vaughn's "Dressed in Black." Tip to collectors: the 12-inch single of "Teenage Pussy from Outer Space" is the very best thing Buck and the Bare Bottom Boys ever did and it's entirely different than the CD version. A crazy man shot and killed Buck before this record ever came out. If you missed seeing him live, then you missed a revelation. (David Smay)

WILLIE NELSON
Phases and Stages (Atlantic, 1974)

Nashville's reaction to Willie Nelson recalls Fred Astaire's infamous screen test: "Can't sing. Can't play. Can write a little." Willie's idiosyncratic singing and guitar playing didn't take Nashville by storm, but his songs did, providing Faron Young ("Hello Walls") and Patsy Cline ("Crazy") with signature songs. It took a decade and a half for Willie's own commercial breakthrough, *Red Headed Stranger* and its hit single, "Blue Eyes Crying in the Rain."

Just before that breakthrough he recorded *Phases and Stages*, a break-up album with Side 1's songs written from the woman's point of view and Side 2's from the man's. I believe it is his finest set of songs and, with his Lefty Frizzell tribute *From Willie to Lefty* and his Great American Songbook tribute *Stardust*, among his best recordings. Produced by Jerry Wexler, it features the Muscle Shoals Rhythm Section and fiddler Johnny Gimble; Willie's guitar, the beautiful beat-up Martin known as "Trigger," is front and center as always. The arrangements are full, yet still very spare and restrained.

There's less bitterness and anger in the songs than on *Red Headed Stranger*, and little Hank Williams or George Jones–style high drama, probably because, whatever his faults, Willie's not a highway wreck of a human being. In fact, he's very much like us, and so are his characters, who in the midst of upheaval, mostly seem stunned. There's a lovely balance between melancholic resignation and maintaining a sense of humor, between slow heartbreakers and up-tempo dance-away-the-blues numbers, between Side 1's "I'm falling in love again/And if I lose or win/How will I know?" and Side

MIKE NESMITH
Nevada Fighter   (RCA, 1971)

The second side of this album features an incredible "suite" of songs that will leave you feeling pretty desolate, but happier for it. Red Rhodes does wail fine on the pedal steel.

(Ed Ward, *Flash* #2, June–July 1972)

2's "Sometimes it's heaven and sometimes it's hell/And sometimes I don't even know."

Phases is full of little quirks that sound odd at first, but once you're on his wavelength seem ineffably, definitively right. As with Thelonious Monk, when listening to Willie Nelson one is amazed at how right and wrong it all is simultaneously. "Ugly beauty" as Monk put it. This is Willie at his ugliest beautiful. (Joe Boucher)

NEUTRAL MILK HOTEL
In the Aeroplane over the Sea
(Merge, 1998)

Less than six years old, it's already crusted in the kind of speculation and lore that only a handful of recordings inspire. *In the Aeroplane over the Sea* is one of those rare records that can buoy you in dark times; small wonder its fans have latched on to it so fervently. And now that fervor seems to have driven poor Jeff Mangum into a Salingeresque retreat.

It starts off simply with an acoustic guitar. Mangum's voice sounds calm even as the lyrics take their first left turn: "When you were young you were the King of Carrot Flowers/and how you built a tower tumbling through the trees/in holy rattlesnakes that fell all around your feet." The images roil up in a reverie of childhood, tree houses, family violence and the consolation of sex.

Then, "I love youuu Jeee-susss Chr-iiiiist"—funereal marching bands led by Scott Spillane's trumpet wander into folky laments that blast off in furious thrashings of guitar pushed to distortion until your speaker cone's blowing a raspberry. Jeremy Barnes rattles and powers the drums, forcing the songs faster and upward until they become windblown scatterings.

But that description makes *Aeroplane* sound discordant in a way it never could be. This is the most organic of records, an oracular rush flooding out of Mangum's mouth in a blissful blur of assonance and association, imagery cohering somehow along the cracks in his voice. It shares *Astral Weeks'* obsessions, but scumbles them, smearing them: sex and death and childhood and mystery. Mangum's lyrics are both dreamlike and harrowingly concrete. He fingers the notches along the human spine and wonders at the unreal corporeality of life. Ghosts hover in the eerie pitchshifting warble of Julian Koster's musical saw. *Aeroplane* plays like the soundtrack to the *Little Nemo in Slumberland* comic strip, but a Nemo grown old, trapped on the wrong side of the twentieth century, falling helplessly in love with Anne Frank decades too late ("Holland 1945" is this lovesong). When Mangum's voice drops into "Oh Comely" he's looking right into the black sockets.

Some records are a benediction. The music here, so pretty, alive, and carnivalesque, digs into dark places. Yet there is a kindness in it, a fellow feeling rushing forward airborne over the sea, over the semen-stained mountaintops, laughing with the ghosts of forgiven suicides. *Aeroplane* is, in its way, a prayerful record. (David Smay)

THE NEW BLOCKADERS

Changez Le Blockeurs   **(Privately pressed, 1982)**

An incisive and timeless album whose mystique only serves to spawn and spew constant rumors, and this is how rumors get started: Emily and Jack work in the mailroom. The boss comes around and tells Emily, "I'm gonna have to lay you or Jack off." Now to dispel some rumors: what you hear (casters twisted, metal plates beaten erratically, slapping) is what you get.

Coming down fast out of nowhere and heading straight back behind curling contrails of crumpling oblivion, the LP was re-issued on CD by the German label Urthona in 1997; originally, it was released in an edition of

100. Imagine being in a room with the 99 other owners of this particular album. Like watching a Down syndrome gangbang, it's an exceptionally spirited series of recordings by the brothers Rupenus (Richard and Philip), marooned in the middle of Northumbria, England, and incessantly vowing that the succeeding live action would definitely be their "Final Live Performance." Cut-ups, grinding, scraping, and much squeaking and rattling—one of the original LPs sold recently on eBay for $366.70, ultimately to Thurston Moore. Hey now! A medieval woodcut illustration on the cover is altered and hassled by new and magic markings. It's a shame that the manifesto ("We vote for nobody … for the right reasons!" etc.) from the back cover of the original LP is missing from the Urthona edition. However, is the anti-aesthetic still part of the aesthetic, going against nature and becoming part of it, too? There is a feeling of genuine fun and amusement that the Rupenus brothers might have enjoyed while realizing these sounds (because, as with some anti-art, it's difficult to discern if the situation is immensely enjoyable or intensely painful). If you use this for fuck music—keep that lover by any means necessary! (David Cotner)

Portions of this piece appeared previously in *Freq* and *NewCreativeMusic*.

ANDY NEWMAN
Rainbow　　　　　　　　　　　　　　　　　**(Track U.K., 1971)**

The phrase "unlikely trio" surfaced repeatedly when critics wrote of Thunderclap Newman. Though guitarist Jimmy McCulloch was barely out of short pants and singer/songwriter/drummer Speedy Keen resembled a blond clone of band producer Pete Townshend, it was multi-instrumentalist Andy Newman the scribes were really describing. Portly, bearded, dressed like a postal clerk, Newman looked a generation older than Townshend, though the two had attended art school concurrently. The trio comprising Thunderclap Newman was a volatile alloy destined to produce only one album, *Hollywood Dream*, which contained the hit "Something in the Air" and several curious songs hallmarked by Keen's reedy, doubled-tracked vocals and McCulloch's blistering guitar. Their melodies were fleshed out with music-hall piano and clusters of orchestral percussion, all provided—via recently introduced multitrack technology—by Andy Newman.

Immediately after the group disbanded Newman completed his only solo album, *Rainbow*. *Rainbow*'s sleeve art defined the lure of English imports to American record buyers desperate for anything of a personal or eccentric flavor in the benighted early seventies. Against a sky of robin's egg blue, Newman strolled along a beach past an abandoned piano, the colors of the titular phenomenon arching overhead. The cover image put one in mind of Alfred Hitchcock making a customary walk-on appearance. A lengthy list of instrumental odds 'n' sods spilled down the interior of the gatefold, atop a photo of Newman, a big man playing what seemed like an improbably small saxophone.

Rainbow's repertoire was divided evenly between English postwar dancehall favorites and Newman's compositions, which were of a piece with the tunes he chose from an earlier era. The record was entirely the product of overdubs; no other players were involved. Its first track, "That's What I Like about You," set a consistent tone, wordless, jaunty, and effortlessly charming, its tune sketched by piano, saxophones and kazoo. In a retail landscape dominated by the Allman Brothers and *Aqualung*, small wonder that *Rainbow* slipped quickly beneath the waves. No matter, though, for even as this appreciation is written, Pete Townshend has announced his own reissue of *Rainbow*, the Little Album That Could (Still). (Richard Henderson) (See also: The Who)

THE NEW YORK ROCK ENSEMBLE
Roll Over   (Columbia, 1971)

When film composer Michael Kamen died, the newspapers provided great cascading lists of the films he had scored, including *X-Men*, all the *Lethal Weapons*, all the *Die Hards*, and *Brazil*. Less frequently did they mention his contributions in the great lost rock records of the 1970s.

In the late 1960s, Kamen set out with a crew of gifted cronies to prove that classical musicians could conquer rock and roll. Early albums were exuberant failures—"Let's turn the Brandenburg Concerto No. 5 into a rock song!" They abandoned classical grandstanding to produce one perfect footstomping extravaganza.

Roll Over opens with a racket of drums and bells, the sound of a man's heart jangling as he flees from the law in "Running Down the Highway." The songs are like a series of mini horror flicks: a man confronts a succubus in "Gravedigger," a huge snake menaces the populace in "Anaconda," a couple witness the end of the world in "Fields of Joy." But the boogie-woogie keyboards have you vamping around no matter how bleak or terrifying the lyrical content. Kamen's singing is the secret weapon. He quakes with pent-up fury on "Traditional Order," pleads on the serenade "Beside You." He even sounds like he's having fun during the demonic "Anaconda."

Architectural Digestion:
More Songs About Domiciles and Habitats

"Come On-A My House," Rosemary Clooney

"A House Is Not a Home," Dionne Warwick

"Hello Walls," Faron Young

"Walking the Floor Over You," George Hamilton IV

"In My House," The Mary Jane Girls

"Ain't Nobody Home," Howard Tate

"Haunted House," Gene Simmons

"Up on the Roof," Drifters

"In My Room," Beach Boys

"One Less Bell to Answer," Fifth Dimension

"Knock Three Times," Dawn

"Our House," Crosby, Stills & Nash

"Up in Her Room," Seeds

"Little House I Used to Live In," Frank Zappa

"Lookin' Out My Back Door," Creedence Clearwater Revival

"Darling Come Home Soon," Lovin' Spoonful

"In Your Room," Bangles

"Little Pad," Beach Boys

"442 Glenwood Avenue," Pixies Three

"This Ole House," Stuart Hamblen

"My Head Is My Only House When It Rains," Captain Beefheart
   (Gene Sculatti)

After the band broke up, Kamen went on to write all those scores, and another member, Marty Fulterman, wrote some famous music too, including the insidious theme to *The X-Files* (as Mark Snow). If you need a minor party trick, put the soundtracks of *The X-Files* and *X-Men* side by side and see who can guess what these records have in common besides their near-identical graphic design.

However, *Roll Over's* most memorable song, the rollicking "Traditional Order," was written not by the future pop-entertainment mavens Kamen and Fulterman/Snow, but by cellist-bassist Dorian Rudnytsky. My fond hope is that this guy is even now concocting the most devastatingly infectious movie/TV anthem you'll ever hear. Consider yourself warned. (Genevieve Conaty)

BILLY NICHOLLS

Would You Believe   **(Immediate, 1968)**

Oft billed as "The British answer to *Pet Sounds*," Billy Nicholls's *Would You Believe* rests in a charmed meadow in London's Itchycoo Park, between the orchestral psychedelia of the Zombies' *Odessey & Oracle* and the pastoral whimsy of the Kinks' *Village Green*. There are echoes, nevertheless, of its California touchstone, which it attempted to trump with a battery of harpsichords, madrigalesque vocals and the Andrew Loog Oldham Orchestra.

In 1966, Nicholls was a sixteen-year-old prodigy who, through George Harrison, recorded a few demos. The demos eventually fell into the hands of Rolling Stones producer Oldham, who signed Nicholls as a staff songwriter to his fledgling Immediate label and installed Nicholls in a studio "full of Revoxes, mellotrons, and the Stones' guitars." Nicholls began laying down demos and falling in with recently psychedelicized labelmates the Small Faces, who provide the musical backbone of *Would You Believe*, abetted by U.K. sessionmen Nicky Hopkins, John Paul Jones and Caleb Quaye. A teaser single, "Would You Believe/Daytime Girl," was released in January 1968 to good notices, even if one blinkered critic called it "the most overproduced record of the '60s." In April, Oldham pressed promotional copies of the album, but in dire financial straits and betting the farm on the Small Faces' forthcoming *Ogden's Nut Gone Flake*, pulled *Would You Believe*, leading to the original LP exchanging hands over the years for silly money. An unintentional concept album revolving around a wide-eyed hipster teen in swinging London—receiving his "London Social Degree" from a dealer on Carnaby Street, smoking Turkish cigarettes on "Portobello Road," falling in love with a "Girl from New York"—*Would You Believe* is a supremely melodic time capsule from a heady era, but, devoid of the Tolkienesque gobbledygook so prevalent in British psychedelia, it remains uniquely timeless. (Andrew Hultkrans)

HARRY NILSSON
Knillssonn (RCA, 1977)

The Beatles had claimed his poignant tenor as a favorite voice during the late sixties and the prolific Harry Nilsson repaid the compliment with album upon album of witty vignettes set to Tin Pan–perfect melodies. Harry entered the following decade with a hit album (*Nilsson Schmilsson*), annexing thousands of new ears to his fan base, but by the mid-seventies had been all but written off as worthless, a casualty of self-indulgence. His singing had deteriorated to a nearly painful extent, as evidenced on the *Pussycats* collection produced by John Lennon; that the pair survived the sessions has become a small marvel to rock historians.

Yet it was a rejuvenated Nilsson who surprised and rewarded his few remaining fans with *Knillssonn* in 1977. Though his vocal range had downshifted an octave, he had recovered the supple timbre and control that so endeared him to listeners a decade before. His wit was intact, as was his unfailing good taste in arrangements. To the latter, the template was clearly delineated: bass, drums, acoustic guitar, string orchestra and—whenever Harry sensed his audience was at their most vulnerable—a boy choir. Nilsson managed the neat trick of constructing spare, nearly minimalist songs from grandiose components, entirely of a piece with the monochromatic artwork of the sleeve containing them. Here and there, homeopathic tinctures of psychedelia would surface, as with the reversed tape loop that anchors "I Never Thought I'd Get This Lonely."

Nilsson's romantic agenda was now colored with regret, the sound of lost opportunities lamented in song. Still, this was Harry's favorite among his extensive catalog. Though his sense of humor could never be denied, the autumnal temper and heart-wrenching vocals of *Knillssonn* stand it in good stead as a worthy successor to a much earlier and equally wistful concept album (possibly the first so): Frank Sinatra's *In the Wee Small Hours*. (Richard Henderson)

THE NOURALLAH BROTHERS
Try to Get Along   **(unreleased, 2003)**

Because of his refusal to perform and inclination to record alone, Faris Nourallah effectively disbanded the Nourallah Brothers over the course of these recordings. A pop virtuoso of sorts, he comes off alternately glib and tender, like his apparent hero Ray Davies. By default, elder brother Salim is more the Dave in this scenario, the throatier-voiced brother who started the band only to be supplanted by his more precocious sibling.

Salim Nourallah, bolder, more romantic (and perhaps more tyrannical) by nature, can probably be thanked for at least trying to pull *Try to Get Along* together. A favorite of mine is his coy "Nothing Ever Goes Right," a bitter-sweet slice of jangle-pop swaddled in some of the trademarks of Nourallah production. Here, a bright, thumpy bass is coupled with individually mixed drums and fearless low-grade synthesizers. His "One Foot Stuck in the Past" is purely jubilant, with acoustic guitars, organ, and a lilting falsetto vocal occasionally reminiscent of *Wild Life*–era McCartney. Also superb is the gutsy delivery of the atmospheric, delay-soaked ballad "Say You Belong to Me," a mélange of early Cure and Prince.

Faris' best contributions tend to a certain lovelorn frankness. His stark piano ballads "Adieu" and "In My Dreams" are built with the same sort of harmonic and emotional layering that made some of John Lennon's early solo music so intimate. On "Someone to Love," Faris repeats the frighteningly honest refrain "all our lives are spent searching for someone to love" to a near rock frenzy, before imploding and reinterpreting the song's main melody on a reverberating upright.

Despite having been "in the can" twice already, *Try to Get Along* may never be released. I got my copy direct from Salim with a note reading, "You may be one of ten people to hear this record…" Instead, look for a pair of solo albums, each snatching up two or three of these tracks, Faris' *Problematico* and Salim's *Polaroid*. (Jonathan Donaldson)

PHIL OCHS
In Concert   **(Elektra, 1966)**

Unless your name was Dylan, 1966 was not a great time to be a folk singer. A year after *Highway '61 Revisited*, it must have been easy to dismiss a live, solo acoustic album of new folk songs. And yet it's here that Phil Ochs' struggle with creative direction received its first public airing. The opening songs are rooted squarely in Phil's *All the News That's Fit to Sing* mode of politically acute, honest-to-god protest songs: "I'm Going to Say It Now," a rant against the constrictive authority of college administrators, and "Bracero," an exposé of the migrant farm worker's plight, so damned earnest he'll try to rhyme "berries" with "bellies."

But it's in the intro to "Ringing of Revolution" that the always acerbic Ochs seeks to marry his talent for topical humor to a song about imminent cultural change. As he spins a description of the Hollywood blockbuster being made from the song you just fall in love with this guy for being so funny and for letting you in on the joke. Ochs' humor is given an even better airing in "Love Me, I'm a Liberal," a screed against mainstream Democrats that still stings, even if some of the references are obscured by the mists of time (you'll get the Sammy Davis, Jr. joke, but Les Crane is probably best forgotten).

Finally, though, *In Concert* introduces three songs of gentle power and indelible quality: "There But for Fortune," with which Joan Baez later had a hit; "Changes," which previews the kind of aching pop ballad he would try again with the title song to 1967's *Pleasures of the Harbor* and "When I'm Gone," a musical epitaph written by a young man who could look far enough into the future to realize that if he was ever going to change the world, there was no time to lose. (Ken Rudman)

OLD 97S

Too Far To Care   (Elektra, 1997)

The opening notes of "Timebomb," the first track on *Too Far to Care*, come off Ken Bethea's electric guitar like some burning call to action, and as the rest of the band comes in, pushing the song into high gear, you realize that's exactly what they were. "Timebomb" is a relentlessly catchy tune with something for everyone: the pogo-stick beat of punk, a chord progression that wouldn't be out of place at the Grand Old Opry and lyrics that match the urgency of the sound with the urgency of desire. If alternative country had ever fulfilled its crossover promise it would've been here, with this brash major label debut.

Alt-country's curse is ironic hipster detachment, but the Old 97s are geeky enough to embrace their source material wholeheartedly and their own songs are suffused with raggedly felt raw emotion. Rhett Miller's lyrics are well crafted but always ingeniously honest, whether he's singing about heartbreak, new love, or even the weariness of constant touring ("Nightclub").

The album's central emotion isn't weariness, but urgency: the pull of the open road, the push to discover if a romance will last, the drunken need for a one-night stand you realize is a bad idea even as it's happening. *Too Far to Care*, despite its title, is a live wire; it cares desperately, and it makes you care as well. The album ends with another explosion: "Four Leaf Clover," a duet that has Miller trading lines about a desperate and unrequited love with Exene Cervenka. An embrace of where they're from and a propulsive leap forward, the song practically jumps off the disc at you. The Old 97s themselves later moved towards a more pop-inflected sound, but this disc is the perfect raucous reminder of why people thought alt-country could be the next big thing in the first place. (Michele Tepper)

THE ONLY ONES

Even Serpents Shine   (CBS, 1979)

Being too charismatic, too good, too "rock" and too literate would all compound to impair the Only Ones as they ultimately faded behind the boring pub-pop and tardy, single-minded punk that highway-robbed the era. The complexity, the romanticizing of bad love and bad drugs, the drummer from

Spooky Tooth … like most of the entries in this book, the artist didn't make enough sense.

This watershed album would jump-start indifference by failing to produce a follow-up to the debut's magnificent "Another Girl, Another Planet." Typically the "darker, mature second album," *Serpents* set the Only Ones closer to a British take on Television than to the common and lazy power-pop classification. Fodder for that parallel is that *Serpents* is what *Adventure* could have been instead of the P.O.S. it was. The cover art is a brushed blotter of red, black and gold that hinted at the shadow of a serpent, with, interestingly, no picture of the band.

There are a handful of songs on *Even Serpents Shine*, namely "Programme" and "No Solution" (though the latter contains the word "fucking"), that might have been engineered as the next "Another Girl." Yep, that could have happened. And "Miles from Nowhere" must be groveled over for a sec: the false ending opening up the middle instro that climaxes with ninefold the bile of the first section—welcome to the reason that superlatives clutter up music writing. Discarded and stepped on, *Even Serpents Shine* unquestionably scarred the post–*Sorry Ma* career trajectory of the Replacements (and many other eighties punk 'n' roll barflies) along its own path to obscurity. In that sense, it helped make (what everyone *else* thought helped make) what's hot. (Andrew Earles)

YOKO ONO

Plastic Ono Band (Apple, 1970)

When I was twelve I discovered the local used record store's 25¢ bin. I'd heard that John Lennon's first solo LP was great, and when I saw what looked like a copy in the racks, I snapped it up. It wasn't until I got home that I realized my error—I had purchased the almost identically covered solo debut of *Mrs.* Lennon—the widely disparaged Yoko Ono.

Though I was initially put off by the extended vocal techniques and un-songlike compositions, there were no returns on the bargain bin. So I listened to it, again and again. The first minute still strikes me as one of the most exciting rock album openings—the swipe of a tape starting up in mid-jam to a strangely jaunty two-step from Ringo and bassist Klaus Voormann, over which Lennon coaxes an ominous cascade of elephant cries from his guitar, which become increasingly fragmentary and rhythmic until they almost imperceptibly mutate into Yoko's trademark caterwaul, wailing the title word "Why?" over and over in various shades from the battle-cry of a bird of prey to a demonic larynx-rattling chortle. Lennon's playing is equally inventive—ranging from slivers of rock guitar quotation to piping feedback mimicry. The whole careening mechanism rattles on ominously for five more minutes, and then stops dead, trailing a few puffs of noise and studio chatter.

While the rest of the album didn't pack quite the wallop of "Why," several tracks come close, like "Greenfield Morning" with its looping electronic drone, slippery non-Western vocal harmonies, and chorus of birdsongs forging the link between my interests in musique concrete and early industrial bands like Cabaret Voltaire before I even knew they existed.

In spite of decades of hindsight and concerted efforts at spin control and remarketing, Ono's music still labors under the reputation of unlistenable self-indulgence that had more to do with her husband's job than anything she laid down. Ono's solo debut was nevertheless a depth-charge primer of audio experimentalism for many—myself included. (Doug Harvey)

ORCHESTRAL MANOEUVRES IN THE DARK
Dazzle Ships   **(Virgin, 1983)**

Dazzle Ships is a mind-blowing, discordantly moving, highly developed sonic abstraction. It's a progressive combination of chords, toys, samples, hand claps, melodies, typewriters, emulators, vocals, synthesizers, sound effects, sequencers, shortwave radio, tones, guitars, and percussion blended to produce angst-ridden ballads or bouncy dance songs. On this record, OMD obsesses about computer science, the politics of the Cold War era and maritime adventure around the world. Despite all this, *Dazzle Ships* was not only underrated and unappreciated in the U.K. upon release, but completely misunderstood and ignored in the States. Sadly, founding member Andy McCluskey was even quoted as saying, "We don't make fillers, just interesting failures."

How can an ensemble of experimental composers and musicians like Orchestral Manoeuvres in the Dark be remembered merely as a new wave novelty act instead of celebrated for their courage to pioneer and push the boundaries of electro-acoustic music in the synth-pop genre? After a string of hit singles in the U.K., their cryptic, creepy, romantic 1981 album, *Architecture & Morality*, had surprising sales success. For some bizarro reason, the follow-up release was just way too heavy, dark, psychedelic and ahead of its time for the teen scene, and too much too soon for the art rock experimental scene of the day.

What a shame! This isn't just music, folks, this is a gripping, timeless audio experience that should be an inspiration for everyone. (Kelly Kuvo)

THE ORGONE BOX

The Orgone Box (Minus Zero U.K., 2001)

Too many bedroom bands drink at the trough of *Evolution* and *Revolver*, fire up the old four-track, and seek to replicate the same, with results typically stiff, unconvincing and a trifle embarrassing. But not this time. Rick Corcoran is the real thing: a massively skilled sixties-influenced songwriter who doesn't need to ape his masters—his own ideas are that good. Corcoran's response to the retro question? "I'm not into memorabilia/I've got a psychedelic mind/Whatever" (which aside comes wrapped in a riff that could be convincingly sold as a lost George Harrison demo circa 1967).

Playing nearly all the instruments, Corcoran creates a gorgeous wall of bittersweet harmonies, heartbeat drums and phased guitars propelling honey-drenched melodies. The lyrics are clever abstractions, shielding emotions that, while guarded in the English fashion, threaten to erupt all over the shop. And ooo, what lovely hooks!

As Orange, Corcoran released the "Judy over the Rainbow" single in 1994, generated lively buzz in the U.K. press, then vanished back into his bedroom. Space does not permit us to explore the impulses that could lead one to make such appealing music, then willfully withhold it from public hearing. These marvelous sounds were barely released in Japan in 1996, and reissued by a London record shop five years later, to rapturous response in the pop zines but little attention elsewhere. A "follow-up" Orgone Box album comprised early nineties material, and it's unclear when or if we'll be permitted to hear newer work. But I'm not complaining. This album is such delicious pop-edelia, its maker can be forgiven anything. (Kim Cooper)

P

DOLLY PARTON
Hello I'm Dolly   **(Monument, 1967)**

This is a wonderful, charming "debut" album—Dolly previously recorded rockabilly sides as a child and a budget-bin Kitty Wells soundalike LP—that introduced America to one of the most dynamic, talented women in pop music history. The lead track, "Dumb Blonde," was a minor hit, and though Dolly didn't write it, it's a perfect song for her and really sets the tone of this album. As she declares, "Just because I'm blonde don't mean I'm dumb, and this dumb blonde ain't nobody's fool," she establishes herself as a growling ass-kicking country diva along the lines of Wanda Jackson. She's not standing by her man, she's stepping up to him (and to rivals for his affection), and stomping! She declares in "I Don't Wanna Throw Rice" that she'd rather "throw rocks" at the girl marrying her love, and lists other graphic tortures she's contemplating. Most of the tunes are written by Dolly and her uncle Bill Owens, and the songwriting is superb. The C&W punnery/wordplay on "Something Fishy" about a husband's alleged fishing trips ("I guess some large mouth bass left that lipstick on your shirt") and the overall craftsmanship of the catchy, powerful tunes is classic C&W, yet hints at something new going on: a youthful understanding of the world beyond the Opry. The material on this fantastic LP, coupled with her fresh-faced beauty which the cover art showcases (Dolly's hair looks downright natural!), make it no surprise that she soon caught the ears and eyes of Porter Wagoner and RCA. (Jake Austen)

THE PARTRIDGE FAMILY

Sound Magazine **(Bell, 1971)**

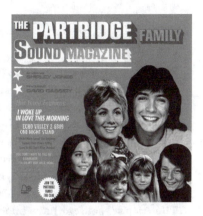

Since you've tried everything else, why not a fierce, impeccable pop concept album about jism pressure?

Released just before *The Partridge Family*'s second season left the egg, *Sound Magazine*, like predecessors *The Partridge Family Album* and *Up to Date* was produced by Wes Farrell, written by songwriters then resident in popdom's upper ether (Rupert Holmes, Bobby Hart, Tony Romeo) performed by L.A. session wizards like Hal Blaine (drums) and Michael Melvoin (keys), backup sung by the Love Generation and, not quite incidentally, vocalized by TV mom Shirley Jones and her brilliantly lovelorn son, David Cassidy. Here, then, is *product*—that base, yet tasty, ore upon which the record industry built its fortunes. Presold to a gigantic preteen audience, there is no conventional rock critic excuse at all for this album's emotional sweep and delicacy. So much the worse for convention and rock criticism.

Cassidy's excuse is ambition. On previous outings, Farrell sped up David's voice to make the star (then in his late teens) sound adolescent. The effect was that of a constipated chipmunk fleeing a series of catgut holocausts. The son of Broadway dynamo Jack Cassidy and step-son of Hollywood musical-comedy star Shirley Jones, David fit poorly the then-emerging model of instant pop star, since *nothing* was above his station, and he had every expectation of a long career once the TV show closed. A song cycle about star isolation and busted love affairs was a rare perfect fit of commerce and art.

Finally, there's the scarcely believable, yet unmistakable intent that post-Beatles preteens might respond to a sophisticated, cleverly wrought whole. The beautiful boy's sore heart, expressed with magnificent brio in "Rainmaker," "One Night Stand," and "I Woke up in Love This Morning" provided kids with tantalizing glimpses of adult miseries they couldn't wait to have for their very own. (Ron Garmon) (See also: David Cassidy)

PATTO

Roll 'Em Smoke 'Em Put Another Line Out   (Island, 1972)

Patto's third album is something different, Not different than their last release, *Hold Your Fire,* which is fairly similar stylistically, but very distinctive indeed in comparison with the general run of present-day musical product. Songs like "Singing the Blues On Reds" and "I Got Rhythm" are unique; seldom have such bizarre musical/lyrical creations seen the vinyl light (in the case of tracks like "Mummy" and the bulk of "Cap'n and The Atto's," seldom have such thoroughly unlistenable nonmusical creations blighted the vinyl scene, but you can skip those after maybe one audition).

Wondrous and mystifying aural delights abound within the rest of the LP; you'll find weird rhythms apparently equally derivative of James Brown and Captain Beefheart plus some heavy rock and a bit of jazz thrown in for good measure. There are frequent interludes of the most aggravating instrumental doodling, as well as recurrent flashes of offbeat but dazzling guitar and keyboard wizardry (by Olly Halsall). Lyrically the standout tracks are probably the presumably autobiographical "Singing the Blues On Reds" (by title alone an instant classic) and the ominously deadpan "I Got Rhythm." From a musical standpoint I'd nominate the crypto-heavy metal "Loud Green Song"; "Flat-Footed Woman," with its wheezing Mott the Hoople organ flourishes, neat background vocals, and coruscating pianistics; and the amazing "Turn Turtle," a complex commentary on sexual frigidity which actually possesses a poignant melody and positively ethereal harmonies (at times most reminiscent of B. Bumble and The Stingers with vocals).

And there's much more as yet unplumbed, I expect to be bemusedly deciphering this album for the next dozen listenings (which may take a year or more, 'cause you've got to be careful you don't overplay this stuff for fear of irrevocable damage to the anterior lobe regions). Patto's come a long way since they covered The 4 Seasons' "Beggin' " in their Timebox days, and you could do worse than check out what they're up to. You won't be indifferent, that's for sure.

(Ken Barnes, *Fusion*, February 1973)

PENTANGLE
Solomon's Seal   (Reprise, 1972)

Of the albums that have been rereleased on CD from this essential British traditional folk group, it's a sin that my very favorite is only available as an
import. Featuring the two pre-eminent guitarists from the sixties London café
scene, John Renbourn and Burt Jansch, Pentangle's intersecting guitar parts
predated postpunk by twenty years. Drummer Terry Cox was jazzy, creative,
and unpredictable, shifting from Moondog to Mingus mid-stroke—but never
prog-y in the overindulgent sense. Pentangle was also the permanent residence
of bassist Danny Thompson, whose muted but rhythmic upright tones should
be well known to fans of Nick Drake's *Bryter Later,* the Incredible String
Band's *5000 Spirits or Layers of the Onion* and John Martyn's *Solid Air* (just a
few of the classic albums he was called upon to help define). That's Pentangle
in a nutshell. If anything though, this album belongs to group songbird Jaqui
McShee, whose intimate still-life reading of the medieval ballad "Willy
O'Winsbury" feels like a child's walk into a cathedral in the middle of the
night, complete with dimly lit rosaries, bleeding statues, and the deep smell of
wooden pews and earthy pillars. McShee and Jansch deliver a brilliant harmony vocal on the magnificent "People on the Highway." The acoustic
blues/folk sophistication of "Jump Baby Jump" is equally satisfying. Note: the
top half of the LP is loaded with much of the serious and sour feudal folk that
mars their early (and highly acclaimed LPs), but the mid-album payload is
their finest hour. Glorious! (Jonathan Donaldson)

PERE UBU
New Picnic Time   (Chrysalis, 1979)

This is one of the scariest albums ever made. Pere Ubu had made scary
albums before, including at least two of the best records of the seventies, *The
Modern Dance* and *Dub Housing,* but those were *before*: before the seesawing
fortunes of the band, before the religious conversion of lead singer David
Thomas, before the political darkness occurring nationally in 1979–1980.
The Pere Ubu aesthetic, at least during the relatively stable period of
1977–1979, was about a tug-of-war between the garage rock grooves of the
rhythm section (Tony Maimone and Scott Krauss and guitarist Tom

Herman), and the keening spirals of synthesizer player Allen Ravenstine and the vocals of Thomas, whose warbling tenor sounds more like a jazz balladeer or Broadway crooner than it does a conventional rock singer.

Here, Thomas and Ravenstine prevail in the aesthetic tussle, and so the album's flavor, when compared to the earlier hits like "Final Solution" and "Non-Alignment Pact," and notwithstanding a couple of great rock songs like "The Fabulous Sequel" and "Small Was Fast," is frankly experimental, with the emphasis on sprung rhythms driven not by drums but by synthesizer swoops or morsels of bass or piano. When this inclination toward experiment is combined with the apocalyptic, millenarian lyrical imagery of "Kingdom Come," "A Small Dark Cloud," or "All the Dogs Are Barking," ("There's a fly in the ointment!" Thomas remarks ominously on "A Small Dark Cloud," before giving way to a shrieked "Don't rock the boat!" with such desperation that you suddenly know well the cost if you *do*), the result is a picture window that looks out on vast expanses of anxiety, confusion, disturbance and eschatological dread. Things seem to be winding down, coming to a dark end, on every song here. Every positive assertion ("Ya gotta have happiness!") is matched by some brooding, doom-laden droning. Even people who like Pere Ubu are justifiably terrified of this recording. With good reason. It even drove the band into hiatus. So why listen to one of the scariest records ever made? Well, because melancholia and dread demand explication. Few have used the popular song as fearlessly to do so. This is a record of true worry from a time that offered many good reasons for worry. Amazing, when you consider that Chrysalis released *Parallel Lines* by Blondie at virtually the same instant. (Rick Moody)

LINDA PERHACS
Parallelograms   (Kapp, 1970)

Linda Perhacs was a Beverly Hills dentist's assistant with a secret life. Strange, potent music flowed through her like a swift-moving stream. In childhood, her creative efforts were stunted. As a young woman, surrounded by the energies of late-sixties Los Angeles and a circle of turned-on friends, the music refused to be denied. Among Perhacs' patients was film composer Leonard Rosenman, who asked to hear her songs. The homemade tapes so impressed Rosenman that he secured an album contract, called his favorite session players (including Shelly Manne and Milt Holland), and commenced the yearlong recording of *Parallelograms.*

Perhacs' songs are delicately layered love poems to the natural world and the charged erotics of youth, smarter and more ambitious than her hippie goddess reputation suggests. The arrangements, by Perhacs, Rosenman and guitarist Steve Cohn, are prismatic three-dimensional wave forms enfolding folk-rock germs, while Perhacs' multitracked vocals entwine into other-worldly harmonies.

The gorgeous title track is an astonishing whirl of minimal, mathematical imagery with an eerie backwards-masked central passage that might represent a journey deep into the subcellular world of numbers. On "Chimacum Rain," Perhacs intones "I'm spacing out/I'm seeing silences between leaves" before admitting that the man who lured her to the place of green moss and water belongs there and can't be possessed. "Paper Mountain Man" is a satirical blues-rock portrait of another sort of inaccessible male, an arrogant canyon king, "half raccoon and half horse trader," with a dozen women on his string. "Porcelain Baked Cast Iron Wedding" skewers rich girls and their fancy rituals, so removed from the real raw stuff of love. *Parallelograms* is an extraordinary record, powerful, delicate and repeatedly rewarding.

Kapp's vinyl pressing was nearly as poor as their promotion; Linda Perhacs never again recorded, and the album became a pricey collectable. Anyone remotely interested in psychedelia and the feminine mind is directed to The Wild Place's 2003 reissue with its superior mix taken from the artist's own tapes. (Kim Cooper)

JOHN PHILLIPS
John, the Wolf King of L.A.   **(Dunhill, 1970)**

Papa John's first solo record is a dizzyingly satisfying artifact of pure song-writing, recording mastery, and the dire after-effects of fame. It makes something jaunty of a miscarriage in the basement and something glum and listless out of lying on the beach in Malibu, waiting for your drug connection. This exemplar of the Hollywood empyrean chooses—maybe out of boredom, maybe because deep down Papa John always felt like a street junkie—to get himself earthy with a sound by superstar studio pros that's canyon pop country at its most languid and lovely, but never, never sweet. This is a record of remarkable sourness for a man who had as many of his California dreams come true as John Phillips.

Michelle once lamented that the Mamas & Papas didn't get to sing on *Wolf King*. It contained, she wisely recognized, some of John's strongest, toughest songs. Still, tough luck, Michelle: the band's sweetness could only have marred this piquant record. Out of print almost forever, for an artist as pop as John its failure meant it barely existed, or maybe shouldn't have. It earns about three sentences in his bazillion-page autobiography.

This is doubly strange, because of all the work John released in his life, *Wolf King* comes closest (even in its front and back cover, which shows sweet, handsome Papa reduced to a lurching, hideous beach bum in the truest sense) to the tales of druggy desperation and degradation that dominate his best-selling self-flagellation. "Those junkie bums are gonna steal your Blackburn drums," his distant, quiet tenor warns; but still, "keep it in mind/for some other time/Malibu people really know how to live." You'd have to listen to this whole record—and after the first delicious pedal steel strains of the classic opener, "April Anne," which maintains a brilliantly consistent A-A-A-A rhyme scheme without seeming strained or silly, you'll definitely want to—to understand the depth and strength of the irony in that. (Brian Doherty)

PINK FLOYD
The Final Cut (Columbia, 1983)

One might think it inappropriate to describe an album by a band with as huge a footprint as Pink Floyd's as unduly neglected. Yes, this dour, haunting album dominated rock radio when it came out and was declared a five-star classic right out of the box by *Rolling Stone*. Still, you never hear it on the radio anymore, and the "official" Floyd has tried to effectively eliminate it from their discography (though it remains in print) since erstwhile leader Roger Waters is very much its sole auteur. (It's identified in the liners as being "by Roger Waters, performed by Pink Floyd.") Guitarist David Gilmour, keeper of the Floyd crown, writes it off as mere rejects from their previous blockbuster opus *The Wall*.

But by being less ambitious and grandiose than that bloated classic, *Final Cut* deepens and purifies its obsession: Waters' hate, rage, and contempt for the politicians who send men (like his father, killed in WWII) off to die for reasons of state. It's a well-written, delicate and forceful record, painful and detailed and taking deep pain deeply seriously. But the largely static music and an abundance of Floyd's classic new-stereo-system-testing sound effects work their understated, sad magic as well. It's for late nights with headphones, sinking into a hoped-for world where "maniacs don't blow holes in bandsmen by remote control" and remembrances of soldiers returning from war "in '45/and no one spoke and no one smiled/there were too many spaces in the line." Waters' unrelenting moral dudgeon bordering on madness is exhilarating; he imagines in "The Fletcher Memorial Home" gathering various war mongering world leaders, and asking them "is everyone in? Are you having a nice time? Now the final solution can be applied." If it hadn't come from someone leading what might have been the most famous and successful rock band in the world at the time, this would doubtless be embraced as a maniacal classic by hip cognoscenti. (Brian Doherty)

PLUSH

Fed (After Hours, Japan, 2002)

Aside from the Great American Novel, there is no shibboleth that haunts our culture like the Lost Pop Masterpiece. If only Brian had finished *Smile*, we say, forgetting it's the mosaic nature of that kind of project that prompts us to chase the ghost. The imagined greatness of *Smile* necessarily exceeds any attainable kind of greatness. Liam "Plush" Hayes's *Fed* is another record laboring under the delusion that more is more, and more-than-that is really more. Orchestras, glockenspiels, xylophones, and God only knows what else labor mightily to construct a sound without bottom, that Phil and Brian might emerge from their respective catatonias to walk the earth again.

Initially, one wonders who forgot the tunes? Hayes's previous efforts (a fab single and so-so album) suggested he had a knack for them, but here his wibbly voice seems to disappear under the weight of the instrumentation; the magniloquent opening track gives way to show-tune stabs-of-brass on "I've Changed My Number," and you think the jig is up. Chalk one up for hubris. But what emerges, on repeat listening, is a fastidious (indeed, of course, insanely so) arranger working out a battle between delicacy and bombast. "My creation has drowned me," Hayes tellingly yelps on "Whose Blues," while the limpid "So Blind" repeats its title phrase in a way that makes it sound otherwise: sublime. If Hayes is a genius, and he may not be, he is one whose gift reveals itself, subtly and slowly, as anguishingly personal. Which may seem self-evident—what other kind of creativity is there?—until we remember the number of pasticheurs and twee pretenders who've made a career of such. From narrow-niche practitioners like the High Llamas to knob-twiddling avatars like Mirwais, it's one thing to imitate brilliance and quite another to attain it. What makes Hayes worth hearing is the on-record struggle with his own limitations, the stroke of genuine, humble doubt—the very thing that crippled his heroes—authenticating the result after all. (Matthew Specktor)

POCO
Rose of Cimarron   **(ABC, 1976)**

Far more vibrant than the Eagles, Poco here combines the audio cinematic grandeur of "Rose of Cimarron" (later covered by Emmylou Harris) with what can now be honorably called bubblegum country-rock numbers sung by Timothy B. Schmidt ("Stealaway," "Starin' at the Sky," "Just Like Me"). Schmidt had previously been with the Glad and played with the New Breed of "Green Eyed Woman" fame. When Richie Furay left Poco in 1973, Schmidt and pedal steel guitarist Rusty Young filled the creative void. The compressed pop of Schmidt's David Cassidy–like vocal tracks was chock full of both bubblegum's and country-rock's most important element: close, warm, rising and tight harmonies. Drummer George Grantham filled out the mix with a high part similar to the Graham Nash role in the Hollies.

What Poco achieved was a bouncy backbeat reminiscent of the Turtles or early Buffalo Springfield. Bluegrass numbers come off with the same kind of rock 'n' roll fun and abandon associated with early Beach Boys singles. Oddly, Schmidt's bubblegum melodicism was couched in that old Buffalo Springfield role played by Neil Young, the soft-toned melodic "Indian" of the group, while lead guitarist Paul Cotton filled the role of the rugged, low-voiced Stephen Stills "Cowboy." Cotton's "Too Many Nights Too Long" (with its middle eight sung in Spanish) portrays a man running from the law and hiding out in Mexico. "Tulsa Turnaround" is a closing Western instrumental with Cotton imposing a few vocal lines out of nowhere.

Rose of Cimarron feels off the cuff, but in fact is some of the most finely arranged pop of the 1970s. It joins *Pickin' up the Pieces, Crazy Eyes*, and *Cantamos* in a series of four neglected Poco masterworks. (Domenic Priore)

MICHEL POLNAREFF
Michel Polnareff   **(Atlantic, 1974)**

Michel Polnareff could have been one of the few sixties French artists to break through in America. Like Françoise Hardy, he was on the Kapp/Four Corner label, and Jimmy Page even played on Polnareff's European hits. But despite lyrics by Keith Reid of Procol Harum, the English-language market remained indifferent to the ex-beatnik's songwriting genius.

In France before 1968, pop culture was not taken seriously by the Gaullist squares. After 1968, it was the radicals' turn to look suspiciously upon anything that sounded entertaining and pop-influenced; they despised it as bourgeois and decadent. With his unique brand of psychedelic, folky, baroque, almost bubblegumesque pop, Michel Polnareff sounded nothing like the local showbiz trade nor the underground. In 1972, Polnareff faced the moral majority after pasting his feces on the walls of Paris, and the following year income tax agents persecuted the maverick composer into polnadepression.

To rise from these depths, Polnareff reinvented himself. Exit his Françoise Sagan-meets-Brian Jones look and in comes a peroxide poodle on steroids (topped with Elton John shades). Polnareff moved to L.A. and signed with Atlantic. He really believed the fame and professional acclaim he deserved would happen. In a frenzy of optimism, the young Jean-Claude Vannier (the arranger of Gainsbourg's *Melody Nelson*) was chosen to help the maestro. But quickly an ego clash broke out between these two, an omen of the record's expensive commercial failure.

What a shame! This ambitious record is unique, the work of a French guy trying to top Todd Rundgren with layers of baroque and continental weirdness. Almost too close to the edge of kitsch, this LP is the last spark of polnagreatness. After this, Polnareff would bury himself in egomaniacal self-destruction and terrible overproduced Californian FM rock crapola (like his awful *Lipstick* soundtrack from the 1976 rapesploitation flick with Margeux Hemingway). Nobody cares anymore about Polnareff, except hardcore Japanese fans. (Jean-Emmanuel Deluxe)

POSTER CHILDREN
Junior Citizen   (Sire/Warner, 1995)

At this writing, the Champaign, Illinois–based Poster Children have been together for sixteen years. *Junior Citizen* falls at the midpoint of the band's career: the fourth of seven albums, it sounds like a breakthrough. Instead, the band had one follow-up on Warner before being dropped. The Poster Children are still going strong, though, and there's justice in that.

What's most unjust about the trajectory of their career is that *Junior Citizen* didn't make a huge critical and commercial splash. Lost in the glut of post-grunge guitar outfits, the Poster Children built their wall of sound not on sneers and controversy but on an assertive sense of melody and straight-forward (if occasionally buried) lyrics. Arguably their best album, *Junior Citizen* plays like the soundtrack to the coolest anime flick never made. The credits flash to the wake-up call of "Get a Life," which segues into the call-to-arms title track, exhorting the listener to join the fight against "the empire of the bored." There's a paean to the heroic virtues of *Baywatch* star David Hasselhoff ("He's My Star"), then the mosh-anthem of "Revolution Year Zero" with its locomotive guitar and ghostly ululations.

"Drug I Need" backs the love-story montage, cutting the tempo but los-ing little of the guitar, while "New Boyfriend" introduces the romantic com-plication, strutting chords capturing perfectly the arrogance of the interloper. Then, just as the prepubescents are getting restless, "Wide Awake" transi-tions back into the action, followed by the fight song "King for a Day." There's a wry piece for the leader of Megadeth ("Mustaine"), and then "Downwind" accompanies the final battle. The film—okay, the album—closes with the moody and tragic "One of Us," and while some might wish for a happier ending, that seems to be the lot of the Poster Children. Still sol-diering on in the indie wilds, fighting the good fight. Listening to this album will make you want to join up. (David J. Schwartz)

THE POTATOMEN

Now **(Lookout, 1995)**

Released during Lookout Records' heyday, this chiming, jangly, and deceptively simple album got lost among the label's bouncy punk-pop. Starting as an acoustic sideshow in the parking lot of an all-ages spot, the Potatomen were quickly cast off to the island of misfit toys for an unfashionable sound that gallantly reached back and pushed forward. From the past, they rounded up the story-song tradition of Johnny Horton and

ELVIS PRESLEY
Elvis Sings the Wonderful World of Christmas (RCA, 1971)

And a merry fuckin' Xmas greeting to you and yours, whether
early, belated or otherwise. And a merry fuckin' etc. to you too
Elvis wherever the fuck you are while the wife and kid do the
unwrapping under the old family tree. There's this old 78 with
an Elvis interview on it where he sez he wouldn't want his kid
to be an only child, this was 195X or something. Well his kid's
still an only child and the least Elvis coulda done was give her
a baby brother for Xmas this year, it's the least he shoulda
done. Even if he's not fucking Priscilla anymore he could've at
least jerked off in a bottle and sent it to her gift wrapped for
artificial insemination purposes. Or is his sperm too valuable
to him to waste it on conception? What's he expect Priscilla to
do, get knocked up by *immaculate* conception or something?

Well anyway time was they used to use Elvis to sell Xmas,
if Johnny Mathis could do it Elvis could do it too if not more
so. Well these days they're tryin' to use Xmas to sell Elvis, his
latest bunch of albums haven't been such hot shit and the folks
who buy 'em would probably just as soon buy a 69–center like
Moldivar Sanchez Plays the Sacred Season on Camden. This
one could have been on Camden but they don't cost enough.
Jesus, just *imagine* usin' the name of God's offspring to make a
fucking profit!

Yeah you'd think so but then the pious sounds of "Come All
Ye Faithful" come wafting thru the speakers and there's good
will to men all over the living room. Bing Crosby never did it
better, in fact Bing Crosby was *shit*. His whole rep with the
20th century is based on Xmas shit anyway, "White Christmas"
to be exact, so he's just a seasonal hack and nothing but.
Elvis's rep's got a little more meat attached to it but it's too bad
he ain't cyclical himself, he could do with a little upsurge in
relevance but for the time being "The First Noel" will have to
do. But what's it do? It doesn't even put him back in the Tupelo
hall of fame but even the whole goddam New Testament could-
n't do that, not if it was as Euro-pee-an as "First Noel."

continued

But then there's the freshness of "Winter Wonderland," that tough mother of a gem that's been recorded more times than "Stardust" or "St. James Infirmary" and the best version is still Johnny Mathis'. Wait a minute, no, I'm thinking of "Sleigh Bells" or "Sleigh Ride" or whatever it is and that's not even on the album. Come to think of it this album *stinks*. And they better stop trying to sell Xmas so early in the year from now on. They used to get the campaign going the week after Thanksgiving, now they start cranking the whole thing up two weeks before Halloween. Polaroid Copy Service has even started pushing Xmas cards in August. Spiritual Xmas died a hell of a long time ago, no way of reviving that worthless corpse nohow. Anyway commercial Xmas is a gas, better than the original holiday ever could've been. But it's gonna have to be safeguarded or pretty soon it too's gonna be headed down the drain. So next year (people at RCA are you listening?) no Elvis yuletide disc until the first or second week of December (and that means review copies too), okay?

(Richard Meltzer, *Creem*, January 1972)

Marty Robbins, the tragedy of Hank Williams, and the pop sensibilities of Buddy Holly. To the ranch shirt past, they added the stripped-down naivete of the C86 movement, and then hooked their Telecaster and Gretsch guitars to jaunty punk-pop.

The overall result had them sounding closer to the Housemartins than the oft-compared Smiths, though Lawrence Livermore's resonant vocals and phrasing recall *Watertown*-era Sinatra and Del Shannon. "Won't You Be" chimes in with giddy anticipation, and by "That Girl" the possibilities have become actualities and unbounded joy because "Tonight She Wants to See Me." "BART Song" provides a click-clack update of "Downtown" from a male POV—promise opening up as the train approaches the spanning skyscrapers in "Summer in the City." Everything comes at a cost, though, and *Now* also documents the grinding old route in "Sam's Song" with the dispirited lyric: "The whistle blows down at the mill/another shift's begun/The workers stumble to their jobs their dreams already done."

These catchy city and western songs resonate because they're rooted in specifics like a page ripped out of *Cometbus* and offered up to the universal. Livermore's personality radiates through these songs, bringing a much needed heartland beat to the leftland. Moreover, he knows how to deliver complex emotions in a straightforward yet poetic way. The rejected and wounded protagonist in "Now" is on the far side of where he started, the curtain is already down, and life slogs along. This may be the oldest story in song, but *Now* declares it's all worth it for those elusive "moments in the sun." (Ted Liebler)

PRINCE AND THE NEW POWER GENERATION

(Warner Brothers, 1992)

On its release, the pundits noticed that this record was pretty hot shit. But history has not been kind, and his biographers have relegated it to part of his supposedly disappointing slow creative collapse. Some mark Prince's alleged fall as beginning with 1988's *Lovesexy* (such people are so misguided one can do nothing but shake one's head and make sure they are seated at the other end of the table at dinner parties), others somewhere among *Batman*, *Graffiti Bridge*, and *Diamonds and Pearls*. But as the nineties wore on, it's widely agreed, Prince became memorable solely for peculiarities and peccadilloes such as changing his name to this record's titular symbol, casting Kirstie Alley as "the nosy reporter" in the disjointed and irrelevant "plot" that theoretically unites ♀'s potpourri of musical riches, and later publicly declaring himself a "slave" to his contractual partners at Warner Bros.

That may be all people talk about, but that's because people can be dumb. One forgets or ignores the shockingly wide and wonderful range of beauty and funk that this album represents at the peril of one's own soul and ass. It is at the same time purely gorgeous and complicated, but also purely pop. One of its loveliest and strangest tracks, "7," was one of the singles. Prince has never been funkier than "Sexy MF," never power-balladed as yearningly and prettily as on "The Morning Papers," never been gorgeously weirder than on "Love 2 the 9s." All the way through its double LP length he and his band sing and play with endless enthusiasm on compositions of

Psychedelic Soul

Funkadelic, *Maggot Brain*: The very definition of the phrase "dropping the bomb." "Super Stupid" is the mother of all funk-metal, an inner-city apocalypse complete in three minutes.

Eddie Hazel, *Games, Dames & Guitar Things*: Maggot Brain's illogical-progression. Kicks off with a heavy-ass version of "California Dreaming," peaks with a heavier-ass one of "I Want You (She's So Heavy)."

Baby Huey and The Babysitters: Three-hundred-pound Huey lived just long enough to record a scattering of crush-rock grooves before dropping of a heart attack. Dig that ten-minute version of "A Change Is Gonna Come," replete with let's-have-a-tab monologue.

Muddy Waters, *Electric Mud*: Muddy was subsequently embarrassed by the record that included a harpsichord-embellished cover of "Let's Spend the Night Together." Not to mention enough wah-wah to give Ron Asheton a run for his money. If that doesn't sound good to you, you're reading the wrong column.

James "Blood" Ulmer, *Blackrock*: Exactly what the title implies: the harmelodic jazz guitarist plugs in and wails. Equal parts Jimi, Bootsy, and Ornette.

Shuggie Otis, *Freedom Flight*: Less reticent than the subsequent "Inspiration Information," Shuggie's second record contains the majestic space-rock title track: twelve minutes of liquid electric grace.

The Isley Brothers, *Givin' It Back*: No strangers to giving a good freaking to, erm, more AOR-style material, here Ron, Ernie, and Reg put paid to James Taylor, Stephen Stills, and others. Includes their kick-ass medley of "Ohio" and Jimi's "Machine Gun."

Cymande, *The Soul of Rasta*: Bafflingly titled compilation of this great London funk outfit, with nary a dreadlock in sight. Curtis Mayfield was an obvious inspiration, as—on tracks like the eleven-minute "Dove"—were the Grateful Dead.

The Politicians Featuring McKinley Jackson: Actually, most releases on Lamont Dozier and Eddie Holland's post-Motown Invictus label would qualify. Lovely, dusted, echoey rock-soul.

continued

Various Artists, *Chains and Black Exhaust* Compilation: Best for last, arguably: a semi-legitimate compilation that appeared, mysteriously, in early 2003. No track, label, or artist information appears on the package, but these eighteen pieces of smokin' punkadelic soul are worth whatever crimes you need to commit to get 'em. Essential. (Mathew Specktor)

multileveled and multi-genred strength. True love of music and life shines through, and I strongly suspect its failure to reach *Purple Rain* levels of success was a big part of Prince's real retreat, which began right after this record. (Brian Doherty)

R

MARK RADICE

Mark Radice   **(Paramount, 1970)**

Beatles singles weren't coming out fast enough for Mark Radice, so he spent his New Jersey boyhood making up new ones as he rode his bike. Being the son of engineer Gene Radice (Hendrix, Vanilla Fudge), no one told him he couldn't do this. He graduated to making demos by age eight, culminating in this album released some time after his thirteenth birthday. Donovan gave his imprimatur and this was considered a prelude to great things.

Among great things, *Mark Radice* is indeed a rarity— a mellow, romantic series of piano pop vignettes in the manner of Elton John, but more languid and sophisticated. Arthur Lee was born to this shade of purple, Billy Joel and Rod Stewart strove for the mantle, but young Radice wears it draped like a Mozart with Napoleon's nerve. The cameos bookending the record give the spurious feel of a concept album, with "Please Don't Blow up the Ship" kicking off with an uneasy

Chiltonian lurch into muted despair. The chic horniness of "Hey, My Love" (covered by Dion on *Streetheart*), "You Knew It Too" and "Your Love Is Like Fire" are set off by character pieces like "Take Me to the Park," a geezer's reverie as minor-key melancholy worthy of Garland Jeffries at his most autumnal. Only at the finale, "Seein' Through My Pillow," does the mask crack for a hint of adolescent fear and wonder at the immensity of life (and love) to escape.

Since Radice was a mere stripling, this album was dismissed as a parlor trick. He resurfaced as a funk/disco artist later in the decade, enjoying the only chart action of his solo career in 1976 with "If You Can't Beat 'Em, Join 'Em" before hitting the road with Aerosmith (at the fervent urging of old chum Steven Tyler) and Cheap Trick. Barbara Streisand and Barry Manilow have recorded his songs. In sum, an honorable career, but far short of this handful of stardust. (Ron Garmon)

THE RAMONES
Subterranean Jungle   **(Sire, 1983)**

The Ramones' seventh album, *Subterranean Jungle* is the most underrated work in their Carbona-huffin' canon. It is the only one of the Ramones' post-seventies works that fully embraces the trash-pop, bubblegum aesthetic that made their first four albums such enduring classics; yet it was the first original Ramones album to be deleted. And its follow-up, 1984's far-less-bouncy *Too Tough to Die*, wound up being hailed (*falsely!*) as the Ramones' return to greatness.

The Ramones wanted to be a bubblegum band, a faster and louder version of the Bay City Rollers and the Ohio Express. With sixties bubblegum vets Ritchie Cordell and Glen Kolotkin producing, *Subterranean Jungle* opens with a cover of the Music Explosion's "Little Bit O' Soul." (A fab cover of the 1910 Fruitgum Company's "Indian Giver" was also recorded, but appeared as a non-LP B-side.) A seemingly incongruous cover of the Chambers Brothers' psychedelic soul touchstone "Time Has Come Today" defies expectations and simply soars. And Dee Dee Ramone's misfit themes "Outsider" and "In the Park" (the latter song inspired—go figure!—by trips to the park to cop heroin) transcend their origins and emerge as triumphant, fist-pumpin', bubblicious delights.

It's not all bubbly. While Joey yearns for "Somebody Like Me" and "My-My Kind of a Girl," Dee Dee's badass "Time Bomb" warns he's gonna kill his mom and dad, and Dee Dee and Johnny's "Psycho Therapy"—ultimately the album's best-known track—is an audio slasher flick, with a horror-film video banned by the weasels at MTV. Behind the scenes, Marky Ramone was fired from the band during the making of the album; the cover graphics show him clearly apart from the rest of the Ramones, looking out a subway window, a brudder-in-arms no longer. This was the last great Ramones album, a bubblegum punk classic, and no one seems to appreciate it. Maybe that time has come today. (Carl Cafarelli)

THE RASPBERRIES
Side Three   (Capitol, 1973)

The Raspberries' first big hits, "Go All the Way" and "I Wanna Be with You," were like gifts from heaven to my Beatles-missin' ears in 1972. Not only were the ex-Beatles themselves producing nothing but crap then (remember John and Yoko's *Some Time in New York City?* Or Wings' debut *Wild Life?* Blechhh!), but hardly anyone else was releasing anything that was worth a damn either. So hearing those Raspberries tunes blaring out of the loudspeakers at our local public swimming pool never failed to send a chill down my spine.

Unfortunately, the same could not be said for their first two LPs, the bulk of which consisted of limp-wristed ballads, or sounded like the drippy dance hall music Ray Davies always had such a weakness for. Not that those are bad

The following is an edited version of the review that ran in the

November 1972 issue of *Phonograph Record Magazine.*

RASPBERRIES
Fresh   (Capitol)

I always held that the next revitalization of pop music would be heralded by a resurgence of interest in the mid-sixties, but I couldn't have imagined a year ago that things would come so far so fast. What amazes me most is that the public is accepting it at face value, welcoming its enthusiasm and unabashed non-heaviness like the breath of fresh air it is to today's stale, inbred rock scene.

The new Raspberries album, which should've been called *Beatles '65,* is the first successful LP in what has already become a new genre. It opens with "I Wanna Be With You" which blends pure vintage Beatles with a dash of "One Fine Day" to make perhaps their most delightfully ingenious song yet. "Nobody Knows" is not the first song on this album to send me shuffling through Beatles albums looking for the song I was sure it sounded just like. Like all the rest, I couldn't find it. The hooks are placed so insidiously that you're never quite sure your memory isn't playing tricks. It's mostly the guitar riffs that gnaw at my mind. "Drivin' Around" is, of all things, a Beach Boys routine straight out of "Heroes and Villains." When it comes to synthesizing ambience, these guys are real pros. This sort of thing opens all sorts of avenues that it would be great to see Raspberries pursue in future recordings. Why limit themselves to Beatles, after all?

In fact, such a move may be to their benefit in more ways than one. I haven't seen any other reviews yet, but it's hard to believe the critics will sit still for an album as overtly derivative as this. The fact that it's simply fun to do songs like this should not be ignored, and by fooling around with other, related styles, I think Raspberries could better put across this side of their intent. If what they are trying to do can be accepted as valid in the first place, maybe then people will

continued

listen closely enough to realize that Raspberries' songs are, beyond any stylistic considerations, really quite superior by any criteria of pop songwriting, and that this album is every bit as enjoyable as the classic Beatles albums. Maybe they didn't invent the style, but their work within it has been pretty nearly equal to that of the Masters. And being as good as the Beatles is, when you think about it, quite an accomplishment. (Greg Shaw)

things per se, but none of it rocked like their singles did, and in a way that my fifteen-year-old self was craving. I wanted some *power* with my pop! Was that too much to ask for?

Eric Carmen & Co. must have read my mind, since that's exactly what they served up—and in spades—on their third release. While all nine tracks were quite melodic and featured fine harmonies, they also all had blasting guitars—Carmen's tunes in particular, which suggests that he'd been listening to a heapin' helpin' of *Who's Next* ("Ecstasy" somehow manages to be a rip off of nearly every Who song ever written). He still croons like an orgasmic loony bird all over this LP, but so long as it isn't to some power ballad I can refrain from wanting to strangle him.

Bassist Dave Smalley and drummer Jim Bonfanti lacked such restraint, apparently, and the band split in two shortly after *Side Three's* release. A real shame, since not only did the members share a pedigree that went all the way back to Cleveland's very first Brit-inspired garage bands, but they had finally combined all the best elements of that pedigree on this one great album. (Peter Bagge)

LOU REED

The Bells   (Arista, 1979)

Absolutely the greatest Lou Reed LP ever, *The Bells* features some of Lou's most inspired wordplay sung over rock 'n' roll music with occasional free jazz tendencies. There's also a hint of the German experimental rock aesthetic that permeated *Street Hassle* and Pop and Bowie's late seventies recordings. *The Bells* is, both sonically and lyrically, a *total* Lou Reed experience, unencumbered by restrictions of genre and expectations of record companies or audiences.

When Lou's voice first appears on the opening track, "Stupid Man," quivering and wheezing in what might be an amphetamine frenzy, you know you are dealing with the *real* Lou. It's followed by the twisted robot cabaret of "Disco Mystic." The tune's only words come when Lou mumbles "disco mystic" over and over as if he thinks he's just joined Kraftwerk. "I Want to Boogie with You" sounds like the Leonard Cohen LP that Phil Spector produced—a massive, chaotic, murky, and brilliant sound. "With You" features Lou's larynx waging a psychic war with Alvin and the Chipmunks. Chaplin's ghost is summoned with Art Ensemble of Chicago–style trumpets and percussion on "City Lights." "All Through the Night" sounds like Springsteen's E-Street Band produced by William Burroughs, mixed beneath tapes of random conversations and funky saxophones.

Then there's "The Bells." 9:18 of synth drone and abstract jazz tonalities evoking a dizzying Fritz Lang skyscraper view of a city. Towards the end Lou begins to sing a particularly sinister lyric about not having a parachute. It's one of his best lyrics. The song ends with what sounds like your stereo being sucked through a black hole in space. All you're left with is Lou's face staring knowingly at you from the LP jacket: an Expressionist image of a weary cabaret crooner or a disco mystic who's been up all night making 1979's most unsettling music. (Matthew Smith) (See also: John Cale, Lewis Furey)

Legendary Hearts   **(RCA, 1983)**

Subtle, unflashy, funny, exquisitely balanced, *Legendary Hearts* displays a number of Lou Reed's less celebrated but very real strengths. Like the third Velvet Underground album, it achieves its effects obliquely, sneaking up instead of screaming "I'M HERE!" When Lou left the Velvets, they were known only to a small audience. By the early eighties, their legacy turned into an 800-pound monkey on Lou's back. Good albums were invariably "his best since the Velvets;" bad albums were greeted with, "Lou's lost it; this sure ain't the VU."

Was *Legendary Hearts* Lou's answer to the crushing expectations? "I can't live up to this/I'm good for just a kiss/Not legendary love." Okay, Lou, let's not fight and lose another night of legendary … uh, listening. *Legendary Hearts* displays quintessential Lou mixtures of awkward and fluid, high and low language like "Romeo, oh Romeo, wherefore art thou Romeo?/He's in a car, or at a bar/Or churning his blood with an impure drug/He's in the past and seemingly lost forever."

Twenty years later *Legendary Hearts* should be the legend, not an album that failed to live up to it. *Legendary Hearts* deserves better. It should be remembered because two of rock's great guitarists, Lou Reed and Robert Quine, were on the top of their game, soloing rarely but playing off each other impeccably, always finding the perfect setting for the material. It should be remembered because bassist Fernando Saunders still manages to steal the spotlight on nearly every song. Because Lou's songs are consistently excellent, Side 1's Comedy triptych ("Don't Talk to Me About Work," "Make up My Mind," "Martial Law") as strong as Side 2's "Bottoming Out" trilogy ("Betrayed," "Bottoming Out," "Home of the Brave"). Because the band is as strong as the material and (like the songs) just as adept at tickling our funny bones as gut-punching us, sometimes in the same song. Listen to *Legendary Hearts* because Lou is one of the greats and this is one of his best. (Joe Boucher) (See also: John Cale, Lewis Furey)

NINO REJNA AND HIS HAWAIAN [SIC] GUITARS
Nino Rejna and His Hawaian [sic] Guitars   (Kappa, Italy, no date)

Nino Rejna and His Hawaian [sic] Guitars is one of the most mysterious Hawaiian records I own. The music sounds quite different from the standard Hawaiian genre, perhaps because the record was actually recorded and distributed in Italy.

One does not expect to hear spaghetti western movie soundtrack music on a Hawaiian music LP, but that is what the best song on this LP sounds like. It is the "Theme from Exodus," done in the style of Ennio Morricone's "Theme from the Good, the Bad, and the Ugly." This version is complete with rapid strumming guitars, wordless vocals wafting in the background but also with the addition of a Hawaiian slide guitar. The result is a fantastic hybrid of musical cultures that absolutely thrilled me when I first heard it, and continues to do so.

The rest of the LP is comprised of instrumentals recorded with a bit of echo and very strong stereo separation. The main instruments are the slide guitar, an accompanying Les Paul-like rhythm guitar, and now and then to stir things up, a heavy vibrato Hammond organ that would sound perfect in a small-town roller skating rink. The overall effect is a changing and swerving of music instruments from one channel to another, a poor man's attempt at matching the artistry of Esquivel's arrangements.

Who was Nino Rejna? A query to some exotica-loving Italian friends brought no answers, only the suggestion that he might have been a minor act in Naples, as Kappa was a budget label specializing in instant cash-in recordings of current hits by second-line no-name sessionmen. To add to the album's mystique, an effort to use a web-based service to translate some of the songs' names from Italian to English resulted in such surreal titles as "The Dead Leaves," "Fountain of Courses," and "Foreigner Between the Angels." If exotica represents a form of mystery, than this record definitely qualifies. (Vern Stoltz)

EMITT RHODES
Emitt Rhodes
(ABC/Dunhill, 1970)

Cursedly blessed with a McCartney-esque singing voice and soulful pop sensibility, the former Merry-Go-Round leader's charming homegrown debut—entirely played, produced, and recorded in the shed behind his folks' house in Hawthorne, California—was a surprise radio hit after engineers Keith Olsen and Curt Boettcher lent a final polish. But a good number of those radio spins were preceded by DJs suggestively implying they had their hands on some bootleg goods from Apple Corps, and when studio brat Rhodes proved less than comfortable on the concert stage, any hopes of Emittmania were allowed to quietly fizz.

He recorded two more fine discs for the label—despite a half-million-dollar nuisance suit for not producing a second album in six months—the ebulliently poppy *Mirror* and the more introspective, jazzy *Farewell to Paradise,* but the 1970 disc, recorded with no contracts and no pressure, is Rhodes at his purest.

On the Merry-Go-Round's A&M record, and the *American Dream* demos cash-in released when *Emitt Rhodes* started to sell, Rhodes was revealed as perhaps the most talented teenage songwriter on the West Coast, one who could have gone head to head with the Left Banke's Michael Brown for national honors. While his palette as he eased into his twenties was a bit limited—sensitive, observational lyrics married to *Rubber Soul*–era rhythms—what Rhodes did with these basic elements was sensational. From the delirious self-recrimination of the opening cut, "With My Face on the Floor," to the quaint silent movie love fantasy of "She's Such a Beauty" to the defining boogie of "Fresh As a Daisy," this is an artist whose facility with a hook is practically lethal, and whose sincerity and gentleness are undeniable. *Emitt Rhodes* is available in every third thrift store in America. Pick up your copy today. (Kim Cooper)

JONATHAN RICHMAN
Modern Lovers 88   (Rounder, 1987)

Modern Lovers 88 is an orphaned Jonathan Richman album, stranded in his long catalog between "Roadrunner" and "I Was Dancing in the Lesbian Bar." Jonathan himself neglects it, rarely performing these songs in concert and excludes it from his numerous "best of" compilations. Which is a shame, because *ML88* captures Jonathan in fine, quirky form with 29 minutes of rattling great music. It reminds us that Jonathan's not just sweetness and whimsy, but a visionary, stubbornly working out his own unique brand of acoustic rock and roll.

The first thing you notice about *Modern Lovers 88* is just how assured Jonathan sounds. "Dancin' Late at Night" bursts open with an exuberant surfabilly chord that bounces you deep into the song almost before you realize it's started. It's the auditory equivalent of a Jane Austen opening sentence, breezy, shrugged off—and, in its soft and cheerful way—almost obscenely sure of itself. He lures you into the second side with a taut African highlife riff that leads you into "I Love Hot Nights," another stay-up-late song. Same theme, same rough structure—it ought to be dull and repetitive, but it works—no surf, no bounce, just a tense, ragged tear across the guitar strings with the drum beat swooping behind, pulling the listener into a humid 2 A.M. downtown worlds away from the first song.

The record abounds with similar flourishes. The shouted "Hey!" that opens "New Kind of Neighborhood" conjures a crowd from his two backup singers (Brennan Totten and Johnny Avila, the other guitarist and the drummer respectively). Jonathan himself blatts raspberrys on the saxophone through "California Desert Party" and his voice curls around each lyric with an audible grin. "Gail Loves Me" repeats the title phrase over and over, ecstatic, wrapped in giddy doo-wop syllables and supported by exquisite guitar work. The shimmering instrumental "African Lady" showcases more of JR's underrated guitar playing, and "The Theme from Moulin Rouge" closes the album, drawing all the raucous energy that's preceded it down into stillness.

You expect the light and exultant qualities in *ML88*, but it also displays a sure, confident musician reveling in the sheer pleasure of making lovely, loud, or lunatic sounds just because he can. (Jacqueline Zahas)

RICO

Jama Rico   **(2-Tone/Chrysalis U.K., 1982)**

Anyone taking the long view of Rico Rodriguez's contributions to Jamaican music would be justified in describing the course of his professional life as "serpentine." Rico was steeped in music while attending the Alpha Boys School, a home for "wayward boys" in Kingston, where Don Drummond, the tragic genius of Jamaica's early music scene, tutored him on trombone. In his post-collegiate years, Rico divided his time between stints with hotel orchestras and life in a rural collective known as Count Ossie's Mystic Revelation of Rastafari, the latter resembling a Rasta equivalent of the communard jazz orchestra led by American iconoclast Sun Ra. A consummate brass player whose tone radiated versatility and self-assurance, Rico's trombone featured in many of the best early ska and reggae records; subsequent years have found the peripatetic Rico experimenting with fusion music based on those earlier forms.

Moving to the U.K. in the early sixties, Rico figured prominently in the nascent ska craze. Nearly twenty years later, he was hailed as an innovator by the revivalist bands coalescing around Jerry Dammers' 2–Tone label. Dammers enlisted Rico as a satellite member of the Specials, exposing a new generation to the veteran trombonist's sound. Dammers also played midwife to two Rico solo releases, *That Man Is Forward* and *Jama Rico*, each a sterling labor of love.

Both albums featured sessions evenly divided between Kingston and London, with no shortage of marquee names among the musicians. Sly Dunbar, Santa Davis, Winston Wright, Robbie Shakespeare and Earl "Chinna" Smith gave career-defining performances on both albums, as did Dammers, the latter contributing piano and organ. The melodies were out-lined, often as not, by a laminate horn sound, with Rico playing unison lines with producer Dick Cuthell's flugelhorn.

TMIF alternated between the ska so beloved of Rico's labelmates and loping, mid-seventies cultural reggae, reaping an enthusiastic reception upon release. Its follow-up received scant notice, possibly a casualty of 2–Tone's imminent demise. The saxophone of Cedric Im Brooks, a fellow alumnus of Count Ossie's commune, surfaces on "Java," a signal to the essential differ-ence in *Jama Rico*'s tone. There, slow, threatening hand percussion—much of it played by Rico himself—comprised the primal heartbeat of many tracks. He successfully had updated, in a multitracked format, the rhythmic signa-ture of Count Ossie's band, the latter in turn drawing direct inspiration from liturgical drumming heard at Rastafarian "Nyabinghi" gatherings. The results, as heard throughout *Jama Rico*, were dark, spiritually potent and most dread indeed. (Richard Henderson)

ROCK FANTASY

Rock Fantasy   (K-Tel, circa 1977–1978)

Here's a mystery. K-Tel was known more for its condensed repackaging of AM pop radio hits than for making, as the back cover of this album states, "Original 'Funtastic' rock music."

Rock Fantasy is a concept album—and what a concept! "The Land Where Animals Are People" is the song that lays down the mandate. The

Dogg Family suggests the listeners "Just think … how easy life would be if all of you were pets of the Dogg Family." This record does not focus on humans becoming carefree, chewing on bones, being "brushed and petted all the time" (a commonplace thing in my existence, anyhow). No, it spotlights the anthropomorphic. *Rock Fantasy* is not just an exploration of animal traits, but also of psychological character traits. Sniff Sniff Poo Pah Pah Doo is a bloodhound spy (see his songs "Sniff Sniff Poo Pah Pah Doo" and "Bloodhound"). Horace Howell The Wise Old Owl is the advice giver. Harry O'Hare is a creepy perv with a British accent who asks, "Eh, love, would you like some fish and chips?" Jack Kass must be wearing a poly jump-suit strutting around singing and braying, "Fantastic! Fantastic!" Check out the glum aside of Sidney Klunk The Friendly Skunk, "I didn't use my deodorant yesterday and I may not use it today. What good does it do me?"

I know little about the story behind this record, but at least five songs are reworkings of Jewel Akens compositions, to which K-Tel owned the rights. "Georgie Porgie" gets so reworked that it becomes "Long Tall Georgie" by G. Raffe! Source material for the rest of *Rock Fantasy* is uncertain. Was it recorded at a K-Tel staff party with session musicians? It's pretty lively! Colorfully catchy songs with top-notch playing. Upbeat cartoon soul. (Robert Dayton)

RODRIGUEZ
Cold Fact   (Sussex, 1970)

Cold Fact first caught my attention in the early nineties, when the mysterious Sixto Rodriguez was still rumored to have met with an early seventies heroin-fueled demise. It's since been discovered that Rodriguez is alive and well and living in Michigan. If you happen to encounter a tall, sharp-dressed Mexican guy walking down some desolate Detroit street, it could very well be Rodriguez. When he's not playing packed stadiums in Australia and South Africa, he spends his time in the Motor City, where he enjoys a certain kind of anonymity. Rodriguez is Detroit's most enigmatic urban acoustic rock and roll troubadour.

Like *What's Goin' On* and *Maggot Brain*, *Cold Fact*'s vision of the sixties' aftermath is also a time capsule of the end of the Motown era. It begins with

"Sugar Man," the ultimate in psychedelic seventies Mexican junkie street opera. A shopping list of drugs is recited in Kurt Weill fashion while swirling, hallucinatory voices worthy of Sid and Marty Krofft draw the listener into a vortex of madness. On "Only Good for Conversation," the band achieves one of the all-time heaviest Detroit rock moments. Session ace Dennis Coffey's fuzz guitar buzzes like an electric razor while Rodriguez sings about cookies, Kool-Aid and a refrain of "You're the coldest bitch I know." Songs like "Crucify Your Mind" and "Hate Street Dialogue" are pleasant folk-rock meditations on the death of flower power. "I Wonder" is the most upbeat and anthemic of Rodriguez' songs. It was apparently a big hit in Australia and South Africa. Why it never clicked in America, who can say? The street vibes continue with "Gommorah" [*sic*], "Rich Folks Hoax," and "Like Janis," culminating in "Jane S. Piddy," which finds Rodriguez singing a lyric of the disappearing sixties that stands up to anything by Dylan or Leonard Cohen or Van Morrison. (Matthew Smith)

GEORGE RUSSELL
Jazz Workshop   (RCA, 1956)

It's hardly surprising that a man who has dedicated his life to developing a theory called the Lydian Chromatic Concept of Tonal Organization would remain obscure. More surprising is that his name remains known to, and his records heard by, only hardcore aficionados despite the crucial role he played in the development of the two most famous albums in modern jazz, Miles Davis' *Kind of Blue* and John Coltrane's *A Love Supreme*. He also gave Bill Evans his first important exposure. George Russell changed the soundscape of post-bop jazz. His theory, compositions and behind-the-scenes influence led to "modal jazz"—music that is harmonically static compared to bebop but that gives musicians the opportunity to develop melodic themes at length.

Though his Concept may be abstruse and daunting, Russell's music is anything but academic, particularly on his first album as leader, *The Jazz Workshop*. The compositions are diverse, ranging from fast and dense ("Ye Hypocrite, Ye Beelzebub") to slow and full of sonic space ("Jack's Blues"), from ensemble pieces ("Round Johnny Rondo"), to solo showcases ("Concerto for Billy the Kid"). Russell's liner notes describe each piece, much as Evans' did for *Kind of Blue* three years later. The rhythm section of bassists Milt Hinton and Teddy Kotick and drummers Joe Harris, Osie Johnson, and Paul Motian is absolutely top notch. Alto Hal McKusick and trumpeter Art Farmer shine. Guitarist Barry Galbraith is much more aggressive than is typical for a 1950s guitar player or a modal jazz record. But the real star, composer/bandleader notwithstanding, is Bill Evans. The delicate, lyrical style and slow/medium tempi that dominate his playing on *Kind of Blue* and with his classic trios are much less in evidence here than are a fierce attack and dazzling dexterity testifying to the influence of Bud Powell. "Concerto for Billy the Kid"—Russell's nod to Aaron Copland and his soloist—is an Evans classic.

The Jazz Workshop belongs on your shelf because you love music, not because you need a history lesson. (Joe Boucher)

S

SAGITTARIUS
Present Tense   (Columbia, 1968)

Curt Boettcher had already produced the Association's debut and recorded an unreleased LP with his band, the Ballroom, before meeting Gary Usher, with whom he'd make the orchestral pop-psych masterpiece *Present Tense*. During this period Boettcher startled Usher and Brian Wilson with his production work, which the veteran pair heard wafting down the halls of Studio Three West. "I had never seen Brian turn white," Usher recalled. "It *stunned* him." At this point Usher was producing the Byrds' *Younger Than Yesterday*, but he longed to work on his own material. When one of his other production charges rejected "My World Fell Down," a *Pet Sounds*–style number, Usher decided to record it himself, using the entire Wrecking Crew, vocals by Glen Campbell, Bruce Johnston and Terry Melcher, and a surreal interlude by the Firesign Theater.

When Columbia honcho Clive Davis heard the song he excitedly asked for more from this mystery group, which Usher hastily dubbed Sagittarius. In a jam, Usher turned to Boettcher, who was happy to oblige with his unreleased Ballroom songs, future Millennium bandmates, and superabundant musical talent. The resulting album, with its gossamer orchestrations, choirs of Boettcher's gender-indeterminate voice, and hyper-innocent lyricism, is disturbingly beautiful—or beautifully disturbed. There's a David Lynch vibe throughout, mingling big-eye painting sentimentality with a lysergic creepiness (Boettcher gobbled acid but retained a Peter Pan–like innocence). With titles like "Song to the Magic Frog (Will You Ever Know)" and "The Truth Is Not Real," *Present Tense* is certain to clear the room of Black Flag fans. One track, "Musty Dusty," is an unbearably cloying lullaby to the singer's childhood toys that, looped indefinitely, would drive the most hardened terrorist out of his bunker. But those who remain in this magic garden will be taken on a masterfully produced, pleasantly eerie journey down the fine line between schlock and psychosis. (Andrew Hultkrans) (See also: Curt Boettcher)

BRIDGET ST. JOHN
Songs for the Gentle Man   (Elektra/Dandelion, 1971)

Imagine a Nico of the buttercups, all sunshine, smiles and cautious optimism. On her second album, Bridget St. John's voice is eerily similar to Nico's Teutonic burr, with the same warm timbre and oddly precise enunciation. She even brings out the harmonium for the tiny final snatch of a song. Affected, adenoidal, plying a formal language so narrow it recalls Dorothy Parker's jibe about Katharine Hepburn running the gamut of emotions from A to B, the effect is nonetheless quite captivating. St. John collaborated with producer-arranger Ron Geesin (Pink Floyd) on this little sweetmeat for John Peel's short-lived Dandelion label, a set of cool, pastel originals garnished with a pinch of John Martyn and a splash of Donovan.

The chamber group and vocalists that accompany her lilting folk-rock meanders are utilized in unsettling ways that highlight the record's understated weirdness. On the opening track, "A Day Away," the players' subdued burble rises gently like the sound of a band just downstream, while the listener floats closer, not knowing who or what will be seen there. Elsewhere they hum like bees in the garden, just out of reach, sometimes buzzing along with the lady, sometimes in opposition. Through it all, St. John slides along unflappable, a Fernand Khnopff sphinx on the River Cam. A small record, yet one that fills the room and lingers. (Kim Cooper)

SALEM 66

A Ripping Spin   (Matador, 1986)

Salem 66 suffered from a classic case of bad timing. Had this Boston band formed a few years earlier, they might have been celebrated as postpunk pioneers next to the Marine Girls and Raincoats. A few years later, they would have benefited from an explosion of female-led bands. But in mid-1980s American indieland, they were virtually alone on the landscape. Perhaps this is why their work still sounds so singular and mysterious.

Their 1984 recordings—an EP and a track on the *Bands That Could Be God* compilation—blend Fairport Convention's translucent folk with the learn-as-you-go rawness of Rough Trade postpunk. Over Susan Merriam's shambly drum patterns, bassist Beth Kaplan and guitarist Judy Grunwald harmonized sweetly and uneasily; busy, off-kilter guitar lines provided counterpoint. The songs could be dark, yet with an unerring melodic sense.

Their promise was fulfilled with *A Ripping Spin*. Joined by second guitarist Robert Wilson Rodriguez, Kaplan and Grunwald never sounded so self-assured, rocking out on tracks like "Chinchilla" and "Playground." Yet even the most straight-ahead tracks are somewhat fragile and frayed around the edges.

The album's centerpiece is "Across the Sea." Originally released as a 7–inch, it was a powerful statement about loneliness and distance. It's been rerecorded here, losing a little of its emotional wallop in the process. However, it's still bracing to hear Kaplan repeating "I'm not afraid of living on my own now/I'm not afraid of living far from home," as if she's not at all sure that's the case.

Salem 66 never made such a perfect recording again, though 1986's *Frequency & Urgency* was nearly as splendid. Then drummer Merriam left, taking her signature style with her. The band continued for two more albums, which displayed a heavier, more rock-oriented sound. By 1991, they were gone.

A Ripping Spin has not been reissued, although several tracks appear on *Your Soul Is Mine, Fork It Over*, a now-deleted compilation covering their first EP through *Frequency*. Neither Grunwald nor Kaplan has released any new music since the break-up. (Mike Appelstein)

RUSS SAUL
Begin to Feel   **(Tribute, 1977)**

With a stock photo of an ocean shoreline on the front, Russ Saul's hopelessly obscure *Begin to Feel* has all the hallmarks of a vanity-press release. The back cover text is half-baked and vague: "Russ Saul plays and sings with the vision of a man who's seen it all. All Russ will tell you is 'I've been around. My songs tell the story.'" The mastering is perplexingly incompetent, with 30–second spaces and alternating snippets of tape hiss between songs. Side 2 of the album is well under ten minutes long, and many of the song titles themselves seem incorrect and random.

Yet while it may not live up to RIAA standards, *Begin to Feel* is one of the most heart-wrenching albums ever heard. Saul's fragile voice epitomizes complete and utter defeat, and his barroom tales of brazen infidelity are downright bone-chilling. Backed by an appropriately low-rent C&W band, recorded in muffled low-fidelity, and with every self-written line soaked in despair, Russ comes across as an alternate-universe Hank Williams: "You've got some secrets you'll never tell/about the one thing you do so well/you've got those friends that help you unwind/they know you're mine/most of the time."

Years of efforts to find one single piece of solid information about Russ Saul have resulted only in frustration, and the few other LPs tracked down on the Tribute Records label (not to be confused with the Christian label of the same name) exhibit the same packaging and recording peculiarities. In a perfect world, Russ Saul would be a beloved icon of the alt-country crowd. In this one I suspect he is a pickled, broken, anonymous soul, still haunting the rotten bars and being tortured by the repulsive women that he sang about way back in 1977. (Gregg Turkington)

SCHOOLLY D
Smoke Some Kill   **(Jive, 1988)**

A single couplet, from the single "Parkside 5–2," won me over, made me the Schoolly D worshipper I remain to this day. "A little white kid called me a nigger/If I'd had a gun then I'd have pulled that trigger." The multilayered animus in that rhyme could keep Greil Marcus typing for weeks, and it's a perfect encapsulation of Schoolly D—black pride mixed with violent nihilism, over some of the hardest beats of the mid-eighties.

The blend stays that simple on his second full-length album. *Smoke Some Kill* makes *Straight Outta Compton* look like the adolescent fantasy-mongering it was. (Sure, Eazy-E was a drug dealer, but Dr. Dre and Ice Cube grew up in two-parent homes in the suburbs.) The beats are minimalist and mammoth, and the rhymes come straight to the point, except when they don't. Like "Signifying Rapper." Again, multilayered: it's a ghetto-centric knockoff of Dolemite's "Signifying Monkey" bit, built around the riff from Led Zeppelin's "Kashmir" (not sampled; played by a live band), only on the album it follows the song "No More Rock 'N Roll," which is presumably a sequel to Schoolly's old single "I Don't Like Rock 'N Roll," which sampled Joan Jett on the chorus. Ah, postmodern irony.

It was "Signifying Rapper" that made Schoolly, and nearly unmade him. Lunatic gutter-auteur Abel Ferrara picked up the track and used it over the nun-rape scene in his movie *Bad Lieutenant.* That's where Jimmy Page heard it. Shocked as much by the context as by the riff-heisting, he sued Ferrara, the movie company, Schoolly, and Jive Records. The song was cut from the film, the album was yanked from shelves, and now it fetches double-digit prices on eBay. And it's worth every penny. (Phil Freeman)

BRINSLEY SCHWARZ
Despite It All   (Capitol, 1971)
Forget their first album, and forget the one that's due out soon. Something happened when they made this one, and even those who hate goodvibes laid-back hippie acoustic music go for this bizarre combination of all that's good about Van Morrison, the Dead, and the Band.

(Ed Ward, *Flash* #2, June–July 1972)

SCIENTIST
Rids the World of the Evil Curse of the Vampires
(Greensleeves, 1981)

The creation of a dub track is an endeavor worthy of Dr. Frankenstein. Take a raw reggae recording, tear it apart and stitch it back together into something that barely resembles the original. By design, dub makes the stereo sound haunted. Subharmonic bass tones are felt more than heard. Voices, keyboards and horns blur by, distorted with Doppler-style delay and echo effects. And the drums bump and click—noises just beyond the shadow of the melody.

Scientist, a dub mixer who graduated from his job as electrician at King Tubby's studio to upstart dub alchemist, takes the horror undertones of dub to the extreme with this 1981 LP. From the low-budget cover art to the maniacal voice-overs inserted between songs, *Rids the World* plays like a drive-in second feature.

"The Corpse Rises" is the standout for evoking B-movie imagery. The bass slowly crawls to the top of the mix, finally loud enough to shake the earthworms free and lumber above ground. Some of the songs are terrorizing only in title; "The Mummy's Shroud" features a sunny horn riff and what sounds like birds chirping and "Plague of Zombies" disrupts the instrumental gore with hopeful words of unity and love. But then, without the villain there can be no happy ending.

While repairing speakers and soundboards, Scientist obviously paid attention to dub godfather King Tubby at work. His remixing is inventive and confident. *Rids the World* is the effort of a brash young artist ready to make his mark. With this album Scientist reanimated dub as a sort of goofy, noisy monster with a penchant for getting down. In doing so, he crafted a dub lover's album with added appeal for the goth kid, punk and hip-hop fan. (Kris Kendall)

MARVIN SEASE
A Woman Would Rather Be Licked   (Jive/Zomba, 2001)

Forget all those G-boys with the six-pack abs and lo-ridin' baggies braggin' 'bout this and that. In the twenty-first-century R&B scene, nobody serves it up to the ladies like Marvin "Candy Licker" Sease. Since 1987, the Blackville, South Carolina soul singer has championed the cause of gender equality in orgasms in a series of recorded raunch-ups devoted to going down on your date. Beginning with the very direct but wry "Candy Licker," Sease upped the raunch level on every subsequent release.

Blending vintage sixties Stax/Volt-style soul arrangements and in-your-face playa lyrics gained him a solid following in the Deep South and a record deal on—of all labels—Jive/Zomba. Trying to picture this purveyor of Superfly plantation owner chic making his house in the same place as squeakin' clean multiplatinum pop tarts like Britney Spears and 'N Sync is hard to imagine. But that's where this career-topping, ten-track album originated.

From the opening Otis Redding–inspired romp "Money Is What You Want" to the closing get your life together testimonial "We're Still Together," Marvin makes love to a host of honeys and drops pearls of wisdom. With the title track's refrain, "A woman would rather be licked before you do it with your walking stick," it may be one of the most progressive songs to arise from the increasingly misogynist R&B scene in a decade.

More than that, Sease addresses social ills such as the decline of the family in the touching "(She's Not My Wife) She's My Baby's Momma." Can I get a witness that the man knows what he's talking about? And that it's a tragedy more aren't aware of his velvet delivery. Also recommended: *The Bitch Git It All*; *Hootchie Mama*. (Stuart Derdeyn)

Thirteen Odd, Poignant Songs for Cynics Who Harbor Sentimental Tendencies

"Blue and Grey Shirt," American Music Club
"Doin' the Streets," The Stylistics
"Feel Like Givin' Up," Paul Williams (of the Temptations)
"Homely Girl," The Chi-Lites
"I Loved Her," Frank Sinatra
"I Sleep Alone," Brian Wilson
"I Still Miss Someone," Johnny Cash
"Little Black Egg," The Nightcrawlers
"Long Long Time," Linda Ronstadt
"Requiem: 820 Latham," The Fifth Dimension
"Walk Away Renee," Four Tops
"Winter Milk," The Poppy Family
(Gregg Turkington)

SESAME STREET
Born to Add: The Great Rock & Roll from Sesame Street
(CTW-Sesame Street, 1983)

The record's cover art mimics Springsteen's *Born to Run*, leading the listener to expect a derivative rock spoof. Songwriter/musician/producer Christopher Cerf's title track (attributed to Bruce Stringbean) shares the original song's chiming, chugging nature and lyrically alludes to the Jersey shore. Yet, while "Count It Higher" tweaks "Twist and Shout" and "Letter B" winks at "Let It Be," *Born to Add* is more than mere parody. Chrissy and the Alphabeats' "The Opposite Song" is the best bet for crossover adult appeal. The lyrics ostensibly illustrate the concept of opposites, but cleverly outline romantic frustration. Cerf blesses his namesake Muppet with his raspy, powerful tenor, simmering in the early verses only to explode on the bridge: "When I want more, you give me less/When I say no, you say YES, YES, YES!" Pounding piano augments the song's angst, and the Mitch Ryderesque screaming will have you muttering, "Damn, that Muppet can wail!"

"(I Can't Get No) Co-Operation" (credited to Mick Swagger and the Sesame Street Cobble Stones) strikes the perfect balance of pastiche and innovation. Cerf drawls "I cain't find a friend" in Jaggeresque fashion, and the guitar riff resembles a less fuzzy "Satisfaction." The arrangement is not shackled to the Stones' hit, adding tinkling piano flourishes and a flute solo in the middle. Cerf smashes any preciousness, spitting "I'm in an awful FIT/'cause I'm dy-in' to be it" with sneering majesty. The chorus's syncopated "no-no-no-NO-no" evokes the Human Beinz' "Nobody But Me," placing "Co-Operation" squarely in the garage pantheon. Sony Wonder's 1995 CD re-release alters the track listing, sadly diluting the original's punch with pop sheen and overt cuteness. With the garage revival in full swing, I hope that *Sesame Street* brings back the genre's Muppet practitioners. (After all, Chrissy has a much cooler haircut than those guys in the Strokes....) (Elizabeth Ivanovich) (See also: Roosevelt Franklin)

SEX CLARK 5
Strum & Drum!

STRUM & DRUM !

(Records to Russia, 1987/
Beehive Rebellion, 1996)

Hailing from Huntsville, Alabama—the
place where Wernher von Braun traded
rocketry know-how for immunity, but
perhaps more significantly the birthplace
of "Eight Miles High"—these lo-fi pop
wunderkinder had one of the eighties'
great lost discs in *Strum & Drum!*

Their name is one of the broad strokes forming a sly-humored sensibility, this from a group also given to titling a noisy piss-take "Get Back Yoko,"
and producing an electronic loop of the phrase "Girls of Somalia," apparently
a fifth-dimensional play on the Beach Boys' celebrations of regional pulchri-
tude. But these are the oddities on a disc that's 95% ebullient, near-perfect
Beatlesque pop, delivered with careless glee all but unheard of in the power
pop ghetto.

None of singer/guitarist James Butler's twenty songs clocks in above
2:43, giving them the opportunity to charm without boring. SC5 leaves you
wanting more, but with the next unforgettable melody never far away.

Take "Detention Girls," a reductive micro-opera with a cheerleader's
chant giving the if-you-blinked-you-missed-it bridge that extra jolt, sending
the whole marvelous package into sugary hyperdrive. "Modern Fix" is at once
daffy and poignant. The powerfully delivered line "Why don't we take all our
gimmicks, put 'em all in one box/And trade 'em for a bag of tube socks?"
seems (and is) absurd on its face, but in context it's the possibly final plea of
a lover trying to make a rough love work. "Valerie" has a singsong melody
that seems somehow backwards, an exquisite medieval meander fused with a
sweetness straight out of the McCartney songbook. Lightning-paced "Alai"
is blessed with one of those hooks that won't quit, though what the "alai-lai-
lai-lai" the band is on about may never be revealed. Sometimes bassist Joy
Johnson sings in the sweet, slightly flat voice of a serious little kid, but mostly
Butler leads the show, mouth racing to keep up with the shambling, ecstatic
rush of his band.

These dizzy, precise little tunes are like musical meringues, each one a brilliant gem of an idea whipped to soft, gooey peaks. Look for the out-of-print 1996 CD reissue that includes the magical early "Neita Grew up Last Night" EP. (Kim Cooper)

SONNY SHARROCK
Space Ghost: Coast to Coast
(Cartoon Network, 1996)

How did Sonny Sharrock get the job of providing theme music for one of the Cartoon Network's earliest, weirdest shows? Simple: the producers/creators worshipped him, and rightfully so.

Never commercially released, the *Space Ghost* soundtrack EP was a promo sent to TV critics. I got mine by writing to Cartoon Network. Twenty minutes long, it features two versions of a keyboard-anchored space-funk "theme," and four tracks of pure out-skronk joy. Sharrock and an unidentified drummer go at it like two bighorn sheep fighting for the last unoccupied mountaintop.

Sharrock's jagged, jangling brand of noise mingled free jazz, fumblefinger blues and distortion-for-its-own-sake into a screaming (but often beautiful) sound that was totally his. Whether he was out-blaring Peter Brötzmann or roaring behind Herbie Mann's soul-jazz flute, you always knew it was Sonny.

He made a comeback in the late eighties, both as part of Last Exit and as a solo act, with the help of bassist/producer Bill Laswell. As he did it, though, he gradually got further and further away from jazz; albums like *Seize the Rainbow* and *Live in New York* were instrumental hard-rock efforts, exponentially better than anything by Joe Satriani or Steve Vai, but nonetheless primarily appealing to guitar freaks. The *Space Ghost* music is arranged like rock, with no horns or weird chords, but it's much further out than any rock act was going at the time. In fact, it sounds even better in 2004, after hearing recent No Wave/post-hardcore skronk acts like Orthrelm, Botch, and the Flying Luttenbachers, not to mention Gregg Bendian and Nels Cline's guitar-drums reinterpretation of John Coltrane's *Interstellar Space*. This is music that has yet to find the ears for which it was destined. (Phil Freeman)

JUDEE SILL
Judee Sill/Heart Food (Asylum, 1971/1973)

Forgotten among the slew of singer-songwriters that gushed from L.A.'s early seventies canyons like so much February mud, Judee Sill was the first artist signed to pre-mogul David Geffen's Asylum label, the most original, most difficult and likely the best.

Raised in her dad's tavern and later in a stepdad's icy alcoholic version of privilege, the valley girl grew up bright and bitter, turning early to psychological games, armed robbery, heroin and a highly personal form of mystic Christianity informed by Rosicrucianism and failed romance. Just when it seemed like she was going to O.D. or get shot, the Turtles hired her as a staff songwriter, recording the lovely lullaby "Lady-O" before disbanding.

Over two weirdly beautiful albums that hold together like an oft-shuffled tarot deck, Sill orchestrates portraits of cryptic characters who seem to dwell between two worlds: a primal, archetypal realm of moral absolutes, and one more human, suffused with the agonies suffered when others behave badly. The musical dichotomy mirrors the lyrics. Sill sings with a casual, loping Western cadence and she drawls, the slightly dopey/hokey tone in contrast with her elegant symbolist lyrics and the occasional sustained ecstatic incantation, like "The Donor" with its round of "kyrie eleison" and visions of ancient inspirations that come unbidden during sleep. With haunting melodies and powerful language, these songs are strong medicine, leagues from the "laid back" image of label-mates like the Eagles (though a bad scene with J. D. Souther inspired her to write "Jesus Was a Cross Maker").

Both records are extraordinary, though *Heart Food* gets the edge for "The Donor" and "The Pearl," songs that distill Still's unusual obsessions down to their essence. Rhino Handmade's recent expanded reissue includes an alternate "Donor" take that's the finest thing Sill ever did.

Aside from some uncohesive demos, Judee Sill recorded nothing further. She injured her back and returned to heroin, overdosing in 1979. (Kim Cooper)

THE SILOS

The Silos   **(RCA, 1990)**

They were one of *Rolling Stone*'s favorite indie bands in the late eighties, and this marked their sole major label move. Its predecessor, *Cuba*, has taken on the official mantle of their classic, but song-for-song this beats it (admittedly not by much, and your life is poorer without *Cuba* as well). It also has a sound more appropriate for the deeply human, trad-rock of its songs (Buddy Holly, the Band and friends having a beer and getting together to string some chords together and shout the praises of women they are fond of are some possible touchstones). Peter Moore, reproducing his then-hot "live in an empty theater" recording trick used on the Cowboy Junkies' breakthrough, makes a record that breathes with the domestic life and simple human soul that these gentle but insistently chugging rock 'n' roll songs conjure.

This record is genuinely warm and sustaining; you feel like a better, wiser person after hearing it. Singer-guitarist Walter Salas-Humara continues recording as the Silos, minus original partner Bob Rupe and moving away from the simple, soft, and homespun rock of this effort. (Yes, they can "rock out," and do, but it's kinda better when they don't.) *The Silos* feels as monumental and eternal as the characters and scenes it sketches, the music as supple and genuine as the human voices: old Commodore Peter and going to visit a loved one before leaving town, thoughtful drives down country roads, staring wistfully at pictures and vowing to take one's country back. "I started to laugh/And she started to laugh" is a lyrical couplet that captures it all—love, connections, life as it is lived every day. It's an epitaph anyone would want to have after letting this lovely and loving record seep pleasingly into the blood. (Brian Doherty)

FRANK SINATRA JR.
Spice (Daybreak, 1971)

Marginalized by the fact of his famous name, and with an innate and sincere disdain for the rock trends that defined his generation, Frank Sinatra Jr. has long been an enigma in the world of popular music. An amazingly talented and articulate man with a colorful, expressive and above all *honest* vocal style, Sinatra Jr. has toured the nightclub circuit almost nonstop since his performing debut as a teenager in 1962.

Though his album releases have been infrequent, the artistic pinnacle of his recording career thus far was a stint with RCA-subsidiary Daybreak, during which time he cut the album that best showcased his singular musical vision. *Spice* is an idiosyncratic collection of his favorite tunes from the previous forty years, given unique, effervescent arrangements by Nelson Riddle, and performed with absolute mastery by Frank Jr. and his ace group of musician pals. The selections range from the vaguely metaphysical Free Design cover, "Tomorrow Is the First Day of the Rest of My Life," to sparkling new interpretations of pop vocal chestnuts ("Indiscreet") and obscurities ("Fun to Be Fooled"). The best tunes on *Spice*, however, are the ones penned by Sinatra Jr. himself, particularly the stunning track that opens Side 2. "Black Night" is a haunting, evocative song that encapsulates a lifetime of disappointment and yearning. Riddle's arrangement for this song, described as "evil" by Frank Jr. in his liner notes, starts with one simple guitar and builds slowly until it coalesces into an absolutely heart-rending orchestral blast. This track is pure dynamite.

Extensive liner notes referring to songs in culinary terms add to the album's considerable overall charm. Despite having been pressed on the short-lived, extra-thin Dynaflex vinyl, meticulous production and recording techniques help give *Spice* an enchanting sound from start to finish. (Gregg Turkington)

SIR DOUGLAS QUINTET
Mendocino   (Smash/Mercury, 1969)

The first boxed set to ever open my wallet will be a collection of the Quintet's four California albums, whenever that happens. Until then, the curious and uninitiated should look for this, the second and the best of Doug Sahm's ... er ... best. To deflate a misconception, the country, Tex Mex, barroom rock and British Invasion nods outweigh any psych aspirations, barring the weird version of the earlier hit "She's About A Mover" and some distorted vocals here and there. Now, melding styles into his own machine was Doug Sahm's specialty, and there is no finer snapshot of that than *Mendocino*.

The sock-hop Tex Mex of the title track and the pre-boogie chug-a-long of "Oh, Baby, It Just Don't Matter" seem joined at birth with the dirt road laments of "I Don't Want" and "At the Crossroads" without the album having a look-at-me kitchen sink air about it. I've never known exactly what the hell "cosmic country" meant. Slow country rock? Psychedelic country? "I'm A Mediocre Rock Writer?" The Burritos were more traditional than their butt-lickers are willing to admit, and *Mendocino* had *The Gilded Palace of Sin* nailed up, down and sideways when it came to sheer innovation and vision. Perhaps I'm taking it out of context, forgetting the "Tex Mex," but it's not like 1969 offered different classifications of superb left-field country rock (Byrds notwithstanding). A healthy number of *Mendocino*'s tracks had the makings of huge hits. A world with the title track all over AM oldies radio would be a world no different than ours. The album's perfectly crafted good-times nature, devoid of overt drug discourse or personnel tumult, is the disregarded magic. It sounds like the band loved every minute. (Andrew Earles)

SIREN
Siren   (Dandelion, 1969/Elektra, 1970)

The best album I ever picked up for 25 cents would have to be the eponymous release by Siren. Lead singer Kevin Coyne released a bunch of critically acclaimed albums and became fairly popular in Europe. That almost didn't come to pass, however, because *Siren* sold so poorly. I'm not surprised that Kevin found an audience based on the strength of this album, though, because there is no denying his genius. (A few of the bigwigs at Elektra were impressed enough that they picked Kevin Coyne as the logical replacement for an out-of-control Jim Morrison in the Doors at one point.)

There is a lot of variety on *Siren*, as is the case with most great blues records. One of the three remakes on the album is B.B. King's "Rock Me Baby." The band originals, ten rough gems, are just as inspiring, and all seem to be created from the same general mindset, but possess lots of offbeat charm. "Ze-Ze-Ze-Ze" is more fun than the blues is ever supposed to be. Kevin's voice has a peculiar edge and an odd soulful beauty, something I've found lacking in his solo albums. The guitar and piano musicianship is immaculate and intricate without being flashy. I can only assume that fans of British white boy blues were unaware that this was such a unique and primo example of rootsy cool when it came out, or the group would be remembered as worthy contemporaries of Savoy Brown, Peter Green–era Fleetwood Mac and the Groundhogs. (P. Edwin Letcher)

PATRICK SKY

Songs That Made America Famous (Adelphi, 1973)

In 1965, yet another earnest Greenwich Village folkie signed to Vanguard Records and released an album full of pleasing if inconsequential singalongs. While the result can be called little more than *The Freewheelin' Pat Sky*, little did Patrick realize this idiom was all but dead—that Bob Hisself was already haunting music stores for the latest in—gasp!—*electric* Fender gear.

Six years later, by which time Dylan had retired to Tall Tree land, Patrick Sky finally got around to committing fourteen of his *own* special nightmares to tape: a collection of songs so wickedly brutal in their examination of Nixonian America that they were turned down flat by not only Vanguard but every other label in the land. However, thanks to a brave campaign by veteran blacklisted journalist Al Aronowitz, *Songs That Made America Famous* was finally unleashed, two years after it had been recorded, by the tiny Adelphi label.

It was then, and remains to this day, the absolute Grandaddy of All Things Politically Incorrect, its satire as sharp, stinging, but simultaneously entertaining now as the day it was recorded. Songs such as "Ramblin' Hunchback," "Vatican Caskets" and "Bake Dat Chicken Pie" are in no way fit for the feeble of ear, yet ultimately prove Sky was unafraid to put his mouth where his harmonica was when push came to heave-ho. Of course after delivering such an eloquent "Folk you!" Patrick found himself the industry's number one guitarist-non-grata. But years later in Ireland he chanced upon a village pub where the townsfolk gathered, every Friday night, to sing *Songs That Made America Famous* in its entirety, word for wicked word.

I still await this Uneasy Listening classic's rousing vindication right here within the famous America from whence it sprang … and not a minute too soon, the way things seem to be headed. (Gary Pig Gold)

SLEEP CHAMBER
Symphony Sexualis (Fünfundvierzig, 1993)
"This musick waz made exclusively to accompany the fine leisure time spent durring erotik interaction. The pleasure of play aspect ov erotik interaction iz a motivation force in emotional consciousness. Sexuality iz an induvidual emotional atitude. The most important sexually-based emotion iz LOVE. A definition ov LOVE might be 'A growing interest in the desire to possess and to serve.'" So saith the liner notes. There are two kinds of Sleep Chamber records: the heavily atmospheric ones with ritualistic rhythmic undertones and somnambulant sexual overtones—and the ones where they're a rock band that uses lyrics like "lascivious butt." Oh, dear. Sleep Chamber is essentially John Zewizz (née McSweeney), an engineer on the railways in Massachusetts. For twenty years he's made scads of music, done a lot of heroin and fucked a lot of shmokin' hot women. This is the album that inspired my current interest in experimental music and everything that's engendered in the world of making things *happen*. Cast your mind back: it's New Year's Eve, 1993 (going into 1994) and I bought this album while staying in a harpsichord museum in Berkeley. Without any prior frame of reference to this strain of the avant-garde, I turned out all the lights in the attic with the exemplary sound system and put the CD into the player. Ten minutes later, all the lights for three floors down burned brightly and all doors had been flung open. I was terrified by that record. Today, I realize that it's all merely backward-masked violin processed to create one of the greatest conceivable soundtracks for fucking, but back then? It was *real*, and it was

beautiful, and it's one of the only recordings to ever make me viscerally feel something that didn't have anything to do with a pleasurable tingling down my spine. (David Cotner)

SLOAN

One Chord to Another (Murderecords, 1996)

This is the record Sloan wasn't supposed to make. The Halifax band had experienced problems with its previous label, and a permanent breakup seemed likely. After time apart, Sloan's members decided to record some songs informally for release on their own label. From these humble beginnings came a shimmering testament to the band's artistic strength, *One Chord to Another*.

The music overflows with vitality, yet reveals exceptional maturity. Take Chris Murphy's punky "G Turns to D," a break-up song as notable for its lack of lyrical self-pity as for its frenetic catchiness. Likewise, his "Autobiography" combines pun-filled images of memoir-writing, shaving and schoolgoing without forcing its whimsy. His "Take the Bench" effectively contrasts strutting instrumentation with a sweet depiction of childhood music recitals.

The songwriting takes new chances and overwhelmingly succeeds. In the heartbreaking "Junior Panthers," Jay Ferguson demonstrates his aptitude for penning the gorgeous ballads that would grace *Between the Bridges* and *Pretty Together*. Meanwhile, Patrick Pentland contributes his first two classic Sloan singles: the rollicking "The Good in Everyone" and the sprightly "Everything You've Done Wrong" (rivaled only by the Zombies' "Care of Cell 44" in the "girlfriend in prison" genre).

The arrangements hold promise of future delights. Andrew Scott's "A Side Wins" has a deceptively simple piano-based structure, but its unexpected tempo change and rueful lyrics foretell the complex pop songs he'd provide from *Navy Blues* onward. Murphy's glam-rock stomper "Anyone Who's Anyone" features a psychedelic backwards-guitar track and Sloan's first three-part harmony. (On previous records, the group's vocal prowess sometimes got buried under fuzzy guitars; hereafter, the singing would shine gloriously.)

Admittedly, there is no such thing as a definitive Sloan album. Each member writes, sings, and plays multiple instruments, ensuring varied and prolific material. Nevertheless, *One Chord* distills the crunchy guitars and dreamy vocals of Sloan's earlier records, while displaying the playfulness and stylistic creativity that have marked its later work. As a result, it best encapsulates what makes this sorely underrated band wonderful. (Elizabeth Ivanovich)

SPARKS

Propaganda   (Island, 1974)

Propaganda is the standard to which I hold myself and everything else. Overshadowed by its predecessor, *Kimono My House*, I still hold that this is the superior album. It's not like this period of Sparks is sung from the highest mountain, and when it is mentioned the quirk factor has loomed larger than its absolute "kick-ass" quotient. I'm tired of hearing about *Pet Sounds*; jump to this album—*this* is one of the few perfect pop albums I've ever heard. I adore the way the songs are constructed out of traded lines between instruments, a huge wall of sound built out of crisscrossing salvos that land in a monstrous pop explosion. This is true theatre of the absurd, a Gilbert and Sullivan production by the inmates of the asylum of Charenton under the direction of the Marquis de Sade. How can you not love that? The lyrics refine the misanthropy of *Kimono My House* into grinning, deceptive tales of human misfortune. Only Ron and Russell would tell the story of Noah's ark from the perspective of the animals left behind. This record makes me yearn for a time that is sadly past: this music was popular! They had screaming teenage girls throwing themselves at them! *Kimono My House* was their breakthrough after they'd relocated to England. *Propaganda* was followed by *Indiscreet*, which found them breaking into every music box they could find, but *Propaganda* stands for me as their ultimate statement—like being given a fruit basket, and I'm allergic to fruit. (Jim O'Rourke)

Indiscreet   (Island, 1975)

Ron and Russell Mael's curse is that they're usually two or three years ahead of everyone else. The Sparks are sort of the Jacques Tati of pop music—grasping greatness, but often misunderstood as just being eccentric or plain weird. Their fifth album is like a wild ride through the Maels' despair and humor. The songs on the surface are witty, brisk and humorous, but underneath this thin veil are sadness and disappointment. With the aid of ace producer Tony Visconti, they built a landscape that is physically neither here nor there. Sparks always sound like Sparks. There is no way to mistake a Sparks record for a Bowie, Roxy Music, Public Enemy, or whoever you choose—but within that Sparks sound they have consistently challenged themselves and their audience. The beauty of Sparks' sound is Russell's voice matching with Ron's beautiful, no-nonsense melodies, and their ability to poke holes in our comfort zone. *Indiscreet* was their last baroque masterpiece. Next on line was the rockin' *Big Beat* and the electronic crash (before it was electronic crash) of *No. 1 Song in Heaven*. But for me *Indiscreet* represented a farewell kiss to Sparks past and into the deep unknown future. Beautiful! (Tosh Berman)

SPIRIT

Twelve Dreams of Dr. Sardonicus   (Epic, 1970)

As Dr. Gonzo and the Brown Buffalo careened off the Strip for Vegas, five guys from Topanga Canyon were putting the last touches on a concept rock masterpiece on the death of the L.A. hippie dream. Doctor and attorney need not detain us further. Fuck 'em. Baking in the basin's hash and sunshine haze was Spirit, a weld of heavy psych, fusion jazz and druggy mysticism assembled out of a chance meeting during the 1967 Griffith Park love-ins, components being Jay Ferguson, Randy California, Ed Cassidy, John Locke, and Mark Andes. There was no lead vocalist for imprint, band dynamics worked against any central personality and, despite a renowned live show, Spirit was visually a random muster of Malibu tea-heads and leg-breakers. When Jacques Demy used Spirit's music to pump heavenly doom into his 1969 Strip movie, *The Model Shop*, he didn't have to pick through mangy A.I.P. types to play the band. *Sardonicus* was the fourth and final album by the original quintet, who, despite critical acclaim and open theft of their material by such as Led Zeppelin and Traffic, is now considered obscure enough for inclusion in this book. Mystifying.

Each song is an aggressively bent meditation on the limits of sixties freedom. "Prelude—Nothin' to Hide" finds them all naked at home in L.A.

Satyricon, wallowing as the world burns. "Nature's Way," a seventies FM staple, is California's Blakean musings as urban filth washes over him and the song's namesake. Jay roasts in traffic ("Animal Zoo"), explodes over La Cienega ("Street Worm"), and etches drummer Cass as the phallic "Mr. Skin," its snotty chorus worthy of Lennon and McCartney. Randy also turns in his best songwriting ever, blasting "Morning Will Come" up the 405 in an amphetamine buzz, past "Soldier," a sonorous, ironic coda for the LAX departure lounges stuffed with guys bound for Vietnam. Randy called the record a "twelve-part horror movie," but it comes to us now as exquisite Fears and Loathings among the jacarandas.

After this elegant, uproarious, hard-rocking, jazz-jumping funeral procession down Hollywood Blvd. for an O.D.'d hippie prince, Spirit disbanded. Accounts differ, but I think it was rock's first case of *Jesus, we* can't *top this!* No one has. (Ron Garmon)

VIVIAN STANSHALL

Men Opening Umbrellas Ahead   (Warner Brothers, 1974)

In my humbuggered opinion, the Bonzo Dog Band was the greatest rock band ever. They were layered, they were funny, they were good—too good, and too British. A monstrous flesh flower that blossomed from their droppings was this piece by late great eccentric Stanshall. This album is his post-Bonzos catharsis, a murky, layered recording in which the tape lies bleeding. Ominous thudding pulsations entwined with buzzing African chants and percussion bravely mix with his distinctly British wordplay: reverse colonialism, like a cuppa tea with the witch doctor. Jungle mystery, intensely personal, Stanshall is cutting to the bone here. It's all desperate and raw, possibly a last resort.

Songs start and finish loosely; one can hear burps and laughter. This is a man gone booze (and pill) mad in the studio, sputtering, gargling, italicizing, yet with huge flashes of brilliance. This is an utter release of psyche. Country and western to blues takes are included as he ruptures, "… Don't fade me out, don't! Doughwah! You beasts! Don't fade me out, I intended to mention disappearing tigers and commitment. Commit me, mama, they're trying to commit me! Commit him to the garden maudlin, commit commit commit [indecipherable]. Stop the tape I got spittle all over my moustache!"

Primal and witty, some numbers are solely devoted to his penis ("I beg your pardon, I've got a hard-on")—a bawdy body against a faux-reggae backdrop. Stanshall's recorder playing leads deep, dark instros through uncharted turf. It took roughly two years to make the album with the help of pals Steve Winwood, Jim Capaldi, Neil Innes, Eric Clapton and whoever dropped by (including a cab driver!). This is Stanshall at his most unrestrained, running rampant with amusing, uneasy results. And it still has not been released on CD as of this writing! With only 5,000 copies ever pressed, people are clamoring to hear this. There is even an online petition demanding that Warner Brothers make it available again. God willing. (Robert Dayton)

THE STARK REALITY
The Stark Reality Discovers Hoagy Carmichael's Music Shop
(AJP, 1970)

This two-record blunderbuss was the day job of Oklahoman Monty Stark, vibraphone veteran of Berklee School and Chitlin' Circuit. Stark was working at WGBH (Boston public TV) when Hoagy Bix Carmichael came on as a producer in the mid-sixties. The son of the "Stardust" composer and namesake of Biederbecke loved Stark's dexterous mauling of the tonal scale, commissioning a music-ed series based on the Hoosier Mozart's songbook for kids. The Reality's extendo-jams would amusingly dismantle the songs as a learning tool.

The stoners took over Casa Wonka, pounding the fixtures to day-glo rubble and ripping out staircases to make fantastically creaky gazebos and playground slides. The opener is "Junkman's Song," a ragpicker's chant transformed into jazz caress and funk clatter, with Stark honking like every Southern con-man who ever sold poppy juice off a buckboard. Carmichael's lean melody slips sideways every few seconds into hallucinations for guitar and vibes while the drummer cranks one wheel at a time off the bone-merchant's cart. "Shooting Stars" splatters the cosmos before losing itself in an empty pocket. "Rocket Ship" is stripped down to a garage-rock riff before the components reassemble for an interplanetary soapbox derby. Future chamber jazz pioneer John Abercrombie already proves a subtle, snaky guitarist. The band splits the atom on every song, with Hendrix and Miles Davis distant fuzz on an FM dial.

Fade-in thirty years later. Hip-hoppers and crate-diggers discover this stuff, spiking their own shit by tossing in a few tabs of it. Stone's Throw reissues a single-volume edit (minus two songs) in 2003, with incredible unissued tracks and the Reality's debut single. It's like finding a peyote stem in your dad's copy of *Spider Man* # 52. (Ron Garmon)

FRANKIE STEIN AND HIS GHOULS
Introducing Frankie Stein and His Ghouls
Shock! Terror! Fear!
Ghoul Music
Monster Melodies
Monster Sounds and Dance Music   **(Power, circa 1964)**

If every day is Hallowe'en in your world (like mine), then this series of ghastly rockin' howlers should be the soundtrack of your lives. I first found a copy of *Ghoul Music* as a teenager and was hooked. This record has the gruesomely greatest cover of all time, featuring a demented skull-faced screaming guy with fangs and a big bony green hand with long, pointy fingernails. The middle finger raised fuck-you style with the nail going into the guy's eye with blood and goo oozing out made my teenage eyes bug out! Still does!!

These are truly the greatest party records! If you like your surf-a-go-go tunes peppered (more like smothered) with breaking bones, rattling chains, shrieks, hysterical laughter, boiling bubbling cauldrons, crying, gunshots, footsteps, ringing phones, ghostly howls, car crashes, victims screaming, an unusual amount of wailing harmonica and, of course, wild guitars, then these are for you.

My search to find any info on this particular "group" has turned up nothing, unsurprisingly. All I know is that some of these tunes have turned up on other records with different, or more often no, sound effects. Obviously it was the usual musical hack budget-record company scenario, but these songs/LPs all have a coherence, a very particular style, that leaves no question in my mind that they were all performed and conceived by one group of people, which is extremely unusual for hack budget-record company scenarios.

These records are frighteningly fantastic and wonderfully weird, indispensable pieces of any record collection. To quote the notes: "This record was recorded with the fabulously eerie sound of Power Records' new DDT Method, the die-namic sound with the DEAD beat that has everything to make your dancing party a howling success." (Howie Pyro)

MEIC STEVENS
Outlander
(Warner Bros. U.K., 1970)

If there's a stupider introduction by a major label for a potentially major singer-songwriter to the earhole public than "the Welsh Bob Dylan," I'm sure it'll be attempted over at Interscope any minute now. Native of Solma, Pembrokeshire, Meic Stevens was certainly Welsh, played guitar and harmonica, and did honk satirically Bob-nosed a few times on his debut, but he dazzled a disintroduction on the very first track. "Rowena" starts out like another Donovan-ride through inner space, but Stevens comes on with the hectoring magniloquence of a drunken Cardiff MP egging on a miners' strike. Soon the thing lifts into babble, mantra and transcendence, not to return to earth. It's the greatest British folk-psych song you never heard; the like of which Dylan was no more capable of than the overture to *HMS Pinafore*. The feel of this album is much closer to sketchbooks by Skip Spence or Roky Erickson, but with top-end production and the ineffable advantage of Meic's voice. He's like a great actor or con man high with language and stoned on hearing his skull hum. "The Sailor and Madonna" and "Ghost Town" sail over the next three decades into late-nineties alt-rock, superior at that. "Dau rhosyn coch" looks forward to the next thirty-plus years for Stevens as the most influential Welsh-language pop artist. This release apparently did well enough for Warners to offer another try, but Stevens turned them down to sing for his people. Rhino Handmade's edition includes the original album plus nine bonus tracks. It will improve your existence in ways you can't even imagine. (Ron Garmon)

SUCKDOG

Drugs Are Nice   **(Self-released, 1989)**

Forget the hilarious GTOs. Forget even the mighty Shaggs. Suckdog (which isn't really a band on this record, just a gathering of drug-addled friends conducted like an alley-cat orchestra by Lisa "Suckdog" Carver and her friend Rachel Johnson) captures adolescent female adrenaline-fueled angst and aggression like no recording artist I've heard before or since.

This is not a record for the squeamish; in fact, I have used it myself (in one of my most prankish moments) to disturb and annoy random passersby by shooting its screams and hoots down to street level from a safe rooftop perch (dare I say "sonic terrorism?"). If you want to hear the raw, primal energy of raging puberty, you won't get any closer than this LP. It manages to create a sonic landscape that is scary, funny, outrageous and poignant all at the same time, much as Ms. Carver's later output in the small press world (which includes *Rollerderby* magazine and several underappreciated books) did with words and images.

It is not by mere happenstance that *Spin* magazine proclaimed this record "one of the top hundred records of the eighties." *Drugs Are Nice* certainly changed my life, as did seeing Ms. Carver perform a semi-nude roller skating opera with minimalist indie-rocker Bill "Smog" Callahan and French noise guru Costes in 1990. What makes the world of Suckdog work so well is that it never descends into pretension or anything other than pure geeky *life* in its most frightening, silly, ridiculous extremes. And that, for me, is the best kind of art. (Russ Forster) (See also: Costes)

SUPREME DICKS
The Unexamined Life   (Homestead, 1993)

The spookiness of *The Unexamined Life* results from the Supreme Dicks
themselves sounding a notch below scared shitless. In the unlikely event that
I have a ridiculous nightmare or endure a really stupid horror movie about the
Supreme Dicks, this album will be playing and I will be one of four or five
patrons in a crappy club as some ill-defined line-up of the band hunkers over
their instruments, and I will place my hand on the shoulder of what appears
to be the main guy, and ... OH GOOD GOD, THERE AREN'T ANY
EYEBALLS IN THE SOCKETS!!! Or something like that. Or not.

The endearingly meek vocal warbling that sounds like it's coming from
behind a moss-covered rock is the presumed reason some find the Dicks to
be an "acquired taste." This is what you've always wanted Jandek to sound
like. If the ashen Houstonian even approached the abandoned rural psych-
strum of the Supreme Dicks, then the book chapters and documentaries
about him might make a little more sense. Other than being similarly forgotten, this had nothing to do with the badly aged lo-fi movement of the
early nineties. Wall-to-wall ominous nursery rhymes and backlit pop songs,
The Unexamined Life could earn the Dicks secret-handshake boys-club rev-
erence, but don't hold your breath. This album sits buried in the ground
rather than flying under the radar like it used to, as the band's one-time fan
base (such as it was) is now probably more concerned with aggressive bald-
ing, hemorrhoids, custody rights or struggling to write about new bands. Act
now, before winning this album on eBay equals eating toothpaste for a
month. (Andrew Earles)

SWERVEDRIVER
Mezcal Head   (Creation U.K./A&M, 1993)

You *could* dismiss Swervedriver as four British mushroom sots tear-assing in
big American cars down the streets of Cambridge, but then there's just so
much in the broad universe for finite man to be stupid about. Ornaments of
the U.K. shoegaze scene, Swervedriver's first album was 1990's *Raise*, which
won over many a U.S. metalhead who would likely hear a Boo Radleys record

only at gunpoint. "Son of Mustang Ford," which had some play on the mod-rock charts, nicely puts Swervie's case—propulsion in the service of reverie and hallucination. A&M snatched up American distribution and signed for a follow-up.

"For Seeking Heat" sends us on a nineties soundtrack ride through a sev-enties road movie. There's this great, dark, dual-exhaust roar of guitar veloc-ity that never lets up, with Adam Franklin languorously telling us gnomic stories of sleeplessness, sex, violence, fashion, and that horrible burning smell off in the distance. By "Last Train to Satansville," we are far beyond the rage and ambition of *Raise*. "Girl on a Motorbike" is set in a bar off a lonely interstate in Gehenna, NV. The 8:10 of "Duress" has Jim Hartridge's guitar lifting the album into interstellar space, with Franklin giving a final, lordly dismissal to the entire planet in "You'll Find It Everywhere." That finale is one of the great moments of nineties rock, a sweet wasted tear of pity for all those dreadful losers one sees out the car window. The U.S. release tacks on the lush "Never Lose That Feeling/Never Learn" (from a 1992 Creation EP) to push the disc past sixty minutes and bliss eternal.

Ejector Seat Reservation (1995) being merely excellent was a definite comedown and never scored U.S. distribution, and Swervie's last album, *99th Dream* (1997), is an undervalued attempt to retool their fat black Cadillac sound into sporty pop. Thus ended the best four-album run of the nineties. (Ron Garmon)

SYLVESTER

Living Proof   (Fantasy, 1979)

It's March 11, 1979, and San Francisco belongs to Sylvester! The Opera House is packed to capacity to see disco's truest diva. Twenty tuxedoed mem-bers of the symphony join Syl's band and four backup singers. Though as a rule he doesn't perform under the influence, the thrill of donning the first of the evening's shimmering sequined outfits in the Maria Callas dressing room seems a worthy cause to celebrate, so he washes down a hit of acid with a bot-tle of champagne. He is feeling good … and he is feeling r-e-a-l! Sylvester takes the stage to an overture of his disco anthems.

Those who haven't seen him live before, expecting this palace of culture to be transformed into a carnal bathhouse, are about to be pleasantly disappointed. Yes, the concert would end with a rousing medley (a full side of this live LP) of two of the greatest dance songs of all time, "Dance (Disco Heat)" and "You Make Me Feel (Mighty Real)." But the concert also showcases Sylvester's unique falsetto as an expressive, emotional instrument demonstrating pure class completely appropriate for the venue. He shows off his power as an interpreter on the Beatles' "Blackbird," he explores the blues with "Lover Man," and, most importantly, he ends Side 2 of the double LP with a ballad he felt would show the world what he could do. Syl's cover of Patti LaBelle's "You Are My Friend," would become a powerful anthem among his gay fans. Infused with passion and sincerity, it was a moment Sylvester wanted acknowledged as one of his finest, but unfortunately, the album didn't sell well. Apparently the Black radio audience wasn't ready to hear a man singing to another man and failed to see the universality of his passion.

But that night's audience was certainly ready! Sylvester's ease and joy are apparent as he banters with friends, jokes with the adoring crowd and gets bitchy with the light guys. At one point the massive theatrical production halts as Mayor Feinstein gives Sylvester the key to the city and declares it "Sylvester Day." Even if the mayor hadn't made it official, it's apparent at the end of the show that it was indeed Sylvester's Day, as he turns the tables and conducts the crowd's serenade to him that he makes them feel mighty real. He most certainly did. (Jake Austen)

T

TELEVISION PERSONALITIES
... And Don't the Kids Just Love It   (Rough Trade, 1981)
The Television Personalities' general inability to get their shit together is one variable that robbed ... And Don't the Kids Just Love It of acclaim. Had it happened when it should have, in 1977 or 1978, it would be an incessantly name-dropped, shambolic mile-marker held like a security blanket in the man-purses of every twee pop addict this side of the Young Marble Giants—one of the

myriad overrated bands that filched seminal, hush-hush hipster, calling card fire from the TVPs. But again, it might have helped to get this LP out there a little earlier instead of fiddle-fucking around for years on the delusional laurels provided by scant 7–inches and EPs.

Underground or mainstream or in the middle, ... *And Don't the Kids Just Love It* is about as "1981" as a Poco album. The album is the gem deed of hyper-cynical, over-artsy punk rock Situationist hippies with a frightening knack for incandescent postpunk pop. The standouts ("Look Back in Anger," "Jackanory Stories," and "Le Grande Illusion") are not wholly dissimilar from what would be blown apart and upwards by the Pastels, what previously hibernated in the sloppier cracks of early Cure releases, or the style damned forever by the navel-gazing follies of Beat Happening, et al. Every great album has a pack leader, and "La Grande Illusion" is nothing less than chilling, complete with snaky bass and a less-than-sunny outlook for every party's garden variety postpunk stiffy. Pardon the sacrilege, but the root of the band's relative fame (it was released much earlier), "I Know Where Syd Barrett Lives," opens Side 2 with a skippable three minutes of exaggerated nonsense. Other than that one stumble, you have a brimming pop essentiality available on an assortment of CD reissues, consequently limiting your excuses. (Andrew Earles)

THE TEMPTATIONS
1990   (Gordy, 1973)

Norman Whitfield rescued the Temptations franchise after they lost lead singers Eddie Kendricks and David Ruffin. Whitfield tapped Dennis Edwards to step in, found an Eddie soundalike in Damon Harris, and cut the most devastating track in Motown history: "Papa Was a Rolling Stone." It was not only a hit, it gave the Temptations a shot of credibility in the face of *There's A Riot Goin' On*. By 1973, Whitfield had the keys to the studio, the Funk Brothers on call, and the best vocal group in the world to play with.

1990 is a lost record in the Tempts catalog, their only collaboration with Norman Whitfield never issued on CD. You can see Norman ticking off the potential singles as he wrote and produced this record. The Tempts blend their incomparable harmonies on "Heavenly" and throw down hard on "You've Got My Soul on Fire." Damon Harris' high, pleading lead on "I Need You" glides over the kind of light conga groove that Curtis Mayfield patented.

Toward the end of the A-side, though, the mood turns with the song "Ain't No Justice," and that darker tone carries over to the two songs that take up the entire B-side. On the title track, "1990," Whitfield creates a ghetto landscape of insinuating dread. James Jamerson's bass dollies back in a long tracking shot, picking up the congas hectoring from the street, and the guitar pulls up wreathed in sweet ropes of wah-wah—perfectly setting up the Temptations entrance.

The last long track, "Zoom," opens with the Tempts bullshitting in the studio about UFO conspiracies. You can imagine Norman lighting up and staring out the window, tired of the business, tired from the long struggle— just plain tired. He drifts and the song takes off with him, a funk-stoned excursion that floats away as the group chants "Zoom zoom," absenting the whole planet in disgust. It's not in a class with "Runaway Child Running Wild"—it's too diffuse, too abstract, too full of shit—but, damn, it sounds great. (David Smay)

10CC

Sheet Music   (UK, 1974)

This is the second LP by this studio-based U.K. art/pop band—a band that consisted of former Mindbenders Eric Stewart, songwriter extraordinaire Graham Gouldman, and experimental techno geeks Kevin Godley and Lol Creme. The latter two contributed mainly to the "art" aspect of the band, while the former two served up the bulk of the "pop." That division was not as discernable on their first few LPs, though, where all four members wore their love of the Beatles, the Beach Boys, Bowie and Frank Zappa on their sleeves.

Trying to create new musical sounds while attempting to be witty and clever lyrically is a dangerous game. If you fail, you wind up creating annoying, worthless shit. Yet here is an example of a band attempting and succeeding at both, and with flying colors. Every track is catchy, flawlessly constructed, and features very sophisticated and amusing lyrics. I'm hard pressed to highlight any favorites since every cut is terrific, though I'm somewhat partial to the Stewart and Gouldman-dominated tracks. Stewart has such a fine McCartneyesque voice (and the guitars on "his" songs, such as "Wall Street Shuffle" and "Silly Love," always have the greatest *sound* to them), while Gouldman's compositions are sheer perfection to my ears. He's one of the best composers ever, one of the all-time greats. (Peter Bagge) (See also: Graham Gouldman)

JAKE THACKRAY
The Last Will & Testament of Jake Thackray   (Columbia, 1967)
Whenever another underwhelming songwriter is described as acerbic and droll; whenever another undeserving mopester is chained to the pillars of Brelian legend; and certainly whenever you feel the need to hear a song about a dour housewife who falls in love with an ugly cactus, you should listen to Jake Thackray's debut. Though chronology placed him amid that same explosion of wry acoustic troubadours that expelled Al Stewart, Bert Jansch and Davy Graham, Thackray's eye for the mundane minutiae of everyday life and his ear for the sleaze and morbidity that lurks beneath its façade had no peers whatsoever.

Signed to Columbia as a most peculiar companion for the Pretty Things and the Pink Floyd, Yorkshire-born Thackray released *The Last Will & Testament* in 1967, and his label's nervousness remains palpable. Uncertain what the general public would make of pure, undiluted Thackray, he was paired with a succession of arrangements. Two songs featured Thackray crooning to a simple piano accompaniment; three more linked him to rhythm arrangements directed by Geoff Love; six others saw him fronting the Roger Webb Orchestra.

It did not take a musical genius to determine that, whatever the setting, Thackray was irrepressible. With his air of lugubrious anti-star honed by a lifetime spent on the northern English working-men's club circuit, and the blunt colloquialisms he encountered there, an evening spent listening to Thackray was an evening in the company of gruesome Auntie Susans, itinerant drunkards, and the sad little people who search for love in the personal columns of the local newspaper—in other words, he sang about precisely the people he was singing to. And, though Thackray himself has since passed on, those people still thrive in the world he left behind. His *Last Will & Testament* is a reminder that he is probably still watching them. (Dave Thompson)

THIN LIZZY
Thin Lizzy   **(Decca, 1971)**

Thin Lizzy is the band of curses: self-destruction being the popular one, and trying to break into seventies classic rock as a highly original band fronted by a seven-foot black dude, well that's another one. And then there were the hits. The hits sucked. There was no incentive to look any deeper into a band known for such pedestrian work as "Whiskey in a Jar," "Jailbreak," and "The Boys Are Back in Town." And because the album tracks from the hard period (roughly 1974–1980) are so incendiary and influential (Iron Maiden wouldn't sound like Iron Maiden had it not been for Lizzy's Gorham/Robertson combo), the early albums are forgotten; still crapped on by critics as amateur and unfocused lead-time.

The self-titled debut may be confused, but the album is multiform at a time when eclectic tiptoeing through styles was more likely to work. This is the early seventies hard-rock-folk wunder-album that your e-mail group forgot to mention in the "Good Boogie Rock?" string. There's something here for everyone still kicking themselves for checking out Bloodrock, Cactus or Atomic Rooster. You get hard funk ("Ray-Gun"), power-trio riffers ("Look What the Wind Blew In"), the scraps of whatever U.K. psych-folk was laying around in 1971 ("The Friendly Ranger at Clontarf Castle" and "Honesty Is No Excuse") and epic crescendo proto-metal ballads ("Diddy Levine" and "Remembering"). At this writing, Thin Lizzy's debut can be found on CD, but if someone wants this and the two Decca LPs that followed (*Shades of a Blue Orphanage* and *Vagabonds of the Western World*), well, good copies can fetch at least twenty bucks. (Andrew Earles)

THE THREE SUNS
Movin' 'N' Groovin'   (RCA, 1962)

The Three Suns have a series of recordings that are so hypnotic and kooky that
if their records were candy bars they'd be
straight out of Willy Wonka's Chocolate
Factory. Over the course of twenty years,
I have managed to obsessively thrift
score at least 37 albums and 8-tracks by
these prolific dynamic space age pop
instrumentalist innovators. And, as impossible as it may seem, I have a single
favorite out of all of them: the stereo action masterpiece *Movin' 'N' Groovin'*.

This boldly unusual psychedelic album was arranged, and one song was
composed, quite jarringly for its time, by the versatile musical maestro
Charles Albertine. This is a man who not only composed "Bandstand
Boogie," which ultimately became the theme song to Dick Clark's *American
Bandstand*, but was also commissioned to write an original wedding dance
number for Japan's Crown Prince Akihito, entitled "The Happy Prince
Waltz." So, for a guy used to being hired to produce mainstream instrumental pop music, he must have been completely *insane* when he made *Movin' 'N'
Groovin'!* Far be it from me to ruin the mystique and reveal every instrument
or object used in its creation. But, along with the Three Suns' signature
axes—guitar, accordion and organ—here's a sample: tuned temple blocks,
chromatic cowbells, Jew's harp, tap shoes, harpsichord, bamboo wind bells,
jaw bone, etc., etc. This is mad science made in the recording studio, people,
but please don't be afraid! (Kelly Kuvo)

CAL TJADER
Mas Ritmo Caliente   **(Fantasy, 1957)**

In spite of his lack of pigmentation, Callen Radcliffe Tjader Jr., better known
as Cal Tjader, was the coolest cat in Latin Jazz. The multitalented percussionist recorded dozens of albums over the years, most of them exploring his
sincere and profound interest in this genre.

Mas Ritmo Caliente captures, exemplifies and defines that magic moment when cool jazz met hot North American rhythm met Caribbean and East Coast met West. Culling talent from each locale, Tjader divided the album among three separate recording sessions in San Francisco, Chicago and New York. In 1957 these musicians were in peak form and exhibit the youthful exuberance that was a part of the nascent Latin jazz explosion.

The album opens with "Perdido" (1942), one of the first Latin jazz tunes ever written. Other highlights include "Poinciana Cha Cha," an upbeat number that allows the groove to move you and "Mongorama" by Mongo Santamaria, who at the ripe old age of thirty-five is the senior member of this group! The song is an excuse to wail, and wail they do as Mongo and Willie Bobo share the limelight.

The final cut, "Perfidia Cha Cha," begins with Jerry Sanfino on flute and Cal on vibes playing the opening bars. Then "Chombo" Silva takes the lead with a masterful improvisation. Eventually, each soloist takes a turn while Mongo, Luis Kant and Willie Bobo churn out beats that you cannot sit still to. At 8:12 the engineer pulls down on the faders because he has run out of vinyl. The musicians keep playing as they always do, and I would give the world to hear the rest of that jam session. In the meantime, I'll savor what we have on *Mas Ritmo Caliente* by Cal Tjader Con Amigos. Are you sure that cat is white? (Sean Carrillo)

JOHN TRUBEE AND THE UGLY JANITORS OF AMERICA

THE COMMUNISTS ARE COMING TO KILL US!
John Trubee and the Ugly Janitors of America

The Communists Are Coming to Kill Us! (Enigma, 1984)

Mr. Trubee is best known as the man behind "Blind Man's Penis," a demented poem with lines such as "Warts love my nipples because they are pink/Vomit on me baby, yeah, yeah" that was sent to a song-poem mill and turned into a deadpan country song that subsequently became an underground novelty hit. Lesser known, but far stranger, is his fol-

Big or Little, Labels Come and Go

Focus, Arthur Blythe (Savant): Tiny label + odd lineup (marimba, tuba, alto) = Soon-to-be OOP. Delightful music. Grab it if you see it.

Spiritual Unity, Albert Ayler (ESP): One of the highwater marks of free jazz. cf. Lester Bangs's "Psychotic Reactions & Carburetor Dung" for more on one of the oddest labels ever.

Of Human Feelings, Ornette Coleman (Mango): Harmolodics goes electric. Out of print despite Ornette's stature and Mango's island connection.

Jazz Poet, Tommy Flanagan (Timeless): Mainstream jazz, even by the greats, goes out of print too. Available now, so get it while you can.

Tonal Weights and Blue Fire, Ku-umba Frank Lacy (Tutu): Innovative trombonist/physicist, idiosyncratic singer, backed by the late, great Fred Hopkins on bass ("Apostle Man").

Odds Against Tomorrow, John Lewis: Good film, better score. Soundtrack on United Artists and MJQ version on Atlantic both out of print.

Town Hall Concert, Charles Mingus (Jazz Workshop): Featuring Mingus liner notes about how labels suck so he decided to release it himself. Eric Dolphy at his peak and near his end ("Meditations on Integration").

Thelonious Monk Trio (Prestige): Post-Blue Note, pre-Riverside. "Blue Monk," "Reflections," "Bye-Ya," "Just a Gigolo" solo. Essential.

The Legendary Dial Masters, Charlie Parker: Possibly the greatest session ever ("Moose the Mooche," "Yardbird Suite," "Ornithology," "A Night in Tunisia") by one of the two or three biggest figures in jazz, but still in and out of print. Currently on Jazz Classics.

Revue, World Saxophone Quartet (Black Saint): Strong performances by all four as composers and players. (Joe Boucher) low-up album. Trubee got the ball rolling by sending a fake suicide note to several associates, including *L.A. Reader* rock critic Matt Groening and Enigma's Bill Hein, who agreed to meet with Trubee and negotiate a record deal.

In Trubee's words: "It was no negotiation. I wanted to do the record badly—that was obvious. It was similar to a horny teenage boy negotiating with a supermodel to lose his virginity. There is no deal—he just gets with her *fast* before she changes her mind. I told Bill I'd do it for no money. He set up mastering time at Capitol and I walked in ... with a brown paper bag full of reel tapes and cassettes of teenage poetry rants, prank phone calls, aborted horn chart recordings from music school and other weirdness. I had the flu and I sat with Eddie Shierer for six hours editing all this madness into an album."

What resulted was an extremely unique and, well, odd record. I came across it in a used bin shortly after it came out. It was both annoying as hell and insanely captivating, a collage of atonal avant-jazz, primitive electronic compositions and spoken rants against stuck-up college girls and the suave men who slept with them, plus those juvenile prank calls, a revelation long before the genre became a pop cultural phenomena.

If the record that was attached to the Voyager space probe had contained the sounds of all the alienated, pissed-off, shat-on people on earth, it would sound something like this. (Chas Glynn)

THE TUBES

The Tubes   **(A&M, 1975)**

They came from Phoenix, appearing first as a one-off amalgamation of two bands that decided to go theatrical for a night, cajoling a roadie into costume as lead vocalist. You may know them for bland, insubstantial eighties MTV fare, by which time Fee Waybill, former roadie, had prevailed in the internecine struggles within and embarked on the courtship of such collaborators as Steve Lukather of Toto. Accordingly, you may think you know what to expect here. I urge you to reconsider. Produced by Al Kooper, and featuring a dazzling array of strings, horns, novelty synthesizer blips, relentless time signature changes and vocal harmonies, *The Tubes* is the best and most ambitious album the Tubes produced during their fertile A&M years (1975–1979).

The sound may have been kind of prog or psychedelic back in Phoenix, but under the tutelage of Kooper the Phoenicians blossomed into deranged but coherent generic dabblers. There's a soul song here ("Haloes"), a stirring piece of Tejano ("Malinguero Salerosa"), some metal ("Mondo Bondage"), some sci-fi prog ("Space Baby"), a punk rock epic called "White Punks on Dope," which, despite being proto-punk, featured chorus, strings and a three-minute fadeout. Still, these idiomatic designations don't really describe the cinematic and theatrical range of the music.

Meanwhile, the lyrics are tossed off, hilarious and moving at the same time, most of them the skewed perceptions of one Bill Spooner, guitar player. And he is indeed related to the guy for whom *spoonerism* was coined. During the period when the Tubes mattered, however obscurely, it was Spooner who had the vision, and when he gave in to his considerable demons the Tubes faded like ghosts, despite lingering anemically on MTV. For a brief couple of years they were nearly as inventive and singular as Beefheart or the Mothers of Invention, and in this bizarre and shining moment, they were vaulters at greatness. (Rick Moody)

VARIOUS ARTISTS
Wanna Buy a Bridge?   (Rough Trade, 1980)

Label samplers are, by their nature, a low-priced means to flog whatever product happens to reside on a record company's current roster. Sometimes, however, whether by accident or design (and it's rock 'n' roll we're talking about, so it's probably a bit of both), these lashed-together promotional tools wind up hanging ten on the street waves of the *Zeitgeist*. This attempt to introduce the early denizens of Geoff Travis's Rough Trade label to an American audience captures an absolutely delicious moment in pop-cult time: the moment when those punks who decided to stick around after the gob dried began getting a touch more proficient on their instruments, a little bit more sophisticated politically, removed enough from the scene to make fun of it (and sufficiently self-referential to name-check the song right next to it on the compilation while doing so), and open-minded enough that the keyboard player from a prog band covering Chic can fit in beautifully. Punk calcified into orthodoxy with depressing speed, and the raucous, messy sound of these bands—the blatts of no-wave brass, the spaced-out thumps of borrowed dub reggae, the heretical embrace of electronics and dance beats (albeit ones no one could safely dance to), the vocals that go from crazed and wailing to chilly and detached in the jump of a stylus—is the sound of punk's mutant offspring kicking the chalk out of its corpse before spazzing off into rock-guide footnote oblivion. With each passing year, *WBAB?* seems less like a collection of marginal sub-pop anomalies than the manifesto for a revolution that couldn't even get televised on public access if it tried, which no one much felt like doing anyway. For a collection of bands so relentlessly angry, hysterical, and grim, they sound like they're having too much fun to care. Featuring: Stiff Little Fingers, Delta 5, The Slits, Essential Logic, Television Personalities, Swell Maps, The Pop Group, Spizz Energi, Cabaret Voltaire, The Raincoats, Young Marble Giants, Scritti Politti, and Robert Wyatt. (William Ham)

V-3

Photograph Burns   (American/Onion, 1996)

There's no avoiding the gray hair growing on so-called anger, bitterness, cynicism and "intensity" in the rock music vehicle. An elusive hat trick is performed when those feelings translate as humane rather than as a contrived cloud of negativity. Jim Shepard knew this trick, and he pulled it off with grace on *Photograph Burns*. Though Jim used the predictable "nothing different this time around" angle in interviews, *Photograph Burns* screams that he put some unprecedented (for him) moxie into it. The pieces floating around in the mess of earlier Shepard albums fit together like a weapon here. Two decades of emotional catastrophe, blue collar hate, drinking, raw intellect, hangover paranoia, the underbelly of postpunk pretension and who the fuck knows what else, all come to a nasty head that should teach the dilettantes a thing or two about real problems. Yeah, the class baiting ("American Face," "White Caucasian") beats a worn one, but there's no question that Shepard's sentiments were sincere (and earned) when they hit the paper. The album is almost divided, odds and evens, between force and balladry. The slower songs are the best that Shepard ever recorded—brain burners that the No Depression/Bloodshot crowd could structurally grasp, but would never have the grapes to make or enjoy. Positive feelings are a hard sale when it comes to the Shepard saga, but the man did knock out a masterwork before he tragically passed. If you want to promote the longevity of a worthy voice, *Photograph Burns* is waiting, cheap, in a nearby used bin. (Andrew Earles)

VULGAR BOATMEN
Please Panic   **(Safe House, 1992)**

The Vulgar Boatmen was a band with one endearing peculiarity that the few who ever wrote about them liked to point out: its two songwriters each led his own version of the band in his respective hometown of Gainesville and Indianapolis. This is interesting, sure, but mostly because it becomes astonishing when you hear how the singers and musicians seem to breathe and move like one pair of lungs, one set of strumming arms.

This was the second of their three albums; the first, *You and Your Sister*, was on an even more obscure indie, and the third, *Opposite Sex*, released on a Warner affiliate label in Europe only. All are lovely, and the first and third have some tracks that might well be better than any here. So there's a certain arbitrariness to my choosing this one, but nothing arbitrary about the Vulgar Boatmen themselves; they are as inevitable and full of wonder and depth as childbirth. When I hear the way singers Robert Ray and Dale Lawrence charm so quietly but intensely on songs like "Calling Upstairs" and "Fool Me," I know this record *has to* make the history books.

A bunch of things it might remind you of without really sounding like them include: the fifties when country, rock and soul hadn't yet calcified into separate geological strata; the Everly Brothers; the country-folk side of the Grateful Dead; great, quiet Paul Simon solo songs. These guys clearly have heard a lot of great records and instead of imitating them they've incorporated them effortlessly into their own genetic codes. The drummer is as heroic as Charlie Watts, and the emotions are as huge and encompassing as the most over-the-top doo-wop while still sounding martini dry and as dense with dropped, unmannered details as the best Raymond Carver story. Simply: this record achieves a solid and seemingly effortless perfection that neither lets up nor palls. (Brian Doherty)

LOUDON WAINWRIGHT III

Last Man on Earth (Red House, 2001)

This is a very delicate and pretty record, punctiliously played, avidly arranged, sensitively sung. It can be listened to on that level with quiet early evening pleasure. But what makes it stand out is its paralyzingly depressing twilight subject matter, relentlessly worried over with a folky intensity that in the end is more disturbing than the most maniacal dark metal.

It's a concept album about a partially successful singer-songwriter's slide into a lonely old age, without parents or spouse, children and friends distant. His language is direct and mostly unmetaphorical and has no calculated Dan Fogelbergesque tear-jerking. It takes some thought to realize how dire and upsetting it all is. Its sonic surfaces are so inviting that you are encouraged to set a spell and think about the days his mom was around to drink wine with him on the porch and get into disturbing conversations about dad; about who you might want to name as the person to be notified when you die in an accident when family isn't an option; about the teeth-grinding yet numbing conversations you have with old loves with whom you are determined to "keep in touch."

This queer and wonderful record—with the real dope on what it means to be too old to rock 'n' roll, but too young to die—came out in the post-critical age of abundance, when no record that isn't lead-featured in *Rolling Stone* could be said to have been "noticed" by the culture at large. Ones like this, on obscure indie labels by artists of strong career longevity, but lacking legendary status or major label backing, are guaranteed to light no new fires and at best keep banked fires in the hearts of long-term fans. Discovering it—the best damn album I've heard from any Wainwright—makes you wonder what else everyone is missing. (Brian Doherty)

MUDDY WATERS
Electric Mud   (Chess, 1967)

HOWLIN' WOLF
The Howlin' Wolf Album   (Chess, 1967)

First time I heard Shannon's great "Let the Music Play" (1984), the first thing the massively dense track reminded me of was this pair: two of the most widely denounced LPs of all time. Here's the backstory. In 1967, Chess Records junior honcho Marshall Chess thought he'd "update" the sound of the label's two blues giants. He hired arranger Charles Stepney, fresh from Rotary Connection's psych-soul hits, and the two put Muddy in front of an eight-piece band featuring flute, amplified sax and mad ger-tar-slingers Pete Cosey and Phil Upchurch.

The result was a delicious noise-stew, thick with polyrhythms and fonked-up solos. Think David Axelrod's *Songs of Innocence*, with more focus and meat and fat on its frame. Muddy—and later Wolf, whose set the same crew built—became mere bricks in the wall, like Darlene L. or Ronnie S. But what a wall!

Electric Mud's better, opening with a thunderous "I Just Want to Make Love to You" (it sounds like Cream and Sabbath jamming). On "Tom Cat," Gene Barge runs Coltrane riffs through a jungle of burry fuzz and wah-wah. Muddy catches the spirit on "Herbert Harper's Free Press News" (a salute to an underground paper), barking joyously as the guitarists hurl Hendrix and Cipollina licks against pulverizing piano, bass and drums. The rhythm seems to anticipate hip-hop by three decades. *The Howlin' Wolf Album* is something of a replay of *Electric Mud*, with a few twists ("Smokestack Lightning" gets a flute and an echo chamber). The album, though, if you can find one, is worth its price for "Evil." Wolf's mean blues is reconfigured around a descending bass line and screaming guitar riffs that drop and scatter like a bag of marbles hitting the sidewalk. Talk about multitasking: the whole track wobbles, swings and rocks mightily. (Gene Sculatti)

In Praise of Big Women

Billy Ward and His Dominoes: "My Baby's 3D"
Joe, Ron & George: "Half Ton Mama"
Lee Pickett & the Screamers: "Fatty Patty"
Sonny Hall: "Big Fat Baby"
Fats Waller: "Egyptian Ella"
The Rockabouts: "She's a Fat Girl"
Otis Redding: "Fat Gal"
Ray Gersden: "Fattie Hattie"
Ronnie Moleen: "Fat Mama"
Louie Jordan & His Tympani Five: "I Like 'Em Fat Like That"
Bill Mack: "Fat Woman"
Roy Young: "Big Fat Mama"
Brownie McGhee: "Big Legged Woman"
Buddy Sharpe: "Fat Mama"
Don McKinnon: "Fat Fat Fat"
The Heptones: "I Need a Fat Girl" (Richard Henderson)

JIMMY WEBB

Letters   (Reprise, 1972)

Like fellow hyphenate Burt Bacharach, Jimmy Webb's distinctive brand of melodrama isn't for everyone. The baroque excesses of "MacArthur Park" didn't just top the singles charts (twice), but also columnist Dave Barry's poll of his readers' most hated songs. The music simply inspires powerful responses.

Far below the radar of hits sung by others fly a series of fascinating, neglected solo Jimmy Webb discs recorded for various labels. They all have their bon bons, but *Letters* is satisfying straight through, a sad and funny bus tour of Webb's heartbroken psyche with sidetrips to the San Fernando Valley and Galveston. It's the writer's own version of "Galveston" that opens this set, a fragile, tender performance framed by acoustic guitars that underscores the narrator's vulnerability in ways Glen Campbell, with his superior vocal skills, can not.

The album's heart is "Campo de Encino," an expansive imaginary portrait of the Los Angeles suburbs from an adolescent POV, full of naïve ambition ("I wanna wipe out VD/And set the animals free") giving way to exquisitely sung yearnings for nullification and escape ("But most of all/I wanna soar away"). No Angeleno can listen to this song without having his or her vision of the Valley permanently made a little magical.

A deep vein of sadness and mental confusion runs through the rest of the disc, from the elegant reading of Boudleaux Bryant's "Love Hurts" to the I-hope-you're-satisfied midnight letter of "Hurt Me Well." "Once in the Morning" is a deceptively silly pill-popper's lament with a hollow core, while "Song Seller" (a minor 1972 hit for the Raiders presented here in unexpurgated form) is a cynical psalm to the industry that made Webb rich and threatens to engulf him. Burned out on humans, *Letters* closes with a tender ballad to the writer's piano, which sits reliably up with him all night when the agents, groupies, and hangers-on have all slunk away. (Kim Cooper) (See also: Glen Campbell)

TONY JOE WHITE

... *Continued*   (Monument, 1969)

Tony Joe White was the epitome of what used to be called "swamp rock," an earthy mix of soul, gospel, country and early rock that had a minor vogue around 1969–1971. Creedence Clearwater Revival had hit after hit in this style. Tony Joe only made the pop Top 40 once (with "Polk Salad Annie" in 1969), but his influence reverberated for a few years as a songwriter. He's still at it today, with several excellent albums issued. ... *Continued*, his second, remains the definitive TJW experience.

First, let's get one thing out of the way: if you're looking for The Album With The Big Hit, you want *Black & White*, his debut. Even though two songs on ... *Continued* are straight-up "Polk Salad" clones, Tony Joe is not somebody you judge by The One Big Hit. This album is among his most well-rounded; songs like "I Want You" and "Woodpecker" establish the swamp-funk sound he's known for, but the album also contains some of his most tender ballads, like "The Migrant," "I Thought I Knew You Well," and "For Le Ann," which was written for his wife. This also includes his original version of "Rainy Night in Georgia," which was a hit for Brook Benton the next year. Unlike his first album, this follow-up is a bit more relaxed and doesn't sound like it came from a Nashville assembly line. As the late Sam Phillips, the man behind Sun Records, once allegedly said about a Tony Joe record: "Goddam ... that's so good, it don't sound paid for." He was talking about a later TJW album with a different producer, but he might as well have been referring to ... *Continued.* A bunch of guys getting their swamp on without watching the clock too closely. (James Porter)

WHITE NOISE
An Electric Storm (Polygram, 1969)
This pioneering electronica album was recorded in 1968 and released in 1969. I picked up the Antilles reissue when it came out sometime in the mid-seventies based on rave reviews from a fellow Pink Floyd fan. This became a favorite weird album to go to sleep to. The closest group I know of to compare this music to is the United States of America, but there were a number of other early experimenters mining the field of synthesizers, found sounds, vocal gymnastics and tape manipulation, such as Vangelis, Tangerine Dream, and Joe Meek. I believe this project was probably the least successful of the aforementioned, and I find it the most satisfying. Group leader David Vorhaus was responsible for most of the eerie sound collages. Wisely, he utilized top-notch tunesmiths, vocalists and instrumentalists around which to build his creations.

Four other White Noise albums were released between 1974 and 2000. Most of them are virtually Dave Vorhaus solo projects, though, and lack the input of various members of the BBC Radiophonic Workshop, which helped make the debut so stunning. There are many factors that raise this recording to the level of legendary status. The most obscure is the fact that "Love Without Sound," "My Game of Loving," "The Visitation" and "Your Hidden Dreams" are great songs beneath the layers of fanciful exotic fluff. Another is the sophistication of the use of all the new technologies. This album did for sixties pop what Esquivel did for square lounge music. But perhaps most significant is the depth of feeling this music imparts to the listener. There is a twisted melancholia that permeates the classics I've already mentioned, that underscores the lighter works, "Here Come the Fleas" and "Firebird," and runs amok on the evil closing track, "Black Mass: Electric Storm in Hell." (P. Edwin Letcher)

THE WHO

Face Dances   **(Warner Brothers, 1981)**

Sterling Publishing's 2002 "complete chronicle" on them doesn't even mention the Who's penultimate studio record, and you know the fact that Moon's not on it is why. Well, they can hide in rewritten histories, but you'll find a Who heart at its most vulnerable in 1981, coping with their drummer's overdose through complete denial and a (human) resolve to proceed like nothing was wrong.

Despite typical rock god gestures (overblown rock operas, elder-statesman posturing), the Who's greatness was their warts. Albums loaded with filler (their only "flawless" record is that played-out yawner *Who's Next*), feedback that was actually out of control (not the harnessed veneer of chaos of Hendrix or Page), and a sexual politics based on insecure ambiguity, all allowed glimpses into their inner workings in ways that were positively radical. And if warts are rad, then this "least effective Who recording" (quoth Who biographer Dave Marsh) is a distended cyst of revolt.

Daltrey's vocals aren't wince-inducing for a change. Forced to soften in response to the increasingly strange spill of babble from Townshend's pen, Rog here resembles a real human being more than at any time since *Sell Out*. Also, why doesn't anyone know "The Quiet One?" This faux-metal staple of their 1982 tour rates among John Entwistle's greatest songs, and when he yowls "I ain't nevah had the gift of the gab" he actually, for a moment, sounds like Bon Scott!

The golden lariat of synths and voices opening "You Better You Bet" is the key to this late single: they're done trying to pontificate *Tommy*-style from the mountaintop. Marsh's problem with *Face Dances* is that "the lyrics [are] too personal" and that it's not a concept album. He's stupid. There's a warmth and humor here that all the "Baba O'Riley"s in the world don't touch. (Gene Booth) (See also: Andy Newman)

DENNIS WILSON
Pacific Ocean Blue   (Columbia, 1977)

Those of us who grew up in Los Angeles during the late seventies did so in the middle of a war. Between the glassy cocaine-sleaze of the Eagles and the answering grenade lobbed by the Dangerhouse stable, it was generally understood—even by those of us geopolitically closer to the former—that the latter represented all things righteous. Only as adults did we slink back and admit (grudgingly still, protected by residual irony) that *Rumours* wasn't too bad after all. Such grudgingness wasn't just postpunk orthodoxy. It hurt, growing up at the epicenter of all that narcissism. And no record I know captures that better than *Pacific Ocean Blue*, which welds the studio grandeur of the West Coast's finest—and weakest—pop wizards to an emotional rawness the punks could scarcely imagine.

Dennis had always been misunderstood as the Beach Boys' own dumb angel, the good-looking one who didn't really do anything. In fact he'd been writing some of the finest, overshadowed numbers on the band's records for some time, as well as tunes (like the devastating "Carry Me Home") rejected as "too dark." Finally, Dennis put it all together by himself, with the stratospheric "River Song"—a soaring, white-gospel masterpiece out-Spectoring its inspiration, and predating the likes of Spiritualized by about thirty years—establishing a template his bandmates were too deaf to follow. It's a peak so immediate that you initially hear the rest of *Pacific Ocean Blue* as a letdown, sort of. But the "letdown" is rather a comedown, and it's the dark, scarred orchestral trouble of the rest of the record that bewitches, with attention. The way the Stevie Wonder–like clavinet of "Dreamer," for instance, collapses into moody piano-murk, or "Thoughts of You" reverses the transcendental bliss-out of "Feel Flows" into a frightening meditation on mortality. It's tempting to say brother Brian never wrote at this level of unprotectedness and sheer vulnerability; what's sure is that Dennis shared his brother's gift, and left us this record to prove it. (Mathew Specktor) (See also: Beach Boys)

ROY WOOD'S WIZZARD

Wizzard's Brew   (United Artists, 1973)

When Roy Wood, Jeff Lynne and Bev Bevans formed the Electric Light Orchestra, it was meant as a musical experiment to run alongside their crunchy pop band, the Move. The Move soon stalled and ELO's musical melding of rock and classical survived. Roy Wood's vision for this melding was far too eccentric and bombastic, so, amidst murky mumblings, he departed the group. Wizzard was formed to further expand upon Wood's desires unhindered. After a few catchy hit singles, *Wizzard's Brew* was released (without said singles), and it is an ungodly mess. The liner notes attest to this: "In this group there might be cellos and such, but never would they give forth the sound of a chamber music quartet. This group was to be coarse, loud, and unruly, and it would never lose sight of its dedication to primal rock 'n'roll. Yet it would still be experimental, because Roy Wood was a man of many ideas." Roy Wood is also a long-bearded, wild-looking man with red and blue jagged striped makeup that perfectly matches his outfit. The gatefold features him super huge with his shaggy band at his feet. Another version of the album cover shows him throwing his band into a large cauldron—or, rather, a large melting pot—making for a charmingly disreputable grotesquery. An ultra-heavy fifties pastiche that has one of its club feet locked into the glam of the time, this *Brew* is completely unpredictable; the eight-piece band sounds like they're falling down a flight of stairs, occasionally cushioned by a lengthy sax or cello solo. Their unwieldy stomp is guided by Wood's proto-metal vocals constantly screaming about how "You can dance your rock 'n' roll!" The song "Meet Me at the Jailhouse" is almost fifteen minutes long and never boring. The hodgepodge of instruments that complement the doomsday bass, cowbells and wailing guitars prove it so. That, and the entire right channel is coated in flange. The kind of planning involved to make such sublime vomit must have been intense. Huge, rollicking rockers. A ripper! (Robert Dayton)

THE WYLDE MAMMOTHS
Go Baby Go   (Crypt, 1987)

I can't imagine that there were more than a few thousand copies of *Go Baby Go* ever pressed, and this album surely went virtually unnoticed by anyone who wasn't a devotee of the underground garage rock scene of the mid-eighties. The band put out a handful of singles and a second album, *Things that Matter*, which I haven't heard yet. As far as I have been able to determine, the album has never been released on CD and there are no plans to rectify this situation in the near future. Various members of the band went on to other bands, the most notable being the Maggots. The group was from Sweden, but lead singer Peter Maniette could pass for an American from just about any punk upstart outfit from 1966. This brash, cheap Mick Jagger wannabe quality is applied to twelve original, driving rhythm and blues gems and a remake of the Spitfires' moody "I Never Loved Her." The songs were recorded in Peter's basement. The ambiance is the closest thing I know of to the low-budget production sound of the most inspiring of the nasty blasts found on the various *Pebbles*-style comps. Unlike a lot of the first string of tough guys from the Sonics' era, this quartet had the gift of hindsight, which enabled them to release all killer and no filler. There are no ballads or covers of smarmy pop hits. Rather than being manic or heavy, however, the music is soulful, artfully arranged, and memorable. I have played this album for friends who love retro bands such as the Gravedigger V and Thee Mighty Caesars. All, so far, have agreed that the Wylde Mammoths were extra special. They had a sound that was both authentically sixties and highly individual. (P. Edwin Letcher)

XANADU
Blackout in the City EP   (Black Hole, 1979)

Detroit in the late seventies was an exciting, gloomy, demented void. It was the nuclear aftermath of the Motown era. You could hang out at Bookie's Club 870 and go to record stores where you'd meet all kinds of acid-blasted walking ghosts still recovering from the shock of seeing, or being in, the Stooges, MC5, Funkadelic or countless lesser-known groups. Great music

still existed, but it was destined to fall into the same black hole that had swal-
lowed ? and the Mysterians. While Ted Nugent ruled the airwaves, people
couldn't have cared less about "City Slang" by Sonic's Rendezvous Band. At
a record convention in 1980, I came across strange magazines by the Ann
Arbor–based collective Destroy All Monsters. I already owned their *Days of
Diamonds* EP, featuring founding member Cary Loren. Having read various
accounts of his mysterious disappearance, I asked the guy behind the table,
"Whatever happened to Cary Loren?" "I am Cary Loren," he replied. I told
him how much I loved *Diamonds*. He said, "If you like that, you'll probably
like this" and handed me the Xanadu EP. I think it cost $4.

Xanadu featured Cary and longhaired siblings Larry and Ben Miller. The
Miller brothers played in countless bands, including Sproton Layer (1969–1970,
featuring their brother Roger, who later formed Mission of Burma). The
Xanadu record is all acid flashbacks, atom-age uneasiness, fuzz-guitar storms,
slithering prog-grooves and lyrics that describe a panorama of astral destruction.
In an interview (*Yeti* #1), Cary explains that the lyrics to "Blackout in the City"
were inspired by a vision of "an expressionistic black Jesus dripping blood from
the sky." Twenty years later, Cary Loren explores similar vibrations with acid-
folk improvisers Monster Island and a reunited Destroy All Monsters. Still,
nothing quite captures the "darkness before more darkness" that was Detroit at
the end of the seventies the way this vinyl artifact does. (Matthew Smith)

Note: Seventeen years after obtaining the Xanadu EP, Matthew Smith
was invited to play the sitar and various other instruments with Cary Loren's
Monster Island ensemble.

ZALMAN YANOVSKY
Alive and Well in Argentina   **(Buddah, 1968/Kama-Sutra, 1971)**
Time has not been kind to the Lovin' Spoonful. Their albums languished out
of print for years with only shoddy hits packages available. The record that
unlocks my heart, though, is not even really a Lovin' Spoonful album. Under
stumblings and shady circumstances, Zalman Yanovsky left the Spoonful and
went straight to this solo album.

It opens with a snippet of "Oh Canada" and right into a perfect pop song by Zal and Jerry Yester. Yester? Yessir, the man who replaced him in the Spoonful collaborated on this album! Lucky that, because Yester is a great pop arranger/producer who throws all sorts of instruments and effects into the mix.

"Raven in a Cage," blends falsetto backups with keyboards, all getting higher until the kettle flies off the stove and through the ceiling; an ominous guitar solo briefly cuts through the chipper mood and calliope. Lots of well-chosen covers are rendered here in a psych-is-just-around-the-corner gloss: "You Talk Too Much," "Little Bitty Pretty One," "Brown to Blue," "I Almost Lost My Mind." Zal even covers the Spoonful's "Priscilla Millionaira," which they recorded after he left the group.

Zal's sole solo album has infectious energy. Not the strongest vocalist, he has such character, like a wiggy young uncle, scatting, tongue twisting and mock-German singing to boot ("They was throwing frisbees and hula hoopen, heiling Hitler, and Betty Boopen"). When not playing distorto guitar was he flapping his arms wildly around the studio? The 1970 reissue throws on the Bonner/Gordon romp "As Long as You're Here" that opens with a Jew's harp and ends with female vocals asking, "Is it a hit or a miss?" Both. The mock bravado of "Hip Toad" leads into the ornate ever-changing orch-instrumental "Lt. Schtinkhausen." If you want to cast this album off it can be chastised as novelty. It certainly is novel, a zany pure pop delirium.

Whimsical irreverence is not so easily found in pop anymore. To me, this album plays like a counterpoint to Jerry Yester and Judy Henske's brilliant *Farewell Aldebaran*, a dark poetic album borne out of fever dreams, with which Zal was also involved. (Robert Dayton) (See also: The Mugwumps)

YES

Tormato   (Atlantic, 1978)

Though rock was "cool" in its way in high school in the seventies and eighties (can't speak for the nineties), being into it the way budding rock writers are was not. In that predictable but still sad way in which the underdog looks for someone even meeker to piss on, rockcrit geeks turned around and beat on the even geekier: prog rockers, the rock equivalent of ren-faire lovers, SF fans, and role-playing gamers.

It's a stupid prejudice, especially when applied to the most successful of the proggers, Yes. Weird—often uncomfortably so—by normal rock standards, Yes were also masters of unique beauty and power. Detractors can't get to Yes' virtues—the dazzling, slippery bursts of Steve Howe's intensely skittish guitar and Chris Squire's ceaselessly limber and imaginative bass playing, two of rock's most unique instrumental voices—because their faces get all scrunchy at the mere concept of linking rock to long compositions and pop-spiritual concerns.

Tormato is pretty much at the bottom of the already shallow barrel of respect for Yes. The cover is silly and provided an irresistibly stupid hook for critics: it showed the band spattered with tossed tomatoes on the back. But on this last go-round the almost definitive Yes lineup harnesses its virtues to short, punchy tunes—nine songs on a single LP instead of one stretched over four sides. Without the "bloat" that those with short attention spans decry, Yes put their biggest and most forceful rock foot forward and it lands solidly and satisfyingly. Sure, the songs are about UFOs and future times and saving the whales and the circus of heaven and the promise of a new age of human enlightenment; it even mentions unicorns and the word "celestial" is admittedly uttered often. But they are beautiful and heartening optimistic visions all and the band rocks them like they're all full of beefsteak. It's okay to invite the geeks to the party. You might learn something new from them. (Brian Doherty)

DWIGHT YOAKAM

Hillbilly Deluxe   (Reprise, 1987)

There is a type of record that music geeks relish since they are so few and far between. And so, every time a new one comes along, it's like a bloody freakin' miracle. Behold—another *perfect* record! Consequently, I proclaim that Dwight Yoakam's *Hillbilly Deluxe* is such a record. Each song is a hit and is tracked perfectly from one to the next so that you never want to skip anything. Every song supports the other by lifting you up and then taking you down, but either way, making you look forward to the next. And, by the time you reach the end of Side 2, you want to start the beginning of Side 1 all over again.

Hillbilly Deluxe is a record I own on vinyl, cassette and CD, and I can sing it *a cappella* because I've listened to it a billion times and know it by heart. When it was released, not one kid I knew that was my age (and I was seventeen years old), liked country western music, let alone gave two shits about the future of country western music. Therefore, I had to listen to the record alone or be shunned by every stuck-up "alternative music loving" snob rocker within fifteen miles of my record player. Needless to say, not much has changed among my cohorts to this very day. I didn't care then, and I don't care now, because the music on this album fucking *rules!* It gave me more than hope. It gave me living proof that country music can be fresh and cool and sexy and smart and kick-ass *and* be done by a contemporary artist. Dwight Yoakam continues to transcend the genre in a positive way, and he *still* can't get consistent radio play. (Kelly Kuvo)

Key Comps for Subgenres

Rig Rock Jukebox: Catches an early nineties country rock and honky tonk scene in the Lower East Side. It's all good, but essential for the two Go To Blazes cuts and Stephen Heynman's god-ripping riffs on "97 Miles" and "Why I Drink."

Velvet Tinmine: Ridiculously obscure and fabulous Glam nuggets anchored by the sugarrocket of Brett Smiley's "Va Va Va Voom."

Pictures from the Gone World: Rare Beat poetry-jazz hybrids. Not kitsch, not crap, unuttterably right on Jack Hammer tracks, "Big High Song For Nothing," Moondog, Shel Silverstein and pre-Muppets Jim Henson.

Bad Music for Bad People: Essential comp series arguing the Cramps' position that rock and roll is fetid, nasty, bizarre and warped. All are fantastic, Volume 2 more so.

Hillbilly Music ... Thank God!: Marshall Crenshaw raided the Capitol vaults and rewrote the history of country music to include the west coast. White-hot instros, hardass honkytonk, Louvin Brothers, Jean Shepard and Faron Young. (David Smay)

YUNG WU
Shore Leave   (**Twin/Tone–Coyote, 1987**)

Those of us who were lucky enough to see the Feelies live, I'm sure, all won-
dered the same thing: "This band is great, but what is up with that spaced-
out percussionist?" That percussionist was one Dave Weckerman, who was a
member of the Feelies and Yung Wu, which basically was the Feelies with
Weckerman singing and Speed the Plough's John Baumgartner on keyboards. Whether he was shaking a tambourine, hitting a snare drum or spacing out, Dave Weckerman was definitely out there. Was he stoned? Freaked
out? Dead tired? I guess we'll never know, but he and his bandmates made
one hell of a record in *Shore Leave*.

Needless to say, Weckerman was the least likely frontman you were ever
going to see (and just for the record, I never saw Yung Wu live, only the
Feelies). But he did it. They got him to sing in a recording studio—and on
stage, though not very often—and while the covers of Roxy Music, Neil
Young, and the Rolling Stones are all fine enough, it's the originals that
astounded me. The opening title track is "On the Roof" on 'ludes, "Spinning"
has some of the choicest lead guitar work this side of a Flying Nun band (any
of 'em), and on "Strange Little Man" Weckerman is going off about "It's 1989
and her daddy's gonna lose his mind" while Baumgartner's keyboards add
some pizzazz to the proceedings.

Thanks to this little essay I have had the pleasure of revisiting this record
quite a bit over the past few weeks. Suffice it to say if the Feelies ever made an
impression on you, or you think New Zealand's Bats were a big deal, then this
should be on your "need to find" list. (Tim Hinely) (See also: The Feelies)

Z

WARREN ZEVON
Mutineer   (**Giant, 1995**)

Carl Hiaasen's *Basket Case* had a world-class gimmick: Warren Zevon sang a
song they cowrote, ostensibly the work of the novel's fictional band, on his
album *My Ride's Here*. But to hear their musical mischief at its best, go
straight to *Mutineer*. Its strongest songs are Zevon–Hiaasen collaborations.

"Seminole Bingo" stars a fugitive junk bond trader losing at late-night bingo on an Indian reservation, flanked by alligators and flamingos. He could have stepped out of a book by Hiaasen, Florida's hardest-working chronicler of misadventure. Gambling gangsters have also graced dozens of songs by Zevon ("Lawyers, Guns and Money," "Mr. Bad Example"). The swagger of the out-of-luck outlaw is matched by the pounded piano riff and martial electric guitar.

"Rottweiler Blues" wants to be left alone: "Don't knock on my door if you don't know my Rottweiler's name." This isolationism is shared not only by Hiaasen's swamp-dwelling ex-governor of Florida but also by a goon squad of Zevon anti-heroes ("Splendid Isolation," "Leave My Monkey Alone"). The Rottweiler himself is a familiar figure: Hiaasen loves to whip up chaos by releasing a pit bull or black Lab into the mix, and some of Zevon's best songs feature characters of the canine persuasion ("Even a Dog Can Shake Hands," "Werewolves of London"). Zevon sings this slow-burning, slightly discordant rocker with the laid-back authority of a man sitting on his porch with a mad dog on one side and a big gun on the other, and even manages to wring a piercing animal yelp from his guitar at the end of the bridge.

So what's cooler: that these guys with twin artistic temperaments wound up writing songs together, or that the songwriting grew out of their real-life friendship? I like to picture them at some point in the mythical past, fishing off a Florida pier, the sun at half-mast. Suddenly a beat-up pick-up rockets by, chickens flying out the back and a beautiful woman leaning out to wipe some sinister goo off the windshield. Carl says, "There goes my next book," while Warren is already scribbling the vision on his little notepad. Amen to that. (Genevieve Conaty)

ABOUT SCRAM MAGAZINE

In 1992, Kim Cooper photocopied the first issue of *Scram*, a journal of unpopular culture. Since then, *Scram* has distinguished itself by its passionate devotion to artists that otherwise fly beneath the critical radar, and a series of exquisite covers designed by Peter Bagge, Daniel Clowes, Dave Cooper, and others. Please visit *Scram* online at http://www.scrammagazine.com, and http://www.lostinthegrooves.com for info and downloads from the artists featured in this book.

ABOUT THE EDITORS

When Kim Cooper was wee, a friend of her parents gave her some albums he'd found in a trash can, among them Biff Rose's *Children of Light*, with which she became obsessed. The notion that great music might more easily be found amongst refuse than in brightly lit shops proved impossible to shake, and eventually led to this book.

David Smay was the co-editor of *Bubblegum Music is the Naked Truth*, and has contributed to *Scram*, among many other zines and magazines. He lives in San Francisco with his son and wife, where he is a fan of Los Bros Hernandez, Joss Whedon, Barry Zito, Nathanael West and the New York Dolls. You may not borrow his *Film Noir Encyclopedia*.

ABOUT THE CONTRIBUTORS

Brooke Alberts writes for L.A.-based *Folkworks*, plays whistle in as many Irish traditional sessions as possible, and loves hot whiskey and a great bowl of New England clam chowder.

Mike Appelstein lives in St. Louis, Missouri. For more information on his various writing and musical projects, please visit http://www.appelstein.com.

Jake Austen edits *Roctober* magazine and produces the dance show *Chic-A-Go-Go* (www.roctober.com). His work appears in *A Friendly Game of Poker*, *The Cartoon Music Book*, and *Bubblegum Music is the Naked Truth*.

Peter Bagge is an "alternative" cartoonist, best known for his comic book *Hate*, although he has many other credits to his name. Please refer to http://www.peterbagge.com for further details.

After writing for *Phonograph Record, Rolling Stone, Bomp, Creem*, and more, plus editorial stints at *Radio & Records, ICE*, and Microsoft, Ken Barnes is currently music editor at *USA Today*.

The Bengala is a matrimonial art collective consisting of Benjamin Tischer and Gala Verdugo. They're also key players in *K48 Magazine*, which is way rad. Contact: bengala@verizon.net.

Tosh Berman is a publisher and editor of TamTam Books and recently published Boris Vian's *Foam of the Daze*. http://www.tamtambooks.com.

Jon Bernhardt has been a DJ on WMBR-FM since 1983, and plays theremin for The Lothars and The Pee Wee Fist (CDs available at http://www.wobblymusic.com). He lives in Somerville, Massachusetts.

Gene Booth is a Chicago-based writer.

Although Derrick Bostrom's forays into music journalism and rock history are far from legendary, the same cannot be said about his work as the drummer for the Meat Puppets.

Joe Boucher lives in Brooklyn and plans to name his son Thelonious. Maybe his daughter, too.

Carl Cafarelli writes for *Goldmine* magazine and co-hosts (with Dana Bonn) *This Is Rock 'n' Roll Radio* on Sunday nights from 9 to midnight Eastern time at http://www.wxxe.org.

Kevin Carhart is a freelance writer based in the San Francisco area. Music, comics and women are his preoccupations, nay, obsessions. Check out his writings, drawings and comics at http://carhart.com/~kevin.

Born and raised in East L.A., documentary filmmaker Sean Carrillo was a member of the guerilla art group ASCO and co-founded Troy Café. He is married to artist Bibbe Hansen.

Hayden Childs edits, writes for, and sometimes pimps *The High Hat Magazine* (http://www.thehighhat.com) from an undisclosed secret location that some call "Austin, TX."

Genevieve Conaty has been a staff writer for her own imaginary magazine for twenty-three years. She lives in Reading, England.

David Cotner, keeper of Hertz-Lion—the mighty vault of information concerning the avant-garde—established the literalist method of composition in tandem with the discipline of subjective surrealism.

Robert Dayton is a writer, an actor, a performer in the musical acts Canned Hamm (http://www.cannedhamm.tv) and July Fourth Toilet, and is also a man for all seasons. Moustachedpainless@yahoo.com.

Jean-Emmanuel Deluxe (a.k.a. Dubois) is a pop journalist, writer for several top magazines (*Citizen K, Standard* ...). He is the mastermind with Xavier Alves of euro-visions records. http://www.euro-visions.net

Stuart Derdeyn is a music junkie/journalista whose cell runs out of Vancouver, Canada. His columns run in the *Province* paper and elsewhere. Contact him at sldd@shaw.ca.

Deke Dickerson is a Los Angeles–based writer, musician, and Renaissance man. http://www.dekedickerson.com.

Brian Doherty is a senior editor of *Reason* magazine and author of *This Is Burning Man* (Little, Brown).

Jonathan Donaldson's writings have appeared in *Scram, Dagger, Pop Culture Press,* Junkmedia.org, Tangents.co.uk, and Opuszine.com, focusing on sixties pop and current releases. He also records music as The Color Forms.

My bologna has a first name it's P-h-i-l-i-p. My bologna has a second name it's D-r-u-c-k-e-r. I love to eat it everyday and if you ask me why I'll say, 'cause Philip Drucker has a way with b-o-l-o-g-n-a.

Musician, writer, record producer, and media blowhard SL Duff lives in the Hollywood Hills with his Roller Derby–star wife and his cat Lizzy Borden.

Andrew Earles writes and lives in Memphis, Tennessee. He is working on a medical neo-thriller about comic malpractice and decommissioned rotating restaurants. To find out more about Andrew, visit: http://www.failedpilot.com.

Becky Ebenkamp, a Hollywood based entertainment/pop culture writer, has never paraded around in an aerosol-dispensed dairy product (in public).

Russ Forster resides as an aging hipster in the Midwestern U.S., land of thrift stores and bratwurst. Blame him for overpriced 8-track tapes on eBay.

Phil Freeman is a New Jersey–based freelance writer who contributes to *Jazziz, The Wire, Alternative Press, The Cleveland Scene* and *The Village Voice.*

Ron Garmon edits *Worldly Remains* (http://www.worldlyremains.com) and is an L.A. boulevardier/rock journalist bearing the nickname "the punk rock Paul Lynde" with easy grace. He asserts no moral responsibility whatever.

Doug Gillard is a Cleveland, Ohio–based songwriter and musician not currently seen on any reality TV shows.

Chas Glynn is a San Francisco–based writer, musician, and gadabout. His past employment includes stints as postman, used car salesman, dishwasher in a casino and bachelor party clown.

Gary Pig Gold has been called nearly everything from "rock music's all-time hardest-working man" (All Music Guide) to "cooler than Elvis!" (*Tragedienne*). Find out why, at http://www.tomlou.com and/or PIGPROD@aol.com.

William Ham is a carbon-based writer whose work has appeared in *McSweeney's, Ben Is Dead, Lollipop,* and *The Cambridge Book Review,* among others. He can be reached at whambino@hotmail.com.

Doug Harvey is art critic for the *L.A. Weekly* and played spring strung bass for Tenacious Mucoid Exudate in the 1980s.

Max Hechter is an epidemiologist at the UCLA School of Public Health. He used to host "The Fringe Element" at KPFK-FM in Los Angeles. He owns a lot of records.

Born in Detroit in the second half of the twentieth century, Richard Henderson's writing on music has appeared in *The Wire, Billboard, The Beat, L.A. Weekly, Escape, Psychotronic, Soma* and *Murder Dog.*

Elizabeth Herndon lives in Los Angeles and makes her living neither by writing nor playing music with the punk chamber orchestra WACO. She also supposes that is to be expected.

Tim Hinely lives in Portland, Oregon, and has been doing his own zine, *Dagger*, for seventeen years. Write him at P.O. Box 820102, Portland, OR 97282–1102 or daggerboy@prodigy.net.

Jay Hinman is a San Francisco–based longtime music writer. His writing can be found at http://agonyshorthandblogspot.com.

Andrew Hultkrans is the author of *Forever Changes* (*33 1/3* series, Continuum, 2003). From 1998 through early 2003, he was editor-in-chief of *Bookforum* magazine.

Elizabeth Ivanovich has written for such publications as *Student Guide, Back of a Car, Student Traveler* and the editors' previous anthology, *Bubblegum Music is the Naked Truth*.

Kris Kendall lives in Seattle. His writing has appeared in *Resonance*, Jaguaro.org, and *6 Is 9* magazine.

Kelly Kuvo makes art and music and has written for *Lumpen, Roctober, Index, Oui, Scram* and *Vice*. She proudly attended Englewood Beauty College and received a cosmetology license in 1987.

P. Edwin Letcher is a writer/cartoonist/musician. Current projects include *Garage & Beat, Misty Lane,* Stubbo the Cat with No Paws, The Fleagles and Bangers & Mash. http://www.garageandbeat.com.

Ted Liebler grew up listening to Midwestern oldies radio while riding along in his parents' 1968 AMC Javelin. He currently lives between palm trees and mountains in the Western U.S.

Michael Lucas is available to discuss Mexican rock and roll at weddings, board of directors' meetings and bar mitzvahs. Rates available upon request.

Michael Lynch, a New York garage/pop singer-songwriter, writes for *Ugly Things* and Fufkin.com, and deejays at Manhattan's monthly 1960s party "Pop Gear!" Follow Michael's adventures at http://michaellynch.blogspot.com/.

Erin McKean is the Editor-in-Chief of U.S. Dictionaries for Oxford University Press and the editor of the only magazine for word geeks, *VERBATIM: The Language Quarterly*. http://www.verbatimmag.com.

Richard Meltzer has been to school and is a fool (and he is not cool).

Rick Moody's most recent book is *The Black Veil*.

Tom Neely is a painter/cartoonist in Los Angeles. His work has been featured in galleries, comics, magazines and album covers. He is currently writing his first graphic novel. Visit http://www.iwilldestroyyou.com.

Jim O'Rourke does stuff in music and films, but prefers to watch movies and listen to "propaganda" daily.

Alec Palao is a Bay Area–based musician, writer, reissue bozo and full-time rock 'n' roll fanatic.

George Pelecanos is a screenwriter, independent-film producer and the author of the best-selling series of Derek Strange novels set in and around Washington, D.C., where he lives with his wife and children.

James Porter is a Chicago-based writer who has written for *Roctober, Blender, The Chicago Reader, Scram, No Depression* and other magazines about the blues, rockabilly, bubblegum and other extremities.

Mark Prindle is the CEO of http://www.markprindle.com, the most ridiculously profane and off-topic record review guide on the Internet.

Domenic Priore is the author of *Look! Listen! Vibrate! Smile!*, *Riot on Sunset Strip: Rock 'n' Roll's Last Stand in Hollywood 1965/1966*, and the AMC documentaries *Hollywood Rocks the Movies*.

Coauthor of Big Daddy Roth's *Confessions of a Rat Fink*, Howie Pyro has played bass/collaborated with D Generation, Danzig, J. Thunders, Genesis P. Orridge, Rancid, J. Malin, Electric Frankenstein, etc.

Ken Rudman wishes to remain anonymous. Please visit his website at http://www.kenrudman.com.

Metal Mike Saunders: Hall High (Little Rock), 1969. University of Texas/Austin, 1973. Twenty-two full-time years in the accounting profession, semi-retired 1999. Contact c/o "Angry Samoans" page on http://www.myspace.com via (e-mail lookup) mike_in_oakland@yahoo.com.

David J. Schwartz writes fiction and likes to pretend he knows a thing or two about music.

Gene Sculatti's books include *The Catalog of Cool*, *Too Cool*, and *San Francisco Nights: The Psychedelic Music Trip*. With Kim Cooper, he runs the Web site http://www.catalog-of-cool.com.

Greg Shaw was copublisher (with Marty Cerf, RIP) of *Phonograph Record Magazine*. He is also known for editing *Bomp* (1970–1979) and launching Bomp Records, which has recorded countless bands. http://www.bomp.com.

Jack Shay has written for Citysearch, Livedaily.com, *CityPaper*, and the *Washington Post*. He lives in New York with his chanteuse wife, but he left his heart in mid-nineties Chicago.

Matthew Smith is a musician, record producer and writer based in Detroit, Michigan. He plays in various rock bands, including Outrageous Cherry and the Volebeats.

Matthew Specktor lives in London, for now, with someone else's record collection. He finds one of these conditions more trying than the other.

Vern Stoltz lives in the Washington, D.C., area and has written for several music magazines.

Deniz Tek grew up in Ann Arbor, Michigan. He has been guitar player and songwriter in Radio Birdman. Now lives in Sapphire Beach, Australia. http://www.deniztek.com.

Michele Tepper is a Brooklyn-based writer. Her website is at http://www.micheletepper.com.

Dave Thompson is the Seattle-based author of 70+ books on rock and pop culture.

Gregg Turkington has produced recordings by Neil Hamburger and Anton LaVey, and is the coauthor of *Warm Voices Rearranged: Anagram Record Reviews* (Drag City Books).

Jillian Venters, when not writing the Gothic Miss Manners columns (http://www.gothicmissmanners.com), spends her days trying to achieve balance between her Perkygoth and Cranky Elder Goth philosophies, and plotting world domination.

Elisabeth Vincentelli was born in France and now lives in Brooklyn, New York. She's a senior editor at *Time Out New York*; her book *Abba Gold* (Continuum) is in stores now.

Ed Ward has been writing about music since 1965, and currently covers music, art, food and plenty of other stuff from Berlin.

Steve Wynn's voluminous record collection includes the twenty he has made since breaking on the scene in 1982 with the Dream Syndicate's *The Days of Wine and Roses*. http://www.stevewynn.net.

Jacqueline Zahas lives and works in San Francisco. When things get rough, she likes to ask herself, "What would Buffy do?"

Index